PASSION LENDS THEM POWER

But passion lends them power, time means, to meet,
Temp'ring extremities with extreme sweet.

Romeo and Juliet

DERICK R. C. MARSH

PASSION
LENDS THEM
POWER

A study of Shakespeare's love tragedies

MANCHESTER
UNIVERSITY PRESS

BARNES & NOBLE
BOOKS · NEW YORK

Published by
MANCHESTER UNIVERSITY PRESS
Oxford Road, Manchester M13 9PL
ISBN 0 7190 0625 2

USA
HARPER & ROW PUBLISHERS INC
BARNES & NOBLE IMPORT DIVISION
ISBN 0 06 494562 6

76-375729

Printed in Great Britain by Eyre & Spottiswoode Ltd
at Grosvenor Press, Portsmouth.

TABLE OF CONTENTS

THE TRAGIC STRAND IN THE COMEDIES

MY CHIEF INTENTION in this book is to explore the relation between Shakespeare's three tragedies on the theme of love, *Romeo and Juliet*, *Othello* and *Antony and Cleopatra*, and to look as well at *Troilus and Cressida*, which, like the three tragedies, provides an account of an unhappy love, but which by differences of emphasis and perspective becomes (in my opinion) a play of a very different kind, though it too is concerned with something of the nature of the experience we call being 'in love'. Unlike the other three, however, the nature of the love it depicts is not its central theme. This is both more general, and presented in an altogether more satiric way, than are the chief themes of the other three plays. I shall discuss these differences more fully later, only observing here that I believe that Troilus' love is used, like the pride of Achilles, like Hector's quest for honour or Ulysses' use of reason, as an example of the ways in which men's desires lead them into self-deception. Finally, I shall consider the treatment of love in the Romances, where, in *Cymbeline* and *The Winter's Tale*, the threatened tragic outcome is almost magically reversed. These are comedies and not tragedies, and therefore a second chance is granted to the potentially tragic figures of Posthumus and Leontes, but they also have to prove their worthiness for that chance, through their capacity to learn from their mistakes.

In considering all these plays it is not my intention to try to arrive at some neatly-formulated abstraction which will represent Shakespeare's attitude to love. The plays are sufficiently interesting in themselves; moreover, they span most of Shakespeare's creative life. Even more importantly, they complement each other and therefore illuminate each other remarkably well, and together they make us aware of the profundity and complexity of Shakespeare's continuing exploration of this most human of human emotions.

Norman Rabkin[1] has argued eloquently for seeing what he calls a 'complementarity' in apparently mutually exclusive attitudes to situations within single Shakespearean plays. If, for example, we are asked on the one hand to accept that Othello is essentially noble, it is nevertheless possible, perhaps even necessary, simultaneously to be aware of the opposite opinion that he may also be egotistical, self-regarding, flawed in a way that he does not himself recognise. It is Shakespeare's essentially comprehending genius, Rabkin argues, that allows him to present these many aspects within the same play without any radical imaginative disruption. I shall return later to some of his accounts of the individual plays, but for the present I would like to argue for the recognition of this sort of complementary relation between all the plays that deal centrally with the theme of love. They do not invalidate each other, though they may say very different things. To take a fairly obvious example: one of the points made by *Troilus and Cressida* is that Troilus is mistaken in the purely subjective value his love confers on Cressida, but in *Antony and Cleopatra* it is arguable that nobody outside the love relationship can hope to judge what the lovers mean to each other, that their value for each other is both subjective and absolute. And against this must be set a third play, *Othello*, one valid reading of which can surely be that an absolute commitment in love may be absolutely disastrous. Yet considered in its own context, no single one of these propositions is invalidated by the fact that it is contradicted elsewhere. It is only the attempt to distil a simplified and universal wisdom from Shakespeare's plays that strikes us as being untrue, never the variety and diversity the plays themselves exhibit.

In none of the cases I have cited would I like to be held to the simple view of the plays that these brief remarks may suggest; what I hope to do is to give some indication of how closely they are interconnected, of how the same concerns keep reappearing in different situations, and are examined from different points of view, not only within single plays, but in plays written at different points of Shakespeare's development. My hope is that an expansion of this process of cross-reference, of comparison and contrast, will prove helpful in an understanding of each of these three great love tragedies.

There could hardly be a more important subject than Shakespeare's treatment of the theme of love. In the narrative poems, the sonnets, the comedies, the problem plays, the tragedies and the Romances, Shakespeare returns to it over and over again, and if one excludes the histories, the number of plays in which love between man and woman, or parent and child is not, to say the very least, an important element in the dramatic design, is very small indeed. There is, of course, no one simple point of view, never a simple summing up. The investigation ranges freely over the nature of affection, of passion, of lust, the ability of men and women to experience their greatest happiness and greatest misery. It explores their extreme vulnerability in caring for someone other than themselves, and this is combined with an awareness of the difficulty of seeing clearly, of distinguishing between what is so and what one wants to be so, as well as an awareness of the need to recognise individuality in others and to dominate the concerns of self. The violence of grief, the passion of jealousy, the pain of disappointed love, and the despair that sees all of life as poisoned at the source if one is sexually betrayed, are all seen as equally a part of love. Examined too are the possibilities of the whole state of being in love being only a monstrous illusion; after all, any attempt to put the world aside and live wholly for love, excluding everything else, can only end in the inevitable failure and destruction that death must bring. As Guiderius and Arviragus sing in the famous dirge in *Cymbeline*

> All lovers young, all lovers must
> Consign to thee, and come to dust.
>
> (IV, ii, 262)

Particularly in the three love tragedies, there is an overriding insistence on man's mortality: the lovers die, as all lovers must, but the central critical question is whether they are to be seen as being destroyed by their love, in the sense that their weakness in yielding to the pull of sexual attraction puts them in the situation that destroys them, or whether they are more justly to be seen, at least in part, as winning a brief but splendid victory, through their love, over the eroding forces of life and time. Different plays offer different situations, different answers, and as has already been suggested, sometimes there are different answers within the same play.

There is so much critical disagreement about so many of Shakespeare's plays that it seems almost presumptuous to claim a lion's share of it for the love tragedies, but it is certainly true that both *Othello* and *Antony and Cleopatra* have attracted what might be called powerfully romantic and powerfully anti-romantic readings, while *Romeo and Juliet* has been very frequently called an immature and unsuccessful tragedy and has, perhaps for that reason, not been given anything like the critical attention it deserves as an important element of Shakespeare's continuing dramatic exploration of the nature of love. We need only look at the bibliography provided in T. J. B. Spencer's Penguin Shakespeare edition of the play to see how unfashionable it has been to take *Romeo and Juliet* seriously. I believe that both the disagreement, and in some cases, the avoidance of a recognition of these plays' central truths have partly come about because the love situation is so peculiarly intense and potentially so disturbing an area of human experience that it is very difficult to maintain critical balance when talking about plays which are centrally concerned with the nature of this experience. There is a great temptation either to surrender to a sort of swooning affirmation of the transcendental value of Love triumphing over Death, or to go to the other extreme and deny the value of the experience by denying the worth of the participants, so that we may be distanced from the pain of their destruction. Helen Gardner, in a survey of *Othello* criticism in this century, has argued powerfully for the need not to inhibit our response to that play for fear of being thought too sentimental. The traditional view of a noble Othello, she says, has 'laboured under difficulties since it was accused of sentimentality—a fatal charge among the young, anxious not to be taken in; though, since tragedy is concerned with human suffering, it might be thought that an excess of sympathy is a lesser defect in a critic than a lack of it',[2] and the same comment might very well apply to some critical accounts of *Antony and Cleopatra,* and of *Romeo and Juliet,* too. Each play, obviously, has its own system of checks and balances, and we need only to think of a character like Enobarbus to see how his intelligent scepticism prevents too easy a surrender to the glamour of Antony and his Egyptian Queen, while his own fate in the play, dying of a broken heart as a result of his desertion of Antony, ensures against his own sceptical view of the love affair being accepted as the authoritative view of the play.

If we consider how the love relationship has been handled in the comedies and the problem plays, we may be better prepared for the emotional difficulties of the love tragedies, and may more easily see why we ought to be at once insulated from the temptation to take them too romantically and at the same time prepared to allow them a proper imaginative sympathy. Because the comedies make a number of points that are valid for all of the love tragedies, it seems useful to take these plays out of their chronological order, and consider comedies like *Much Ado About Nothing, As You Like It* and *Twelfth Night* before looking at the earliest of the love tragedies, *Romeo and Juliet,* which precedes them in date of composition. I need hardly add that in the brief analysis of some aspects of these plays that follows, I shall be emphasising elements in them that look forward to attitudes that are developed in the love tragedies, rather than attempting any balanced account of them as comedies. That they are both amusing and delightful I hold to be self-evident truths, needing, on this occasion, no demonstration from me.

It is surely reasonable to begin such an investigation by looking briefly at what is known of contemporary Elizabethan attitudes to love, and here, books like Muriel Bradbrook's *Themes and Conventions in Elizabethan Tragedy*[3] and F. M. Dickey's careful study *Not Wisely But Too Well*[4] are of great value. What emerges very clearly is that, as might have been expected, the Elizabethans, to say nothing of Shakespeare himself, can hardly be thought to have held one mind on so complex a subject as love. Ruthlessly to apply a twentieth-century-derived consensus of sixteenth-century opinion to the interpretation of any single play is to run a risk as great as to approach that play in complete ignorance of what Shakespeare's contemporaries may have felt. The dangers as well as the rewards of a critical approach based on a reconstruction of the Elizabethan sensibility are well illustrated by Professor Dickey's book, which bases its argument on the premise that Elizabethans would see the dramatic presentation of love as weakness, destructive of admirable behaviour, though not for that reason, he is careful to add, necessarily destructive of sympathy for the hero. Applying a special instance of the argument advanced by Lily B. Campbell in her book *Shakespeare's Tragic Heroes, Slaves of Passion*,[5] Professor Dickey maintains that the lovers in *Romeo and Juliet*, *Troilus and Cressida* and *Antony and Cleopatra* all progress to catastrophe because of what Elizabethans would recognise as clear transgressions of moral law, through excessive or mis-directed love. *Othello* is excluded from the discussion because Professor Dickey does not believe that it is centrally concerned with love.

It is easy, I think, to see from the plays themselves the folly of imposing such limitations on the critical response; moreover, some subsequent criticism has argued that it may in any case be a mistake to attribute to the Elizabethans an absolute faith in the superiority of reason.[6] It is certainly true that in a play like *Troilus and Cressida*, the wilful abandonment of reason in favour of what is, in Troilus, a willed passion, is shown to be an abrogation of the higher human faculties, but it seems mistaken to try to impose the same thematic structure on the love tragedies. It is part of my intention to show that what makes these three plays tragic (whatever that term may mean) as opposed to the more astringent effect of *Troilus and Cressida*, stems at least in part from a denial of the logic of reason when applied to love. (I have elsewhere argued something like the same sort of case with regard to the Romances.)[7]

In *Romeo and Juliet* and *Antony and Cleopatra* the point is repeatedly made that the lovers, because of the value at which they prize their love, reject the world's ways of judging their situation, and follow the demands of their love, even to death. It is true that by so doing they are destroyed, but I shall argue that the effect of this destruction is very far from being the teaching of a moral lesson. In *Othello* it is precisely because Othello allows himself to be trapped into accepting the 'reasonable' arguments of Iago that his faith in Desdemona is destroyed. The tragic ending shows that he should have trusted his love, not that he has loved excessively. It may be that the difficulty of avoiding this conclusion was among those considerations that led Professor Dickey to exclude this play from the illustration of his thesis.

But there is no doubt that it is useful to bear in mind that Elizabethans would have made a distinction between love and lust. As usual, the absolute differences between the two apparent opposites are not as great in practice as they appear in discussion, even when we remember that while it may be more accurate to think of the Elizabethan meaning of 'lust' as being somewhat less pejorative than it is now, something closer to a phrase like 'physical attraction', it nevertheless carried the whole-hearted condemnation of the Christian Church, which taught that those who surrendered to its almost irresistible strength risked damnation. Lust, rather than love, is the subject of both Shakespeare's long narrative poems *Venus and Adonis* and *The Rape of Lucrece*; unbridled lust is the subject of bitter denunciations in the words of Hamlet to Ophelia and to his mother, Othello to Desdemona, Troilus to Cressida, Lear to Gloucester, Leontes to Hermione, Posthumus to Imogen, and Prospero to Ferdinand and Miranda, but to equate the emotion contained in these scenes with what Juliet reveals of her feeling for Romeo, Rosalind for Orlando, or Othello for Desdemona when they meet, safely arrived in Cyprus, or any number of other passages, is surely to be as perverse as one can possibly be. The moods and the contexts are wholly different. Against the bitterness of 'The expense of spirit in a waste of shame' we must set a sonnet like 'Let me not to the marriage of true minds admit impediments', which celebrates a quality of feeling still subject, it is true, to the forces of time and death, but in its intensity rising triumphantly above them by making them seem irrelevant, the celebration of perhaps the greatest joy that an individual can experience. We ought to remember too, Ferdinand's own reply to Prospero on this subject

> . . . the strong'st suggestion
> Our worser genius can, shall never melt
> Mine honour into lust, to take away
> The edge of that day's celebration
> When I shall think, or Phoebus' steeds are founder'd
> Or night kept chain'd below.   (IV, i, 26)

It seems almost possible to find the whole spectrum of this human feeling in Shakespeare's work, from lust, through self-love, to monstrous delusion, sometimes ludicrous, like Titania's passion for Bottom with the ass's head on his shoulders, sometimes ugly and violent, like Leontes' trial and condemnation of Hermione, to the tenderness, the passion, and the complete interdependence of spirit that makes a Romeo, an Othello or an Antony ready to welcome death in preference to a life without love. Just as love in life is infinitely varied, so it seems in Shakespeare's plays, and so, it must be acknowledged, it is recognised as being in all that we can glean from the poems and plays people wrote in the sixteenth and seventeenth centuries, from the books they read, the sermons they heard and the songs they sang. Even a cursory glance at those repositories of folk wisdom, the commonplace books,[8] shows what mixed feelings love inspired: the saws alternate between the need for caution and the need for total commitment. It is in the nature of men to feel this ambivalence towards love, and we would be quite wrong to impose on any single one of Shakespeare's plays a single-minded reading which conforms closely to some externally derived point of view. To approach all or any of the plays believing that Shakespeare shared with his audience a disapproving view of excessive love is as distorting as to maintain that strength of passion alone is to be endorsed as the great Shakespearean positive.

Shakespeare's serious interest in love is apparent from very early in his writing. His models, the classical authors, thought love a subject fit for comedy rather than for tragedy: the typical Plautine comedy, for instance, showed lovers as ludicrous in the grip of their passion, but Shakespeare, even in that early play which conforms most closely to the Plautine model, *The Comedy of Errors*, is serving notice that he is not content to remain within the Roman formula. The plot, of two identical twins brought up apart, but so alike that even a wife cannot distinguish her husband from his twin brother, and unbeknown to each other, brought by chance to the same place, gives opportunity for multiple mistakings. The intricate plot is an amalgam of two Roman plays, and is in itself sufficiently funny to hold the attention, but Shakespeare is not content to leave the mood undeepened. Running through the play is the suggestion that our notions of ourselves depend very largely on the reflections we receive back from those around us, and that this is nowhere more crucial or potentially more wounding, than in the sexual relationship. The relevance of this sort of consideration to *Othello* is obvious. I am not arguing that in *The Comedy of Errors* this concern emerges with the dramatic force and human insight that are the triumph of the later plays (though we should bear in mind Harold Brookes's contention that nowhere else in the drama of the period, except for *The Spanish Tragedy*, is there the complexity and integration of theme and situation that one finds in even the early work of Shakespeare)[9] but it is worth considering a few of the speeches and incidents that bear upon this theme.

Antipholus of Syracuse is mistaken for her husband by Adriana, his brother's wife: the rightful husband is shut out and rejected. As the confusion multiplies, each of the central characters is made to doubt his or her own identity. In the case of Antipholus of Syracuse identity is what he has come to Ephesus expressly to seek, since in his isolation, with no family ties, he feels himself lost.

> I to the world am like a drop of water
> That in the ocean seeks another drop.
> Who, falling there to find his fellow forth,
> (Unseen, inquisitive,) confounds himself . . .
>
> (I, ii, 35)

This acknowledgement of the lack of a point of reference may remind us of that great scene of Antony's when, convinced by the desertion of his fleet that Cleopatra is unfaithful to him, his musings show him losing all sense of himself, of his own identity, when it is not defined by the ties of love.

> ANTONY . . . thou hast seen these signs;
>   They are black vesper's pageants.
>   EROS   Ay, my lord.
> ANTONY That which is now a horse, even with a thought
>   The rack dislimns, and makes it indistinct,
>   As water is in water.
>   EROS   It does, my lord.
> ANTONY My good knave Eros, now thy captain is
>   Even such a body: here I am Antony;
>   Yet cannot hold this visible shape, my knave.
>   I made these wars for Egypt; and the queen,—
>   Whose heart I thought I had, for she had mine . . .
>
> (IV, xiv, 7)

In *The Comedy of Errors*, the rightful husband, denied his identity by his wife, is in real danger of going mad, until the resolution of the comedy allows to all the recognition and reconciliation that characterise the form. This is not only a fortuitous mistaking of identity produced by the plot mechanism. Adriana, with her groundless jealousy, has in a real sense already failed to recognise her husband, and has fostered the situation she fears even before her unwitting rejection of him precipitates it. In this earliest of the comedies, Shakespeare seems fully alive to the dangers that lie in a soured love relationship. I am not, I hope, attempting to hang too heavy an emphasis on this single aspect of what is after all a fairly light-hearted comedy of situation,[10] where the possibilities of misunderstanding are squared by having identical twin servants serving identical twin masters. Nor is there, in my opinion, much attempt to use the convention of the identical and indistinguishable twin as anything very much more than a convenient plot mechanism. In *Twelfth Night*, by contrast, the implications of Olivia's acceptance in marriage of a man she has not even seen until a few hours previously, are woven into the total view of love that the play presents.

It would be difficult to deny that the central theme of all the comedies is love. What may be more open to discussion is the way in which Shakespeare treats the subject in the different plays. Frequently he seems to take as his starting point a point of view which he knows his audience will readily recognise and then uses the concomitant presuppositions they may justly be expected to have to make points which will force a reappraisal of that initial point of view. As we shall see, *Troilus and Cressida* makes use of a similar set of preconceptions, those which we may call the orthodox Elizabethan attitudes to the story of the Trojan War. In the early comedies, the starting point seems to be one which sees the lover as somebody so defeated and distracted by his emotions that he is laughable, both in his absurd admiration of his love, and in the self-deceit that is necessary to sustain his idolatry. But, the point is always made, no exercise of reason or intelligence can make men and women immune to the disease; the best that can be hoped for, as plays like *Love's Labour's Lost*, and *Much Ado About Nothing* seem in part to be saying, is that they will exercise these qualities of discrimination once they are in love. In the necessarily brief account of some of the major comedies that follows, I would like it to be remembered that I am not attempting to give anything like a summary of their total effect as plays. What is of interest to me is the awareness they show of the dangers and disasters inherent in any love situation, here in the comedies largely conquered and avoided both by the qualities the lovers discover in themselves and each other, but most of all avoided because the conventions of comedy demand that they prove ultimately avoidable. If my account of the comedies seems too sombre, it is because I am giving, for the purpose of my argument, too great an emphasis to the element of potential tragedy which I believe Shakespeare's work shows, even here in the comedies, as an unavoidable part of the love relationship.

The whole situation of *Love's Labour's Lost* is made credible by the recognition demanded from the audience of the folly of attempting to shun love. Berowne speaks for everyone when he is sceptical of the four friends' ability to abide by their vow to avoid the society of women. Indeed, there is a repeated iteration through the whole series of comedies, usually voiced by the clowns, of the irresistible pull of sexual attraction, of the need to recognise it as a natural thing; there is also an intense awareness on the part of the heroines, particularly Viola, Beatrice and Rosalind, of the necessity for accepting this aspect of love, including it as a proper part of love, in a relationship which needs the qualities of affection and understanding besides. Throughout the comedies, there are four main conflicting pressures on the lovers which need to be brought into some sort of equilibrium: the force of physical attraction, the possibility of so strong a wish to feel the emotion of love that this is mistaken for love itself, the fear of committing oneself too far, and the need to commit oneself completely. The balance which is striven for is an understanding of all these forces, not a denial of any of them.

In the comedies, the world outside, the external situation, is not centrally important: what is needed for a happy ending is a human awareness by the characters of one another's feelings, and of their own. This is what the heroes, and to a lesser extent the heroines, who seem to possess this knowledge more intuitively, need to learn. If such an awareness can be achieved, then the world puts no final bar to happiness, though there may very well have been bars before, which have helped in the educative process. But I shall argue that in the tragedies, though the newly-gained awareness may only have been won through great suffering, the world still intrudes. Quite simply, in the tragic plays we are considering, the lovers are destroyed *because* they choose love above all other considerations; our tragic sense of loss, as well as that elation which comes from having been made more aware of the potential greatness of humanity, depend on our awareness of the quality of the relationship that the lovers have shared. It is worth noticing, though, that while tragedy makes a more obvious claim for importance, neither comedy nor tragedy can claim the greater share of authority; what they offer are related but different truths.

To return to *Love's Labour's Lost*: if the play starts by showing the impossibility of life without love, a truth that is apparently hidden from these seekers after wisdom, it soon moves to a consideration of the difficulties that stand in the way of a true love relationship. The folly of that convention of behaviour that makes young men pretend to scorn the society of women is only matched by the folly with which the same young men hurl themselves at the feet of the French Princess and her ladies, the moment they appear. The sexual urge, coupled with the desire to feel themselves to be in love, makes them as extravagant in their verbal love-making as ever they were in their vows of celibacy. The point is clearly made that this convention too must be broken down before any honest awareness of each other as individual human beings can be reached. Berowne is the point of growth in his little society: he and Rosalind are dramatically and thematically the most important pair of lovers, for through her he learns what she appears to know instinctively, that in order to love, man must break free from what is merely conventional in feeling, and in the language that expresses that feeling.

The set-piece of his speech on love, when he is asked by his friends to justify the breaking of their vows, lists the qualities that being in love confers on the lover, but is perhaps less impressive as a testimony to love's power than is his earlier wry admission that he, Berowne, the witty, sceptical, intelligent young nobleman, can be in love, and with a woman who isn't even the fair beauty of convention:

> And among three, to love the worst of all,
> A whitely wanton, with a velvet brow
> With two pitch-balls stuck in her face for eyes . . .
>
> (III, i, 192)

Berowne may still have a long way to go, but he is becoming aware of himself and of his feelings in a way that the others are not, and knows that it is Rosalind, with all her imperfections, that he loves, and not some idealised image.

The ending of the play, the sudden darkening of its mood with the news of the King of France's death, and the dismissal of the lovers to a year's penance amidst the harsh realities of that life from which their plans for an Academy were only a retreat, offers a look ahead to what is to be a great distinguishing characteristic of Shakespeare's comedy. The emphasis on the risk of love, its pain, its need to be anchored in reality, even if that reality is ugly and dangerous, is what makes it impossible to take even the most Arcadian of these comedies as a romantic escape or to see in them a facile belief that love itself will solve all difficulties. Here a conventional happy ending might not have been difficult to accept, but Shakespeare sounds a profounder note. These couples are only learning how to love; their careless cruelty, light-hearted though it is, to each other, and at the end, to their social inferiors in the presentation of the Worthies, their constant readiness to score verbal hits at the expense of true feeling, show how much they still have to learn.

Love's Labour's Lost in some measure emphasises the difficulties that stand in the way of achieving a true love-relationship, but many readers feel that *A Midsummer Night's Dream* comes close to denying that such a thing is possible. The absolute interchangeability of the two pairs of lovers, reinforced by the broad symbolism of the fairy juice, and by the visual image of Titania adoring the ass-headed Bottom are at once very funny, and very close to the classic prescription of demonstrating how ludicrous lovers in the grip of their brief but blinding passion really are. Hermia and Helena, childhood friends, are alternately scorned and adored by Demetrius and Lysander, in an almost farcical series of changes of partners resulting from Puck's mistakes with the devotion-inspiring juice. Eventually the confusions are sorted out, the lovers marry, and presumably live happily ever after. But a great number of qualifications are introduced into the way this merry-go-round action is presented: it is important, for instance, to notice that the changes start before the couples even reach the enchanted wood. Demetrius loved Helena before winning Egeus' consent to his marriage to Hermia. Hermia loves Lysander and loathes Demetrius. Yet as Theseus, himself a lover, points out, to the outsider there is nothing to choose between the young men.

> THESEUS Demetrius is a worthy gentleman.
> HERMIA So is Lysander.
> THESEUS   In himself he is
>   But in this kind, wanting your father's voice
>   The other must be held the worthier.
> HERMIA I would my father looked but with my eyes.
> THESEUS Rather your eyes must with his judgement look.
>   (I, i, 52)

The emphasis on eyes, so soon to be given an ironic twist by their anointing with the juice of the magic flower, shows how subjective are the lovers' judgements, and yet how impossible it is for them to be made in any other way.

If, as some critics have contended,[11] *Romeo and Juliet* comes close, at least until the death of Mercutio, to being a comedy, *A Midsummer Night's Dream* must be allowed to have a number of potentially tragic undertones. Hermia must make the most personal of choices at her father's command (as Bertram must do at the King's command in *All's Well That Ends Well*) and if she follows her heart and ignores him,

she must either die, or be forced to enter a convent and, as Theseus
warns,

> . . . live a barren sister all your life
> Chanting cold hymns to the cold fruitless Moon
>
> (I, i, 72)

Lysander's comment on the star-crossed quality of their fate, which in
his despair he sees as the inevitable desert of all true lovers, has a
movement and imagery that would make it seem perfectly in place in
that tragedy of young love, *Romeo and Juliet*.

> Or if there were a sympathy in choice,
> War, death, or sickness did lay siege to it,
> Making it momentary as a sound,
> Swift as a shadow, short as any dream,
> Brief as the lightning in the collied night,
> That in a spleen unfolds both heaven and earth,
> And – ere a man hath power to say 'Behold!' –
> The jaws of darkness do devour it up.
> So quick bright things come to confusion.
>
> (I, i, 141)

Nothing that comes later in the play quite bears out the seriousness
and sadness of tone of this, for the lack of differentiation among the
lovers, and the ease with which the partners are changed makes the
notion of a hostile world waiting to destroy those who love too well
seem somewhat remote. But there are other reminders as well, in the
upsetting of the seasons by the sourness of the jealousy in fairyland,
the quarrel between Oberon and Titania. In a sense, this dislocation
of the natural cycle is also natural, just as the cruelty and indifference
shown by the lover to one who loves him but whom he does not love
in return, and the jealousy Oberon feels at Titania's having a part of
her life from which he is barred, are also natural consequences of the
risk of loving. Titania's speech

> Therefore the winds, piping to us in vain
> As in revenge, have suck'd up from the sea
> Contagious fogs . . .
>
> (II, i, 88)

may be a description of a bad summer, but to anyone who is at all
familiar with the English climate, it is not absolute chaos that is being
suggested. Love, too, may undergo a bad season, because the line
between illusion and reality is so difficult to draw, but we must be

careful to distinguish between the 'humiliation' of Titania, who is
blissfully happy with her long-eared lover, and the real anguish of first
Helena, then Hermia, as each in turn is rejected by the man she loves
and pursued by one she does not want. The pain is not allowed to get
out of hand, of course: the interspersion of the scenes with Bottom and
his crew (the play they so happily mangle is itself a tragic love story),
together with the sense of the controlling power that Oberon provides,
see to that. The play remains a comedy, but there is enough, even in
the blunders that Oberon and Puck make, to suggest the possibility of
the roundabout having stopped with Helena paired with Lysander,
and Hermia with Demetrius, and to pose the question of what difference that would really have made.

It is an astonishing play in its balance of mood, and one that deserves
(as indeed any Shakespeare play does) much closer and more detailed
attention than it has been given here. I hope, though, that I have said
enough to suggest that what happens inside the forest casts a doubt on
the ultimate reality and value the lovers claim for their love that cannot
wholly be set at ease by the grace and dignity of the marriage celebration of Theseus and Hyppolita that forms the frame for the rest.
Though this does somewhat restore the equilibrium, Theseus, too, has
been the wild sort of lover, yet if *his* set-piece

> Lovers and madmen have such seething brains,
> Such shaping fantasies, that apprehend
> More than cool reason ever comprehends.
> The lunatic, the lover and the poet
> Are of imagination all compact:
> One sees more devils than vast hell can hold,
> That is, the madman: the lover, all as frantic,
> Sees Helen's beauty in a brow of Egypt:
> The poet's eye, in a fine frenzy rolling,
> Doth glance from heaven to earth, from earth to heaven;
> And as imagination bodies forth
> The forms of things unknown, the poet's pen
> Turns them to shapes and gives to airy nothing
> A local habitation and a name.
> Such tricks hath strong imagination,
> That, if it would but apprehend some joy,
> It comprehends some bringer of that joy . . .
>
> (V, i, 4)

seems to suggest that love is a self-induced state of hypnosis, there is
nevertheless more than a touch of respect allowed to the imagination of
the poet and by association, to the lover. The play opens and closes on
Theseus's love for Hyppolita, and the final, masque-like ceremony,

with its reminder that it is in the marriage bed that life itself is perpetuated, dismisses any suggestion of a simply satiric ending.

In *Much Ado About Nothing* the emphasis is less on the irresistible rush of love's madness than it is on those qualities of awareness, particularly self-awareness, that are necessary if two people, no matter what the power of sexual attraction between them, are to live happily together. In this play, too, there are the possibilities of mistaking, of the difficulty of distinguishing between reality and illusion. The essentially motiveless nastiness of Don John, who springs the plot whereby Claudio is convinced of the unchastity of his Hero, affords the opportunity for a searching look at the quality of Claudio's kind of love, which is so sharply contrasted with the vivacity and quick intelligence of Beatrice and Benedick that it is hard to decide which is the sub-plot and which the main. Beatrice and Benedick have to be gulled into admitting their love for each other, and the gulling makes use of the very quality that threatens to keep them apart, their pride. Each is told that the other loves, and each, of course, is only too ready to believe himself or herself worthily beloved. In their cases, though, this way through vanity leads to a true recognition of each other's value. There have been enough explicit indications earlier that they are attracted to each other, quite apart from the briskness of their verbal exchanges; in admitting their love, they have to face the mockery of their friends, and this they do with a rueful good humour that is very endearing. We cannot say that they are deceived about each other at any stage, for their process of falling in love is shown to be their getting to know each other, and themselves, better, and the recognition (of course in an essentially social and comic situation) that what they mean to each other is more important than anything else in the world. This is a comedy, but Beatrice's 'Kill Claudio' poses a real problem for Benedick, to which his challenge to his friend is a serious response, even though the audience is protected from real apprehension by the comic form. Both plots end happily, but from the point of view of my argument, the course of the wooing of Claudio and Hero is even more interesting than that of Beatrice and Benedick because of all the qualifications to the happy ending that are introduced along the way.

It is sometimes suggested that it is a specifically modern sensibility that feels that there is something equivocal about the happy endings to some of the comic strands in these mature comedies, and also in the problem comedies. Shakespeare's audience, it is argued, would not have bothered much about Claudio's repudiation of Hero at the altar: after all, he was deceived, and in the end he made amends. The same contention is applied to what to my mind is the extreme case of this,

Bertram's behaviour in *All's Well That Ends Well*. He accepts Helena in
the end, and therefore it is argued that as the play's title suggests, all
will be well. My feeling is that if we are to accept this merely conventional happy ending uncritically, then we need to ignore a great deal
else of what is demonstrably present in the plays, and settle for what is
in effect a failure in the organising and integrating power of Shakespeare's imagination. I have no wish to stand this particular argument
on its head, and maintain that the qualifications against simply accepting these endings are so serious that there is no hope of these marriages
being successful: I want rather to point out that all the comedies do
suggest doubts, that not one of these richest of all comedies will allow
an uncritical acceptance of an all-inclusively happy ending.

Claudio, deceived about the unchastity of Hero, provides an instructive parallel with Othello, and with the two later Romance heroes,
Posthumus and Leontes, though Leontes is wholly self-deceived. It is of
course difficult to see Claudio as deeply committed in love at any stage
of the play. He is a not untypical young man, who feels that it may be
time to think of getting married: Hero he remembers as an attractive
girl. He first prudently ascertains that she is her father's sole heir, then
allows his friend and commander the Prince to do his wooing for him.
He fears that he is being cheated by his friend, but is delighted when
Hero is won for him. All through the wooing, there is much of the air of
the merely conventional lover about Claudio, for though he is her
declared suitor, his whole being is not directed toward Hero in the way
that Beatrice and Benedick, with their constant awareness of each
other, even before they admit their loves, are directed to each other.
Claudio, if he loves, does so at a much lower intensity, so that when the
world intrudes, through Don John's plot, he shows little incredulity,
surprisingly little sense of personal loss. (Troilus' real anguish when
faced with evidence of the real infidelity of Cressida provides another
interesting comparison.) It is true that the Prince too, is taken in by the
trick, but then he is not really emotionally involved in the situation. It
is the conventional people of the play who seem unable to recognise the
importance of loving. This, it must be re-emphasised, is a comedy, but
even so Beatrice and Benedick are to some extent set apart from the
others, and there is more than a touch of malice in the way they are
mocked for their love, as if the rest of the world recognises their difference, and has no great relish in acknowledging it.

Claudio and the Prince are both much concerned with honour: this is
clearly an appropriate reaction, for the frequency with which Shakespeare returns to this theme of honour, in particular to the destruction of
personal integrity which a man feels when he believes that the woman

he loves has been sexually unfaithful to him, shows that this strength of emotion should not be underestimated. We may regard it as an ignoble feeling, produced by vanity rather than by love, but to do so is somewhat to mistake the point, for it would seem that for Shakespeare (and the Elizabethans generally) the more deeply the man loved, the more deeply wounding would be such infidelity. The cuckold, as all those jokes about horns testify, is a figure for ridicule, but perhaps so because of the ridiculers' fear of being in a like predicament; the wittold, the willing cuckold, is someone who is felt to deserve only contempt.[12] Nevertheless, despite the emotional charge that the situation itself would seem to contain, there is little evidence of Claudio's anguish or of really strong personal emotion in the rejection scene. The repudiation of Hero is so carefully acted out by Claudio, with so little concern for the feelings of anyone else, and above all with so little regret, that it is difficult to see it as a demonstration of anything but his own sense of conventional honour and of wounded vanity. Even when he hears of Hero's supposed death, there is no word of grief: it is only when the plot is revealed that he regrets what he has lost, but not so much so that he is at all reluctant about taking at once a substitute bride in Hero's supposed cousin.

Such a summary as I have given here clearly overemphasises the inadequacies in Claudio's feelings, and the total effect of the play, with attention at very least shared between these events and the wooing of Beatrice and Benedick, is something very different. But even when we consider the play as a whole it is difficult not to be left wondering. The fact that the villainy has been exposed by such frail ministers of justice as Dogberry and Verges, almost in spite of themselves, helps to suggest a world where the repudiation of Hero could well have been permanent, for those who know her best, Beatrice and the Friar, can trust her in spite of the evidence but cannot help her, while the man who claims to love her destroys her by his lack of trust. Such a situation, the situation of *Othello*, is clearly a potentially tragic one, and as such cannot hold the central place in a comedy, but enough of it is there to make it very difficult to accept uncritically as equal the prospects of happiness of Beatrice and Benedick, whose love is founded on knowledge and self-knowledge, and those of Claudio and Hero. Even if Hero's love carries more conviction than does Claudio's, her case, in love with a man who has given evidence of his readiness to believe ill of her, to forget her and marry another, looks ahead to Helena's in *All's Well That Ends Well*, and begins to suggest the problem of whether individual love, no matter how forgiving and understanding that love may be, is always enough.

As You Like It and *Twelfth Night* are the most mature, the richest and the
most satisfying of Shakespeare's comedies. I am therefore most conscious of the violence I do to them as works of art by abstracting from
them themes and attitudes to help in the elucidation of the love
tragedies. But help they do, for both these plays continue the exploration of the multitudinous facets of the love relationship that the earlier
plays have started, and keep widening their scope.

As You Like It is centrally concerned with the emotional education of
Rosalind and Orlando, this time in a context where malice, and on a
different level, scepticism, are far more direct threats than they have
been before. For Rosalind, it is a largely self-educative process as she
learns to come to terms with what she feels, to establish her love se-
curely in the face of the objections that cynicism, common sense and
external opposition advance, and emerges strengthened because she
can acknowledge the dangers and absurdities of her situation as well as
its ecstasies. In this progress, she leads Orlando along with her.

This play, like *Twelfth Night*, seems to me to differ somewhat from the
earlier comedies, in that it employs a principle of construction rather
like that used in the problem plays and tragedies: a central situation,
with minor situations and characters arranged around in such a way
that each provides a different comment, or a different point of view by
which what is central can be judged. At the centre of *As You Like It*, it
seems to me, stands Rosalind's love for Orlando, and everything else,
including the political situation that has brought the Duke Senior and
his Court to the Forest of Arden, is there to make that love more
comprehensible.

There are all sorts of challenges that Rosalind must meet, of which
the danger inherent in her disguised following of Orlando to the forest
of Arden is in some ways the easiest to deal with. Arden is not Arcady;
man's malice has driven both the good old Duke and Orlando to seek
safety there, but because the forest now holds an assembly of human
beings, it also shelters vanity, pretension and jealousy. Human relationships can perhaps be better sorted out away from the distractions
of court life, but the meetings with Phoebe and Silvius, Touchstone and
Audrey and the melancholy Jacques are hardly likely to allow to
Rosalind a wide-eyed faith in the power of love to conquer all.
Rosalind's situation, as a girl disguised as a boy who is pretending to be
a girl (we may perhaps ignore for the purpose of the argument here that
it would have been a boy playing Rosalind's part) gives her a unique
opportunity to express to Orlando those fears and doubts that must
trouble any lover, and allows her wryly to comment on her own silliness
and infatuation. In this way she learns to acknowledge that her own

love shares something of Phoebe's vanity and desire to exercise power over her lover, something of Touchstone's and Audrey's earthiness

> As the Ox hath his bow sir, the Horse his curb and the Falcon his bells, so Man hath his desires, and as Pigeons bill, so wedlock would be nibbling . . .
>
> (III, iii, 79)

something of Jacques' scepticism. She can see that 'men have died from time to time, and worms have eaten them, but not for love' at the same time that she can long for and accept Orlando's romantic extravagances as no more than her due. And she can achieve this clarity of feeling without any diminution in her love for Orlando; she delights in seeing that the excesses and exaggerations spring from the same intense feeling of desire and longing for possession. It is precisely because she realises this as a general truth that also has application to herself that she can achieve the blend of wit and tenderness, combined with the awareness of all that can go wrong, of her speech in the assumed Rosalind's character.

> ROSALIND Say 'a day,' without the 'ever'. No, no, Orlando; men are April when they woo, December when they wed: maids are May when they are maids, but the sky changes when they are wives. I will be more jealous of thee than a Barbary cock-pigeon over his hen, more clamorous than a parrot against rain, more new-fangled than an ape, more giddy in my desires than a monkey: I will weep for nothing, like Diana in the fountain, and I will do that when you are disposed to be merry; I will laugh like a hyen, and that when thou art inclined to sleep.
>
> ORLANDO But will my Rosalind do so?
>
> ROSALIND By my life, she will do as I do.
>
> (IV, i, 146)

She can be clear-sighted and without illusion, but without the self-satisfaction that Jacques so evidently feels at his 'realism'. Because she can accept that love can go awry, she can recognise the unique value of [1] her own love, and be confident in it.

Again one must insist that this is a comedy, but even so, the precariousness of a perfect love is shown up by the scene that follows, the wearing of the horns and the singing of the mocking song of cuckoldry. But Rosalind is in command, she can resist the confidence-shaking viewpoints of those who do not share her love because her love includes them all. She remains very much the spokesman of this play: the Duke can return to his Court only because of the improbable conversion of Duke Frederick on his way, with an army, to put an end to his brother. Celia can find happiness because of an almost equally improbable conversion in the wicked Oliver on *his* way to kill *his* brother. Jacques can only maintain his jaundiced view of the world by withdrawing from a reality that his philosophy cannot really admit, for the happiness of Orlando and Rosalind is as real as the malice of the play's beginning, but Rosalind, more than anyone else, has proved her right to that happiness by her awareness of its vulnerability.

Twelfth Night, the last of the comedies that I want briefly to examine here, is a marvellous achievement. From my partial point of view, it is also intensely interesting because of the kind of questions it raises. The central situation is the triangular one of Orsino in love with Olivia, who is in love with Cesario, the Duke's page, who is in reality the disguised Viola, herself in love with the Duke. There appears no solution to this problem until the introduction of the new element, hinted at throughout: Sebastian, Viola's twin brother. In one sense, though, his arrival creates almost more problems than it solves, for in the space of a few hours Olivia is married to a man about whom she knows nothing, Orsino has abandoned his heart's quest, which has occupied all the action of the play, and married a girl whom he has previously thought to be his page, while Viola herself is content with a man whom she has loved in secret, and about whom she can surely have few illusions, for he, until that moment, has been diligent in the pursuit of somebody else. Such a bald summary almost suggests that Sir Toby and his Maria have a better chance of a happy marriage than the two central couples, but again, I must emphasise that I would not dream of offering this as my account of the play as a whole. I have merely assembled some of the worrying elements in the plot: in the whole play they cannot prevent the ending from being a joyous one, and yet, throughout the play there has been an undertone of sadness, a sort of resonance of suffering, in which we may laugh at Olivia's wooing of Cesario, and yet be sorry for her, recognise that Viola needs to be lucky if she is not to have her diagnosis of her probable fate, in the recounting of her imaginary sister's history, come true. To reinforce these suggestions, there is Feste, with his songs, to remind us that love does not last, that youth fades, and that this is a more serious thing than the Duke's sentimental luxuriating in their melancholy can realise. Love can cause real heartbreak: there can be no certainty that Olivia and Viola will ever attain their hearts' desires, and the suffering that love may cause, which to Orsino provides only a pleasurably melancholy ending to Viola's story – 'But died thy sister of her love, boy?' – is very real to poor Olivia, trying to gather together her dignity and self-respect after being snubbed when she has offered her love. Even the hapless Sir

Andrew, with his wistful 'I was adored, once' is a reminder that everyone wants to be loved for himself. More so than in any of the other comedies, there are figures who remain unassimilated, unreconciled at the end. Malvolio, with his final 'I'll be revenged on the whole pack of you' is the obvious example, but there is also Antonio, who clearly cares deeply for Sebastian and has risked his life for him; what place is there for him? Sir Andrew is also left out of the reconciliation, and so too is Feste, whose song ends the play on a wistful and in a sense inconclusive note. It is true that both Malvolio and Sir Andrew are victims of their own vanity, and have deluded themselves, but the play at least poses the question of whether the unreality of Malvolio's expectations is any greater than those of Duke Orsino, who simply assures himself that Olivia, who has said repeatedly that she cannot love him, will come around. And at least Malvolio has had the excuse of the gulling letter.

It is a play that is much concerned with the relationship between love and self-love, with the way men can assure themselves that what they want will be so, against all the evidence. For the main characters, things turn out well in the end, almost in spite of themselves in the cases of Orsino and Olivia. Orsino is perhaps the luckiest of all, for Olivia is forced to learn a humility, to pay for her somewhat scornful rejection of Orsino's suit by her suffering at the supposed Cesario's rejection of hers, whereas he is allowed the prize of Viola's love without ever really having to prove himself worthy of it. Viola herself gets what she wants, what she has earned by her suffering and by her ability to put service before self, and if we have a slight nagging doubt that her reward is not altogether worthy of her, it is one to which the play does not allow undue prominence. Nevertheless, we are left with the feeling (as in *As You Like It* and *Much Ado About Nothing*) that this has been a very fortunate outcome, that had not Sebastian appeared somebody must have loved in vain, and as Viola says, to love without the possibility of response is to know the worm destroying the bud from within. It is a measure of the play's greatness that without in any way straining the comic form (for we gladly suspend our disbelief, and rejoice at the weddings that end the play, even if we do feel a little uneasy about Malvolio) we can nevertheless be made aware of the tragic potential of the love situation. All goes well, but these are not such urbane and civilised lovers that they could have shrugged off all disappointments, and started making their lives anew, without each other. Rosalind may declare that 'men have died, and worms have eaten them, but not for love', but she cannot prevent herself from swooning at the sight of the kerchief bathed in Orlando's blood, and her simple words, 'I would I were at home' when she comes round, show that she realises, in spite of all the play acting, how serious her love really is.

Ultimately, I suppose that what I want to say about these comedies is that the principal characters in them, the lovers, are *not* placed in situations which do not admit of solutions. They face dilemmas that are potentially tragic, and from these they learn about the nature of their feelings for one another, but solutions to the problems always appear, as the audience, prepared by the mood and tone of the whole work, is confident that they will. It is the essence of the tragic situation, as W. B. Yeats points out, that solutions are not available. In the love tragedies, these possibilities of broken faith, human malice, mistaking of the illusion for the reality, the clash of conflicting claims of honour and ambition, the operation of sheer bad luck, all these things produce disasters that are not averted by any miraculous intervention or lucky chance. Just as in our time pieces of machinery are tested to destruction, so Shakespeare tests the quality of his lovers' love, by subjecting them to a literally unendurable strain. The tragedies in fact deny that observation of Rosalind's, so apposite to her own play, for Romeo and Juliet, Othello and Desdemona, Antony and Cleopatra do die for love, for the situations in which they are placed make death the only way in which they can finally testify to the importance of that love.

However, before considering these tragedies, we should look at those intermediate plays neither properly comic, nor properly tragic: *Measure for Measure*, *All's Well That Ends Well*, and *Troilus and Cressida*.

CHAPTER TWO

THE PROBLEM COMEDIES AND *TROILUS AND CRESSIDA*

MANY CRITICS have been unable to see the three plays, *Measure for Measure*, *All's Well That Ends Well*, and *Troilus and Cressida*, as belonging comfortably to the category of either comedy or tragedy, and have therefore agreed on the somewhat misleading designation of 'Problem Plays'. This is misleading because in one sense, any play by Shakespeare is a problem play; we are never presented with neatly-encapsulated solutions to human problems. But these three plays demonstrate this open quality to a marked degree. They seem to deny any kind of certainty to the reader, yet most critics are not prepared to dismiss them as artistic failures because of this lack of resolution, though of course that is one possible way out of the dilemma.

It may be useful briefly to run through the principal three critical approaches to the plays. As I have suggested, one group of critics[1] denies to them, particularly to *All's Well That Ends Well* and to *Measure for Measure*, the artistic unity allowed the rest of Shakespeare's mature work. These plays are held to defeat any attempt at consistent reading because they are themselves inconsistent, because Shakespeare has patched a conventionally happy ending on plays that earlier seemed likely to end in tragedy. Such a pattern does not apply to *Troilus and Cressida*, since it does not end happily, but this play is held to be merely chaotic in structure, and therefore confusing in effect.

Those who see the plays as unified can be roughly divided into the optimistic[2] and pessimistic[3] groups. The former sees the happy endings as acceptable, sustained by qualities like justice, tempered with mercy, as exercised by the Duke in *Measure for Measure*, or by the forgiveness and redeeming love of a good woman, Helena, in *All's Well That Ends Well*. *Troilus and Cressida* is usually given the full status of a tragedy, with the gallant, sensitive, intuitive Trojans destroyed by the efficient but heartless practicality of the Greeks.

The pessimistic group,[4] in which I include myself, sees the plays not only as consistent in individual effect, but also strongly related as a group, sharing a distinctive mood that is, to quote Dowden, 'serious, dark, ironical'. In spite of the confidence expressed in the titles of the 'comedies', the ostensibly happy endings focus attention on human inadequacies, while in *Troilus and Cressida* the deliberately inconclusive nature of the ending makes a similar sort of point about the corruption of all human ideals by human self-interest and vanity. We have already identified such a questioning note in the endings of even the earliest comedies, an indication that in less happily fortunate circumstances, some, at least, of the lovers might find their love too weak to withstand internal and external pressures. It is my contention that it is this group of plays that deals with exactly those predicted situations, where love is tested and found wanting. Some critics see this pattern in *Othello* and *Antony and Cleopatra*, but there it seems rather the case that the tragedy of love lies in the fact that the lovers may be broken and destroyed, no matter how strong their love. Finally, in the Romances, as I hope to show, the lovers miraculously survive the apparently tragic situation, and are allowed to continue, stronger than before, made more aware of their value to each other by their suffering and by their experience of the loss of each other.

No responsible critic would, I suppose, deny that the three 'problem plays' are in their different ways, very much concerned with love, in particular with the relation between love, sexuality and some other human ideal or aspiration. In *Measure for Measure* that other quality is justice; in *All's Well That Ends Well* forgiveness, and the nature of honour in a love relationship; in *Troilus and Cressida* the love theme, for all its prominence, is subordinated to the more general picture of the collapse of a whole society when all its values and ideals, love, honour, order, morality, are corrupted by self-interest. All the plays overlap in their concerns, and all are obviously concerned with moral choices, with the nature of right and wrong, and how this varies with varying circumstances. The different states of being in love, what these states do to our perceptions, our judgement, our ability to distinguish between appearance and reality, value and worthlessness, right and wrong, these are Shakespeare's preoccupations here, complicated by his awareness of the terrifying strength of man's sexuality.

All's Well That Ends Well is the most puzzling of these plays, and perhaps the one that is least artistically satisfying. The traditional success story of the virtuous maiden healing the King and being allowed as a reward to choose a husband (the direct source is a story of Cinthio)[5] is given a strikingly different implication in Shakespeare's retelling of it. Though at one time I must admit that I felt there was something remorseless about Helena's pursuit of Bertram, I no longer feel that her actions or her love for him are held up for serious criticism. It is perhaps her misfortune to love a young nobleman who, by his caddish behaviour throughout the play, gives almost no sign whatsoever of being worthy of her. He is nobly born: in the Italian wars he proves to be a dashing leader of cavalry, but unless one is going to adopt an absurdly permissive attitude to the notion that a man's honour will allow him to bed every attractive wench in sight, regardless of the suffering he may cause, there is no escaping the fact that he is a callous, conceited young ass, gullible to a degree, as his trust in Parolles shows, and capable of quite despicable behaviour to Helena his wife and to Diana whom he believes has been his mistress. He shows up at his worst at the very end, in the scene of his unmasking. He is hypocritical in his protestation that he has come to love the memory (as he thinks) of his dead wife, dishonest in the business of the rings, callous in his repudiation of Diana, and, if we think what Shakespeare's accomplishment makes of a reconciliation and recognition scene in say, *King Lear*, or in the statue scene in *The Winter's Tale*, Bertram is perfunctory in his acknowledgement of his fault and in his acceptance of the wife he has rejected and in intention, betrayed.

That Helena loves Bertram is not in question: she, through her modesty and courage, proves her worthiness as a lover, but his has to be taken entirely on trust, and the signs are not favourable. The best things that can be said of him are that he is young, and that he has inspired Helena's love, but if he doesn't really want her, of what use is that? He keeps to the letter of his word. She has fulfilled the apparently impossible conditions of his oath, and so he must surrender, but there is very little indication, if any, that he has learned much from his experience, or indeed that he is capable of learning. The parallels with Posthumus and Leontes are again instructive, for there we are left in no doubt about their awakening to the true worth of love and to the merit of the wives they have previously scorned. There can be no doubt about the change of heart in these erring husbands. Bertram does promise that if what Helena claims is true, he will love her 'dearly, ever dearly' but we are left uneasy. He must concede that he lay with her without recognising her, without the episode even leaving him with the memory of a night of high passion, for the pursuit and conquest of (as he thinks) Diana has already receded from his mind, as an unmemorable affair. Helena's bed-trick has in a sense worked too well, for it has reduced the act of love to a physical coupling where the man cannot recognise the identity of his partner. It seems probable, as is the case with Angelo's

inability to realise that it is Mariana and not the desired Isabella who
has been in bed with him, that it is lust that produces this blindness,
and makes what should be a mutual act into a solitary gratification. In
both cases the result of the successful tricking of the man is enforced
marriage with the woman he did not want; in both cases, if one is to
accept the outcome as happy, this lust must somehow be turned to love,
and there are few, if any, indications that this is a likely outcome, unless
the bare theatrical convention is in itself held to be convincing.

Helena's predicament is that she cannot help but love Bertram;
whether or not he loves her in return, whether or not he is completely
out of her sphere, she loves him and there is nothing she can do about
it. She loves him so truly and selflessly that she can even give him up, as
when, after his indignant refusal to comply with the King's command,
she offers release from the bargain.

> That you are well restored my Lord, I'm glad:
> Let the rest go.
>
> (II, iii, 147)

Her happiness, her honour, her fulfilment lie in being a good wife to
him, but much as she loves him, her love may not be enough to launch
them together into a happy and stable future.

Oddly enough, Bertram himself, unpleasant as he undoubtedly is,
comes in for a share of sympathy in the play, particularly at the point at
which he is being constrained to accept Helena as his wife. The play in
no way excuses his snobbery and his contempt for 'A poor Physician's
daughter', though his case may perhaps have sounded more understandable to Elizabethan ears than it does to ours, but he seems to be
allowed a quite valid point when he protests that he cannot be commanded to love, that he should not be sacrificed in a marriage that he
does not want merely to salvage the King's word.

BERTRAM   My wife my liege! I shall beseech your highness
          In such a business give me leave to use
          The help of mine own eyes . . .
   KING   Thou knowest she has raised me from my sickly bed.
BERTRAM   But follows it, my lord, to bring me down
          Must answer for your raising? I know her well:
          She had her breeding at my father's charge—
          A poor physician's daughter my wife! Disdain
          Rather corrupt me for ever!

> (II, iii, 106)

'I cannot love her,' he says a little later, 'nor will strive to do't,' and it is a reasonable argument, if the matter of individual choice in love has any validity at all. In the end, as we know, Bertram's attempts to escape are defeated. He has to acknowledge Helena as his wife in the exact terms of his insulting sexual repudiation of her, and the very fact that this is a defeat and not a willing change of heart is what must make us sceptical of the literal truth of the play's title.[6]

Mariana's situation in *Measure for Measure* is very like that of Helena, though she does not occupy the centre of the stage to anything like the same extent. She also gets what she wants, the husband who has previously repudiated and abandoned her, through substitution of herself in his bed in place of the virtuous maiden he is seeking to debauch. We are even more uneasy about her prospects for happiness. Her Angelo is to be married to her and then to be put to death as a punishment for his corrupt rule as the Duke's deputy, and for his attempt to ravish the innocent Isabella. His only verbal reaction to this news is to ask for speedy death:

> ANGELO   I am sorry, that such sorrow I procure
> And so deep sticks it in my penitent heart
> That I crave death more willingly than mercy,
> 'Tis my deserving, and I do entreat it.
>
> (V, i, 474)

He has always been a proud man, and death seems to him a lesser punishment than to have to live with the exposure of his frailty. Angelo utters not one word at the news of his reprieve; it is not easy to be as confident as the Duke is, at the outcome of this part of his experiment in making the punishment fit the crime.

The play as a whole, working within the context of the dispensation of justice, is concerned with the way men come to terms, if they can, with their natures as sexual animals. Part of Angelo's way we have already seen: it is first to deny that he is subject to the same desires as other men, then, when this can no longer be maintained, to surrender utterly to his sensual side. Laws to control man's sexuality even when enforced with the severity of an Angelo, cannot be made to work, unless, as Pompey suggests, one is prepared 'to geld and splay all the youth of the city'. Even the Duke, who has earlier denied, in a memorable phrase, that 'the weak and dribbling dart of love' could ever pierce *his* complete bosom, is at the end making a suggestion of marriage to the determinedly chaste Isabella, with what result we do not know. Almost every incident in the play has its connection with the sexual act, and usually with the strong suggestion of copulation as a commercial transaction. Claudio and Julietta have delayed their marriage vows,

but not their lovemaking, to make sure of a dowry; Claudio is condemned to die because Julietta's pregnancy has revealed them as for-
nicators. Angelo has abandoned Mariana because her dowry has been
lost. Pompey and Mistress Overdone are imprisoned because of their
bawdy trade, but all the brothels are not to be closed down—a 'wise
burger' has used his influence on behalf of those in the suburbs, and in
any case the Duke, by his substitution of Mariana for Isabella in
Angelo's bed, is in some sense performing the same sort of bawd's
office.

By exploring the Duke's own motives for his abdication of power the
play as a whole sets up an experiment within an experiment, for if the
Duke's dual purpose, which he, disguised, observes and seeks to control, is to test Angelo's integrity and to reform the corrupt state of
Vienna, the play surely shows the Duke as himself being tested. Various people in the play are given power of various kinds, Angelo the
power of life and death over Claudio, which he callously uses in his
assault on Isabella's virtue; Isabella's attraction has power over him;
the Duke manipulates lives with his power over them all; but what
emerges from all this exercise of power is that nobody uses it well or
disinterestedly. Isabella's speech, when pleading with Angelo for
Claudio's life suggests that nobody *can* ever use it well:

> . . . But man, proud man,
> Drest in a little brief authority,
> Most ignorant of what he's most assured,
> His glassy essence, like an angry ape,
> Plays such fantastic tricks before high heaven
> As make the angels weep; who, with our spleens,
> Would all themselves laugh mortal.
>
> (II, ii, 118)

In the way I read this play, this strongly suggests that it is human
nature to use power to obtain what one wants, and though what different people want varies, as indeed we see with Angelo, the motives for
whose behaviour change from pride in an austere reputation to an
overpowering desire for Isabella, in every case they are led by their
wills. Thus Isabella wants to preserve her chastity at all costs, not
because this is a truly religious feeling, but because she enjoys the
contemplation of her own virtue, while the Duke, anxious to be the
almost superhuman dispenser of justice tempered with mercy that his
soliloquy at the end of Act III, scene iii suggests, convinces himself that
he is this, quite disregarding any damage to human feelings that may
be done in the course of his plot, or in his confident apportioning of

reward and punishment at the play's end. For all his confidence, what has he achieved? Vienna does not seem markedly less corrupt as a result of the whole masquerade of the Duke's departure, his testing and unmasking of Angelo, the condemnation and reprieve of Claudio, and the subjection to stress of Isabella, nor, as we have seen, do any of the principal figures seem to have learned much. Angelo's reformation has to be taken very much on trust, and as for Isabella, her

> I partly think
> A due sincerity govern'd his deeds
> Till he did look on me . . .
>
> (V, i, 443)

in her plea for Angelo's life does little to suggest that she has come to any more measured estimate of what she sees as her moral and physical superiority.

Measure for Measure is a more interesting and disturbing play than *All's Well That Ends Well*; I see it as having a principle of construction, like that of *Troilus and Cressida*, whose purpose is to emphasise the lack of those virtues of concern for others, judgement, unselfishness, love, which can reduce the anarchy of human behaviour to order. It is a play that has what I have elsewhere suggested can be called a disembodied centre,[7] for while the qualities claimed by certain characters for themselves are not shown in the play, their absence points up their vital importance. Man, 'most ignorant of what he's most assured', his own nature, is in desperate need of love and understanding, but in the world of this play, these qualities seem out of his reach.

Troilus and Cressida, which shares this ironic vision of man's imperfections, in many ways offers the most interesting comparison with the love tragedies. I have already remarked that some critics see it as being essentially one of them, a contention that I would deny, because of the division of its interest between the distinct but related concerns of the love story, and those suggested by the progress of the war, as determined by the success of the Greek efforts to get the reluctant Achilles back into the struggle.

It might even legitimately be argued that this play, if tragic, is as much the tragedy of Hector, slain ignominiously by the Myrmidons, as it is of Troilus, who is left disillusioned but alive at the end of the play. The common factor which links the stories of the two brothers, and includes the scheming of Ulysses and the disorder in the Greek camp as well, is perhaps the question of judgement, of the estimation of value in

human actions and of the human difficulty in arriving at such a judgement. Here too, human ideals are examined, and their frailty and their
easy contamination by self-interest exposed.

Within two areas of passionate commitment in human affairs, love
and war, the clashes between self-interest and disinterestedness, between self-love and love for something or someone outside oneself,
between the desire for reputation and truly honourable conduct, are
shown, with in every case the ideal being defeated by human vanity.
Thus for all of Ulysses' intelligence and craft, both his appeals to the
ideal of order and his scheme to play on Achilles' pride are unsuccessful. When Achilles does return to the battle it is for a reason, the death
of Patroclus, that is quite unconnected with Ulysses' efforts, and in any
case Achilles' intervention, which takes the form of the brutality of
Hector's death, though disastrous for Troy, cannot really be seen as
admirable, since it does not even signal the restoration of order among
the Greeks.

Hector has revealed his own flawed idealism in the Trojan council,
when, after acknowledging the moral need to return Helen to the
Greeks, and admitting all the destruction and suffering that the war has
caused, he nevertheless affirms that Helen must be kept, because 'she is
a theme for honour and renown' (II, ii, **199**). This contradiction in his
attitude can only be explained by looking closely at the concept of
honour by which he lives, and as it happens, dies. For Elizabethans, the
conflict between humility and reputation was a complex one, as Curtis
Brown Watson[8] has shown, and the difficulty of a resolution is pointed
up by Hector's fate. His own view of honour is exposed as an absurdly
simple one, closely allied to the notion of fame. His naivety in this, the
central value of his life, makes credible his action in sending the challenge to the Greeks, even when his intelligence and moral sense tell him
that the war should be ended, for he sees the war primarily as an
opportunity for demonstrating his chivalric qualities. As his argument
with Troilus in Act V scene iii shows, he allows himself to be blinded to
what the war really is, so that he may follow his own ideal of it. It is in
keeping with the ironic justice that this play metes out to all its characters that he dies because of this blindness. Pride has prevented him
from doing what he knows is right, in the Council scene, and pride,
symbolised most clearly in the image of the rotting corpse inside the
suit of rich armour that he has so avidly pursued in the field of battle—'I'll hunt thee for thy hide' (V, vi, **31**)—takes him out to his death,
despite the pleadings of his father, wife and sister. He tuts-tuts at
notions of war's savagery when Troilus chides him for giving fallen
Greeks a second chance, but Troilus is right and Hector is wrong, for

the second chance that his chivalric rules allow is not allowed to him, and he is butchered at the hands of Achilles' Myrmidons.

It needs to be said that in spite of Hector's own vulnerable simplicity of attitude, the response to him that the play requires is a complex one, for the values for which he claims to stand, and in part does stand, humanity, mercy, fairness, and courage are not themselves discredited by his fall. We are meant to admire these qualities in Hector, in so far as he can live up to them, and to loathe the cowardly action of Achilles, whose own life Hector has just spared. We are forced to acknowledge, though, the way in which Hector's ideals are put to the service of his desire for glory, for they are contaminated by the same self-interest that taints the reasoning of Ulysses or, as I shall now argue, the love of Troilus.

For this study, it is the love of Troilus, its quality, and its outcome that are of paramount interest: my contention is that he, like the other central characters in this group of plays, is blind to the truths he most needs to know, and that it is his own desire, swaying both will and judgement, that produces the blindness. He may be more clearsighted than Hector in his view of the nature of war and its savagery, but if he is, this makes his argument for the retention of Helen, and thus the war's prolongation the more reprehensible. But it is as a lover that he primarily engages our attention, and indications are not lacking, from the very first scene, indeed from the Prologue, that our awareness of the inadequacy of his ideal of love is to be extended by a method that is very characteristic of this group of plays, a method that makes extensive use of the principle of anti-climax and of ironic juxtaposition.

In the opening scene, Troilus appears in the character of the typical courtly lover, proclaiming that he cannot bring himself to fight outside the walls of Troy, when he finds 'such cruel battle here within' (I, i, 3). His conventional expression of the pangs of disprized love (in tone not unlike the laments of Romeo over Rosaline) is not the chief thing to be noticed here, although the rhetoric does strengthen the impression of artificiality of feeling. What our attention is being directed to is the gap between the way Troilus sees his situation, and what that situation is shown to be. Both he and his emotions are critically presented, for there is a level of meaning in the verse of which he himself is not conscious. After the bawdy exchange with Pandarus, it is hard to believe either that his friend is reluctant to help in Cressida's wooing, or that Troilus himself can believe that she will be 'stubborn-chaste against all suit'. (I, i, 99). No matter what we are led to understand about Cressida's betrayal of Troilus, and of course Shakespeare treats her with very much less sympathy than did Chaucer his Criseyde, any audience must see something comic in Troilus' insistence that she is 'stubborn-chaste'. Even Troilus himself does not give any subsequent indication that he believes that this is really so, but here, in this opening scene, he enjoys the contemplation of himself as the disappointed but persevering lover. His speech, like the opening speech of Orsino in *Twelfth Night*, which expresses a very similar attitude, is not exactly insincere, for it expresses what he feels to be appropriate emotion, but what is also conveyed to the audience is the admixture of self-satisfaction, which prevents the emotion he claims from being taken too seriously, from extending beyond the bounds of convention and convincing us of an actual suffering.

It is, moreover, a dangerous self-satisfaction, for it is only achieved at the cost of refusing to see Cressida as she really is. In the other plays named after pairs of lovers, there is enough to convince us that Juliet's Romeo, or Antony's Cleopatra, can exist, though these views of them are not held by anyone but those who love them. In *Troilus and Cressida* there is nothing, even in Cressida's view of herself, to show that Troilus' Cressida exists anywhere but in his own fancy. Even as early in the play as this our awareness of the extent of his delusion is being built up. The fanciful and delusive nature of his image to describe his wooing, with its commercial basis of himself as the merchant and Pandarus as the ship, sent to purchase Cressida, the pearl beyond price, is later further pointed up by his application of virtually the same image to Helen, here dismissed as a blood-rouged doll not worth keeping. Finally, in the first scene, which like so many of Shakespeare's first scenes seems to suggest so much of what is to follow, there is the alacrity with which he abandons his role of lover for that of warrior, in spite of his previous protestation that he is so much love's servant that he cannot bear to fight. The savagery and destruction of war have already been condemned in the shocking image of Helen, splattered with the blood of the slain

> Helen must needs be fair
> When with your blood you daily paint her thus
>
> (I, i, 90)

but this attitude is quickly abandoned on Aeneas' entry. Now the battle is a 'sport' to which Troilus will hurry, since Cressida's refusal to be won denies him better 'sport' at home. In little, it is a perfect illustration of the way his emotions are directed by what he wants at the moment; the depth of all his protestations of love must be measured against this unawareness that what he feels is determined by what he thinks he ought to feel. He is not hypocritical, but the audience is undoubtedly being given a greater understanding of him than he has of himself, and is being accustomed to seeing him in this critical way. The close parallel between Helen and Cressida, insisted on by Troilus himself, helps to place the whole affair in an unsympathetic light. Diomed's judgement of Helen, when stung by Paris' taunts

> She's bitter to her country: hear me, Paris:
> For every false drop of her bawdy veins
> A Grecian's life hath sunk; for every scruple
> Of her contaminated carrion weight,
> A Trojan hath been slain: since she could speak,
> She hath not given so many good words breath
> As for her Greeks and Trojans suffer'd death . . .
>
> (IV, i, 69)

reflects back on Cressida, for she, like Helen, is in Troilus' estimation, a pearl beyond price, not because of what she is, but because of the value that is set on her. Troilus, in his argument to the Trojan council, and in his own life, puts his trust in his dictum 'What's aught, but as 'tis valued?' Troy is destroyed, and his own life is ruined, because his will constructs a worth where no such worth exists.

It is objected by some who see Troilus as a tragic hero, precisely because of this trust, that this faith in the value that love confers on the loved object is an essential part of the lover's condition. He is not the less in love because his loved object is worthless, or other than what he thinks her to be. We have seen, though, particularly in *A Midsummer Night's Dream*, how Shakespeare can suggest that while this is a part of being in love, it is not the whole story. Bottom remains Bottom, with the ass's head firmly on his shoulders, no matter what Titania may feel, and Bertram for all of Helena's love of him, remains (in the reading of *All's Well That Ends Well* I have suggested) someone of no great worth. So long as the great discrepancy between illusion and reality exists, the possibility of a shocking disillusionment also exists, as Troilus discovers. Antony, by contrast, knows what Cleopatra is, and in one sense, loves her in spite of what she is, though in another he loves her because he knows what she is. In *Romeo and Juliet* the question does not really arise, while in *Othello,* as we shall see, the fact that Othello is *deceived* into believing that Desdemona is corrupt and not what she appears to be, gives a wholly different emphasis to the situation.

I would not deny that if anyone in the play has any right to the status of a tragic hero, that person must be Troilus. He is the most important single character, and unites in his actions and feelings the twin strands

of the play's action, the progress of his love and the progress of the war.
When he is forced into a recognition of Cressida's infidelity he is placed
in a situation in which he might manage that painful progress to
greater self-awareness that is, for me, the distinguishing mark of the
tragic hero. But he learns nothing about himself, and therefore, though
we may pity him, we do not respect him, for he clings determinedly to
that first illusion which has given life to all the other illusions, his view
of himself. We remember that from the first, his estimation of Cressida
has been a hopelessly false one, yet the fact that he has been wrong
about her is much less important than the fact that he has used this
image of her to sustain himself in his roles of courtly lover, of volup-
tuary ('Expectation whirls me round'), of the faithful lover whose lips
are sealed although his heart is breaking when she is forced to leave for
the Greek camp, and at last, in the role of ruthless warrior. The famous
scene in which Troilus, Cressida and Pandarus in turn claim the
characters they will have in history, surely reinforces, among other
things, our awareness of this relish in all three of them in their contemplation of the roles they play. Both Troilus and Cressida, in fact, manage to extract some satisfaction out of all the changing roles through
which their love story takes them, even those of remorse and betrayal.
The central point about Troilus' love is not that it has surface intensity
but no adequate foundation, as Traversi[9] argues, nor that it must be
accepted as strong in itself even if Troilus is unable to see the real worth
of Cressida, nor that his passion lacks reason to guide and control it.[10]
What the play insists on is that Troilus has been unaware of the real
nature of his feelings. When the crisis comes, what he has thought to be
his controlling passion is shown to be inadequate as a value either to
live by or to die for. He has strong feelings, it is true, of shock, bewilderment, disillusionment, but throughout he appears to feel more
strongly about himself, as the faithful but betrayed lover, than he does
about the loss of Cressida's love. This self-regarding quality, which has
been apparent from the beginning, and which has shown his love to be
much less idealistic than he has claimed it to be, becomes hysterically
insistent when he is confronted with the proof of her infidelity. When he
sees Cressida, who has apparently already forgotten him and is
embarking with little show of reluctance on a new sexual liaison with
Diomede, he is also confronted with a choice of reactions, which, in
dramatic terms, constitutes a crucial test of his love, and of his own
integrity. His love is clearly not strong enough to allow him to say, as
Posthumus comes to say of Imogen, that her infidelity does not alter his
love for her, no matter how much it hurts him. One cannot blame
Troilus too much for this (though as the pattern of fidelity he has set

himself high standards), since Shakespeare repeatedly shows us how profoundly disturbing the notion of sexual infidelity is to a man. But leaving that issue aside for the present, we are aware that at this moment of crisis Troilus must either acknowledge that he has been wrong about Cressida, admit, in other words, that he has been wrong in his opinion of himself and of the world around him, or retain his illusions about himself, and look for some other less hurtful reason for his betrayal. To put it plainly, Troilus can either admit that he has made a fool of himself, or he can claim, as in fact he does, that anyone would have done the same. The nature of his confusion, and its basic underlying cause, are revealed in the echoes of his argument at the Trojan court for the keeping of Helen, where his impassioned appeal 'What's aught but as 'tis valued?' was a plea for the primacy of the will. His example, 'I take today a wife . . . ' then made it clear that he regarded the operation of the senses—'traded pilots 'twixt will and judgement'—as properly under the control of the will. Reason is explicitly rejected; a man should see what he wants to see, and form his judgements accordingly. Helen appears to be worth keeping, for she is seen, not even in Hector's terms as 'a theme for honour and renown', but as worth keeping because she was worth stealing in the first place. Though reason advocates her return now, to consent would be to admit an initial mistake, and to do that would be to admit dishonour. Troilus habitually dislocates the normal order, the weighing of information received from the senses by the judgement and the translation of the judgement by the will into action. For him the will may impose *its* judgement on the senses, and see only what it wants to see. A similar solipsistic obsession is to be found in the unregenerate Leontes, who, however, can eventually make the bitter admission that no matter how powerful his will, it cannot refashion the world around him to his desires. Troilus cannot admit this, though he too has his cruel confrontation with reality. He cannot admit that his will has misled him, he cannot question the basis of all his values, his belief in himself, and therefore his will has in sheer self-defence to change direction. His pain and bewilderment are intense, but sympathy for his suffering should not obscure the central dramatic and poetic point of the scene, his continuing self-delusion.

At first he affects not to believe the evidence of his senses, trying still to make his will their master.

> . . . yet there is a credence in my heart,
> An esperance so obstinately strong,
> That doth invert the attest of eyes and ears,
> As if those organs had deceptious functions,
> Created only to calumniate.
> Was Cressid here?

(V, ii, 120)

His language has a clotted quality which reflects the turning and twist-
ing of his mind as he tries to escape from the truth. To deny that this is
the Cressida he loves is a comfort only to his wounded vanity, as is the
hysterical charge that if she is false, then all women are so. Such a
vision of a universal corruption is shared by a number of Shakespeare's
characters when, at moments of intense sexual bitterness and disillusion, they try to evade the pain of the recognition of a particular
sexual infidelity, real or imagined. The difference between Leontes and
Posthumus, say, and Troilus, is that they regain their balance through
recognising their own errors, something that Troilus cannot apparently
do. Cressida, too, has tried to evade individual responsibility for her
actions by blaming her sex, but has done so much more perfunctorily,
as if she can hardly be bothered to excuse her behaviour. The way in
which we are intended to view Troilus' suffering here is surely clearly
indicated by the provision by Shakespeare of two commentators on his
reactions, not only the scurrilous Thersites, whose cynical view of all
life is obviously a partial one, but Ulysses as well, who by this point in
the play has established himself as an acute and reasonable observer of
the follies of others. In this instance, at least, he is a disinterested
onlooker, and his cool matter-of-fact replies to Troilus' frenzied questions tend to point up Troilus' delusions. When he answers 'I cannot
conjure Trojan' to Troilus' query of whether Cressida has really been
there, the implication is that unlike Troilus, he has neither the ability to
conjure up phantoms to deceive, nor the inclination to evade the obvious
reality of the situation by juggling with words. His sardonic question
'What hath she done, prince, that can soil our mothers?' may be
unsympathetic, but besides providing a vehicle for the audience's own
feeling towards Troilus, it also helps to reassert the world of actuality
which Troilus tries to dismiss. Thersites, who as might be expected
relishes Troilus' discomfiture, is more brutally direct in his comments:
'Will he swagger himself out on's own eyes?' (V, ii, 136). He accurately
identifies the vanity ('swagger') that lies behind Troilus' passionate
self-deception. If Troilus can convince himself that fidelity does not
exist, that all men are deceived in love, all women corrupt, then his own
deception, his own error, is less blameworthy. The distortion of a vision
that would rather see the whole world as corrupt than admit its own
mistake is, as we have noticed, not uncommon in Shakespeare, but
whereas characters like Leontes and Posthumus, or even Lear, with
whom Troilus shares the pain of intense disillusionment, learn through
their suffering, Troilus never does. He finds it easier to seek solace in
the belief that all others are deceived as well, that it is the nature of love
to be deceptive, and thus to avoid the risk of any further self-
examination.

The exact sense of the long speech in which Troilus declares that all order, all integrity have been negated by Cressida's defection is not easy to follow, for he is far from clear in his own mind about what he thinks and feels. His confusion may be a shield for him, but it does not prevent the reader from recognising the same obvious and major flaw that his thinking has consistently shown. Because Cressida's beauty has seemed perfect and has been proved false, then he argues, all beauty is deceptive, all truth falsehood and all value in love negated. The whole fabric of the argument rests on the naive premise that what looks beautiful must be good. There is of course no reason, other than that his love for her makes him want to believe it, that Cressida should be sexually honest *because* she is beautiful: Diomedes, and those who welcome her to the Greek camp, recognise her frailty without difficulty. Troilus, in his agony of disappointment, condemns not his own failure to see what everyone else has seen, but love itself. He must still declare that he loves Cressida, for what he believes of the relation between will and honour

> . . . how may I avoid,
> Although my will distaste what it elected
> The wife I chose? there can be no evasion
> To blanch from this and to stand firm by honour . . .
>
> (II, ii, 65)

compels him to do so. But the feeling he now calls love has in it no tenderness, no understanding of Cressida's predicament. It is used solely as a measure of the hate he bears his supplanter, to whom the blame he may not feel himself is shifted. The chaos that he sees all about him is preferable to admitting that he has been mistaken in his point of reference; he makes no attempt to establish another, and all remains chaotic and violent about him to the end of the play. His speeches in their verbal contortions, incoherent rhythms and straining of sense mirror this chaos he creates, the confused despair that is itself a retreat from something worse. His love for Cressida and her fidelity had seemed inseparable, but now they divide 'more wider than the sky and earth'. In an image that combines and confuses the tangling web of the spider, Arachne's vanity and Ariadne's clew of thread, the point is made that he is quite incapable of taking the only way out of the maze of his illusions and vanities. Self-knowledge is the clue, but self-knowledge is what his pride makes him shun, and so, like the spider's victim he is ensnared, and all that remains for him is a struggle and a waiting for death. All the sexual bitterness he feels at his betrayal must be directed at externals, and comes out in the ironic reminder of his earlier, confident

> . . . the remainder viands
> We do not throw in unrespective sieve . . .
>
> (II, ii, 70)

Now the bonds of heaven have been replaced by the knot of Cressida's hand, 'five-finger-tied' to that of her new lover, and she is rejected with revulsion.

> The fragments, scraps, the bits and greasy relics
> Of her o'er-eaten faith are bound to Diomed.
>
> (V, ii, 159)

Some critics, it is true, feel that Troilus' love is strong enough to survive the shock of disillusion, but this crucial scene surely suggests just the opposite. Henceforth Troilus thinks only in terms of a revenge on Diomede, on the Greeks, and on the world that will not conform to his desires. The energy with which he hurls himself into the battle is not that of a man fighting for an ideal (again the comparison with Posthumus is an interesting one) or even for self-preservation, but rather the fury of a mad dog, destroying as much as it can before it too is destroyed.

It is Troilus' impotence that emerges most clearly from these final scenes, his inability to find any purpose in either life or death. Even when the opportunity for revenge offers itself, in the chance meeting with Diomede on the field, Troilus cannot put into execution his horrendous threats, and is denied any kind of satisfaction or resolution. His own wilful blindness to his situation, Cressida's easy infidelity, and Diomedes' cynical opportunism, make the audience not at all disinclined to agree with Thersites' commentary on the inconclusive battle: 'Hold thy whore Grecian!—now for thy whore, Trojan!' (V, iv, 24). When they meet again, Diomede has stolen Troilus' horse as well, and it is now over this loss, and not that of Cressida, that Troilus waxes passionate

> O traitor Diomede! turn thy false face, thou traitor,
> And pay the life thou owest me for my horse!
>
> (V, vi, 5)

Troilus' love could hardly be exposed to a grosser deflation than to have to yield place to this quarrel, with its obscenely ironic suggestions, over a horse.

Nobody in this play seems to advance to a clearer understanding of what he is or what he feels, as do the lovers in the comedies and tragedies alike. In the spheres of deepest personal involvement, love and war, no human quality is discovered strong enough to withstand the corrosion of self-interest, or the corruption of time. The men and women in this world are self-deluding, vain, shallow, futile and contemptible, so that it seems only fitting that the action of the play should tail off into a slack and meaningless disorder, with the last, still inconclusive word given to the syphilitic Pandarus. But in spite of this, the play does not profess a universal cynicism and despair, for it does not claim an exclusive truth. The consequences of corrupt notions of honour, of a lack of order, of a failure to recognise the true nature of love, and therefore of a failure to love truly, are shown with chilling clarity, but to conclude that the play therefore holds that these ideals themselves are corrupt is to miss the point. The need above all for love and understanding is convincingly demonstrated by their absence: in the tragedies, to which we now turn, the lovers learn, too late perhaps, though perhaps in such situations, knowledge can only come too late, what they are, what they believe in and care about most greatly. That they learn this only at their deaths is their tragedy, but at least, in dying for each other they discover a value and a purpose which, if only in retrospect, gives coherence and value to their suffering. It is this sort of value that I cannot find in *Troilus and Cressida*, and its lack is what makes me believe the play is not a tragedy, or that if the nature of its ending makes us feel that it holds some tragic undertones, that they relate to a civic or political tragedy, the fall of Troy through the perversion of its values, a perversion which is shared by Trojan and Greek alike, and of which Troilus, like Hector, is merely an example.

CHAPTER THREE

ROMEO AND JULIET

IN THE PREVIOUS CHAPTER I argued that neither Troilus nor Cressida was presented as a lover who could command the sort of imaginative sympathy and admiration necessary for acceptance as a tragic figure. The more we understand them, the less tragic they become. Pathetic they may be, but though in the end we pity them, we cannot recognise in them that greater awareness to which truly tragic figures attain, and which confers on them their tragic stature.

I do not want to be drawn into an attempt at a precise definition of tragedy: as I have already indicated, I do not believe that such precision is possible, even though we may readily recognise the effect of some plays as tragic, or comic, or satiric, and trace in them the characteristics which are responsible for producing these effects. Thus we may say, I hope, that *King Lear* is a tragedy, without implying a detailed pattern of tragedy to which the play must conform and which it shares with all other tragedies. Too rigid a definition of what tragedy ought to be is one important reason, it seems to me, why a good deal of adverse criticism has been directed at *Romeo and Juliet*: it has been attacked primarily for being an immature or defective tragedy. The dangers of such an approach can readily be seen in some of the criticism of the play written in the first half of our century. By asking the wrong questions, some able critics have blinded themselves to those qualities that are there.

There may be some excuse for looking for signs of immaturity, for this is an early play, written between 1591 and 1597, with the consensus of opinion dating it in the mid-nineties. Of the other plays that can be called tragedies, only *Richard III* and *Titus Andronicus* are reckoned to be earlier. It is followed by *Richard II* and is clearly linked by similarities of theme and style with the Sonnets, with *A Midsummer Night's Dream* and with *Love's Labour's Lost*. If it is noticed that the play shares with these other works a concern with the clash between love and time, with the intense and potentially delusive nature of passion, and, particularly with *Love's Labour's Lost*, an awareness of the difficulty of finding a mode of expression that is adequate to communicate an intensely felt emotion, in a society where not only expression but feeling as well is threatened with restriction by convention, then its real nature is more likely to be recognised. Perhaps most of all we need to recognise in it an obvious and exuberant interest in language, not so much for its own sake, as has sometimes been claimed, but because this youthful energy and vitality itself reflects and comments on the central love situation.

There seems little doubt that A. C. Bradley's work has set the guide-lines for much twentieth century discussion of the play. Committed as he was to a theory of Shakespearean tragedy that depended on the identification of some moral flaw in the protagonist, he was almost certain to find this pattern distorted or partially absent in *Romeo and Juliet*. It is true that he calls it a 'pure tragedy' but he sees it as 'an early work, and in some respects an immature one'.[1] In particular, he notes in it a lack of conflict in the hero, with little if any of that mirroring of an inward conflict in the external struggle, which is for him one of the hallmarks of Shakespearean tragedy. We may note ourselves how his grouping of Romeo with Coriolanus and Antony misses the point of their differences of situation, in order to make the play the 'pure tragedy' he requires. 'How could men escape, we cry, such violent propensities as drive Romeo and Antony and Coriolanus to their doom? And why is it that a man's virtues help destroy him, and that his weakness or defect is so intertwined with everything that is admirable in him that we can hardly separate them, even in imagination?'

Bradley, it goes without saying, is a highly intelligent and sensitive critic, whose detailed accounts of the plays themselves are by no means as distorted as some of the general statements of his theory might seem to suggest. Elsewhere, he recognises that neither *Romeo and Juliet* nor *Antony and Cleopatra* really accords well with his general theory, and it is common knowledge that when he comes to *Othello*, he shifts a good deal of his attention from Othello himself to Iago, in order to render the play more tractable. Certainly Bradley's moral preoccupation seems an unpromising way to approach *Romeo and Juliet*, a play which devotes a great deal of its dramatic and poetic energy to showing how irrelevant the moral judgements of their elders are to the young lovers' situation. Perhaps Bradley's work should lead us to suspect that if a critic of his acuteness and sensitivity cannot make out a wholly convincing case for a noble hero with a tragic flaw in any of these plays, then the organising

principle of these love tragedies should be sought elsewhere. Predictably, it is critics who share Bradley's general approach who are most
worried by *Romeo and Juliet*'s supposed inadequacies. G. B. Harrison,[2]
looking perhaps for some clearer focus of moral interest than the lovers
themselves can afford, thinks that the feud, its course, and its final
abandonment over the grave, are the most important things in the play.
H. B. Charlton calls it a radically unsound play, and one that cannot
bear careful examination, since the Roman idea of destiny, on which he
says it depends, cannot provide 'the indispensable inevitability
required for a true tragedy'. He admits the play's popularity, but feels
that

> . . . as a pattern of the idea of tragedy, it is a failure. Even Shakespeare
> appears to have felt that, as an experiment, it had disappointed him. At
> all events he abandoned tragedy for the next few years and gave himself
> to history and to comedy; and even afterwards, he fought shy of the
> simple theme of love, and of the love of anyone less than a great political
> figure as the main matter for his tragedies.[3]

I can scarcely think of a passage of reasonable criticism with which I
am in more whole-hearted disagreement, though Parrot,[4] too, argues
that Shakespeare was acknowledging failure by the ten-year gap between the probable date of *Romeo and Juliet* and the great tragic period.
Such comments make me wonder whether it is not the particular critic
rather than Shakespeare who has fought shy of the theme of love, and
wonder too, why it should be forgotten that success is an even stronger
reason than failure for a true artist not to repeat himself.

More recently, critics have been more prepared to accept the play on
its own terms; it is not as great a play as *Hamlet* or *King Lear*, but it is an
excellent play of its kind, and one that has its own very important place
in the Shakespearean canon. For this is Shakespeare's account of the
nature of young love, of its intensity and of its terrifying vulnerability.
It is his first taking up and working out of some of those hints which we
have seen in the comedies, the suggestion that no lovers can feel themselves wholly secure from the world around them or from the dangers
within them. In the comedies, such threats are averted, sometimes by
good management, sometimes by sheer good luck. Here, though these
lovers lack nothing in strength and sincerity and passion, the luck runs
against them, and they are destroyed. Romeo and Juliet, particularly
Juliet, are not without those qualities of wit and intelligent self-
awareness the comedies show as necessary for the success of a love
relationship, but these qualities are given little chance to develop or
endure. Within four days Romeo and Juliet meet, fall in love, marry,
part and die: there is no time for slow ripening. What their bad luck

robs them of most of all is time; because their love is the all-consuming passion of first love, they have the illusion that they are independent of time, but, in the constantly repeated paradox of the Sonnets, time is both love's creator and its destroyer. Love cannot exist out of time, but once brought into being, it can only be destroyed:

> Ruin hath taught me thus to ruminate,
> That Time will come and take my love away.
>
> (Sonnet 64)

It is thus the common fate that Romeo and Juliet endure, but it is given terrible dramatic emphasis by the swiftness with which they are destroyed. Yet if this is a tragedy, it is a tragedy of a very special kind, for I believe that this play cannot satisfactorily be accounted for either as what might be called an Aristotelian tragedy, whether successful or not, or a tragedy on the medieval pattern. Romeo and Juliet do not hold important positions in their society, the plot does not arise directly from their characters, and while it may comprise a significant action in Aristotle's sense, it depends too much on chance and coincidence to conform to his requirements. The medieval definition of tragedy as an unexpected fall from prosperity into misery, produced by the operation of fate, the revolution of fortune's wheel, may be nearer to the mark, as Professor Dickey suggests,[5] but even the more complex kind of medieval tragedy, where the human suffering produced by unrestrained passion leads to some moral enlightenment, and is thus included in some greater pattern of divine purpose, leaves too much in this play unaccounted for.

For one thing, the action is so fiercely short, and so shot through with foreboding, that the description of an unexpected fall from prosperity to misery hardly seems to fit the case, and most important of all, attention is concentrated so firmly on the lovers themselves that it is very difficult to see the play as a whole as an example of the way that fortune fulfils God's purpose by turning men's eyes from this world to the next. It is true that even if we are unwilling to feel particularly directed towards a criticism of the excessive passion of the lovers, there is the moral issue of the feud, the external force directly responsible for five of the six deaths in the play, which is only healed over the lovers' grave, but it seems hardly justifiable to see the story of the lovers as labouring to this end. Their love, as the Prologue informs us, and as we are constantly reminded in the course of the play, is foredoomed, yet the final catastrophe depends on a remarkable number of coincidences and mischances. There is the servant who brings the invitation to the Capulet

ball to a party of Montagues for interpretation, the intervention of
Mercutio in the quarrel between his friend and Tybalt, Romeo's well-
meaning obstruction, which causes Mercutio's death and consequently
Tybalt's. After Romeo's banishment, there is the delay in the delivery
of Friar Lawrence's message explaining the stratagem, the Friar's own
failure to arrive at the tomb in time, and the final desperate bad luck of
Juliet's awakening only moments too late to save Romeo's life and her
own. If this is a tragedy that depends on a strong line of causality, it is a
very badly constructed one indeed, for none of these accidents seems
necessarily a result of some strength or flaw in hero's or heroine's
character. In spite of Professor Dickey's careful study, I feel that the
brevity of time spanned by the play, and the extreme ill-luck, both
serve the purpose of directing our sympathy, and in the end our admiration, towards the lovers, whose death is seen as a sort of triumph over
time, as well as a defeat. And this emphasis on bad luck makes the
lovers' choices seem all the more audacious.

Many recent critics[6] have followed Coleridge in seeing the lovers
themselves as the focus of interest in the play. T. J. B. Spencer, in his
Penguin edition of the play argues the case very convincingly, and
Norman Rabkin in his chapter 'Eros and death' in *Shakespeare and the
Common Understanding*, besides much else that is relevant, offers a suc-
cinct argument for seeing the interest in the love affair as central.

In the account that follows, I shall try to show why I think that the
play concerns itself with the nature of a particular kind of love, first
love, that intense sexual attraction that by its very nature cannot long
remain as it is. In the ordinary course of life, this change is accepted
because it is inevitable; either the love withers away, or changes into
some other kind of love, of equal or perhaps even greater value, but
different in kind. In this play, it is protected from change, heightened
and intensified by the sense of doom that pervades the play, but for that
very reason, immune to time's decay, because neither we nor the lovers
are ever allowed to believe that their love can last long enough to
exhaust its first intensity. In that sense their love wins a victory over
time, but since such a victory can only be won out of time, the love
must end in death; in this sense it is self-defeating.

This love, seen against the background of hostility that the feud
provides, is the subject of the play, which within the situation the feud
creates is concerned with the effects of the intensity of their passion on
the lovers themselves, in particular with the way in which their discovery of each other gives a sense of purpose and meaning to two young
people who have, when the play opens, hardly yet begun to live. There
is abundant evidence that Romeo, in love with love in his relationship

with Rosaline, is looking for such a purpose: he so absolutely finds one in his love for Juliet that the boy who lay blubbering on the floor of Friar Lawrence's cell is at the play's end a man who takes the decision for life or death with a mature sense of responsibility and certainty. Juliet, not yet 14 (it is difficult to see any reason other than the stressing of her initial immaturity that could lead Shakespeare to reduce her age from that given in his sources), starts as a girl who regards marriage as 'an honour / That I dream not of'; within a few days she has become a woman who, quite alone, can choose to risk death, and face the most terrifying implications of that choice, rather than contemplate life without her husband. The lovers themselves have neither the time nor the inclination to attempt to come to terms with the hostility and lack of understanding of their world: its hostility becomes the occasion for the destruction of their love, but that love is doomed by its very nature, for as we are reminded by the chain of images of lightning, fire, and gunpowder which runs through the whole play, love of this intensity is a consuming passion which cannot last. Shakespeare heightens its intensity, and its poignancy, by keeping us constantly aware that it will be cut off, constantly aware that though the lovers may love in interludes in a world seemingly released from time, as in the moment when they meet, or in the single night they spend together, even they themselves are made aware that their only real release from time is in death. They are defeated, as all who love must ultimately be defeated, by their own mortality, but by being prepared to die for each other Romeo and Juliet establish a quality of love, of life intensely lived, that becomes its own value. They choose to die, as in their different ways the lovers in the other two love tragedies also choose to die, because each knows that he or she cannot live without the other, and knows this as a simple, literal truth, to be acted on at the first opportunity.

If the play is seen in this way, many of the objections and criticisms that have been directed at it lose much of their force. In any case the finding of wholesale weaknesses, even in an early play, is something that ought to make any critic reconsider the basis of his own reading, for it is always necessary in a play by Shakespeare to look for an organisation that will include in an harmonious whole as many of the play's characteristics as possible. This is not to argue that everything in all the plays is carried out with equal success, for to expect even Shakespeare always to maintain his own highest standards would be absurd. But without wanting to seem idolatrous, it does seem to me that we ought to regard with some suspicion a reading which finds radical flaws in the organisation of a play's material. The point of any scene or incident can generally be discovered, even if on some occasions we feel that the intention has not been perfectly realised. As I hope I shall be able to show, if the shortness of the time spanned by *Romeo and Juliet* is seen both as an expansion of the moment of falling in love, and at the same time as a means of intensification of that love, seen as a maturing force, then many of the charges of inadequacy, of faultiness of plot and extravagance of language that have been directed at the play fall away. This remains true even though, in the special circumstances in which the lovers find themselves, the only operation of that maturity is to choose to live no longer.

Romeo and Juliet has always been a popular play, as the four quartos that appeared before the First Folio testify, and it has continued so. Not only the many performances of the play itself, but the vitality and success of its many offshoots, dramatic, musical and cinematic, pay tribute to the potency of the story alone. Students, nowadays very much on their guard, as Helen Gardner has in another context commented,[7] against anything that can be called sentimental, find it moving and deeply interesting because it is true to their own area of experience. That this area of experience in the play has well-defined limits is not to be denied; Shakespeare by his foreshadowing of the end constantly reminds us of these limits, but within them the play is certainly not simple. The question of the responsibility of the lovers' actions, in particular of the suicides, is thoroughly explored, as is the testing of the quality of their love by the attitudes and actions of all who surround them. Trapped by their love for each other in a world where they can find neither effective help nor real understanding, they are made to inhabit in dramatic fact the sort of illusory isolation that the feeling of being in love confers on its votaries. Because of the hostility of their environment, they are forced to decide whether they really do care more for each other than for the whole world. If the play succeeds, and I believe that it does, then it does so by giving new meaning to the typical lovers' cliché of 'I cannot live without you'.

For me the strongest indication that Shakespeare is in full control in the shaping of this play is the extraordinary skill with which he overcomes the problems that his compression of the time span produces. In the direct sources, Bandello's story as translated by Arthur Brooke in his long narrative poem (1562),[8] and by William Painter, in prose, in *The Palace of Pleasure* (1567), the action occupies a span of some months: the lovers meet at Christmas, Tybalt is killed after Easter, and Romeo spends some months in banishment in Mantua before marriage plans set the feigned death plot in motion. But Shakespeare, presumably to intensify the passion and better to communicate the effect of the first full force of young love, compresses all this into four days, yet at the same time that he conveys the headlong rush of young love as well as the headlong assault of unlucky circumstance, he also manages to give the impression of both Romeo and Juliet growing in maturity, growing in understanding of each other and of themselves, as they become more fully alive under the influence of their love.

As I have already suggested, it is Romeo who has farthest to go: when he is first introduced he clearly cuts a somewhat ridiculous figure. His attitudinising affectation of the courtly lover, as seen in his father's description of him,

> Many a morning hath he there been seen,
> With tears augmenting the fresh morning's dew,
> Adding to clouds more clouds with his deep sighs;
> But all so soon as the all-cheering sun
> Should in the furthest east begin to draw
> The shady curtains from Aurora's bed,
> Away from light steals home my heavy son,
> And private in his chamber pens himself,
> Shuts up his windows, locks fair daylight out,
> And makes himself an artificial night . . .
>
> (I, i, 131)

though in some sense looking forward to his choice of death at the play's end, in tone seems oddly at variance with the much starker introduction given to him by the Prologue, and reinforced by the open-ing scene of the quarrel between the servants of the Montagues and the Capulets. As T. J. B. Spencer points out,[9] the tone of this first scene, with its bawdy jokes, its ignorance and its triviality makes the feud seem tawdry, but not the less dangerous for that. The servants may enjoy the exercise, old Capulet calling for his long sword and being offered a crutch instead by his wife may seem childishly foolish, but Tybalt's arrival

> What, art thou drawn among these heartless hinds?
> Turn thee, Benvolio, look upon thy death . . .
>
> (I, i, 65)

shows how triviality can become an excuse for chilling cruelty and hatred. At no point in the play is the feud dignified by having any reason offered for its existence; dramatically it is there to allow men to reveal their pettiness and malice. As the Duke's judgement indicates,

its consequences are disorder, violence, bloodshed, suffering for the
innocent and for the community as a whole. It can in fact be argued
that this play, in which the hero and heroine are sometimes seen as
wilfully ignoring all good advice in following the inclinations of their
passions to their own destruction, has as its truly destructive force the
feud itself, which is kept in being by the pure exercise of the wills of
those elders engaged in it. At their first appearance both Capulet and
Montague are shown as obstinate and jealous old men; little that
Capulet does later suggests that he is able to show any better judgement in any other area of his life. Even his quelling of the quarrelsome
Tybalt at the masquerade, which has the momentary appearance of a
greater tolerance, soon reveals itself as being a straight clash of wills in
which Capulet's concern is to have his own way.

But to return to this first scene: there is an apparent contrast set up
between the ready acceptance of the destructive hatred of the feud by
everyone at large and the love-sick Romeo's indifference to its existence, as he seeks only to withdraw from the world. The images in
which he is described, however, besides drawing our attention to the
artificiality of his feeling, also begin the fore-shadowing of his fate. The
world of daylight, of the feud, of the concerns of the warring families,
may be love's enemy, but love shares the world of darkness with death,
and love and death draw ever closer together as the play proceeds.

When Romeo himself appears, his enjoyment of his role as the
repulsed and love-lorn suitor of Rosaline is very apparent. His speech is
extravagant, his paradoxes on the nature of love utterly conventional,
his classic cause of disappointment not his rejection because he is the
wrong man, but Rosaline's determination to live a life of chastity. In
short, as Coleridge noticed,[10] he is presented as a young man ripe to fall
in love because he is so much in love with the idea. But when he falls in
love with Juliet, he is protected from any charge of infidelity or incon-
stancy by the very conventional impersonality of his language here, and
by the lack of real concern over his state shown by any of his friends, or
even by himself. His apostrophes to love carry very little conviction,
and his eager readiness to enter into argument with his friends on the
subject indicates how little his true sensibilities are engaged. The point,
in fact, would appear to be obvious; I have gone on at this length
because the criticism that much of Shakespeare's writing in this play
has been more concerned with manner than with matter, is, in part,
based on these first glimpses of Romeo. Romeo himself, in his readiness
to match wits with Mercutio and his friends, is much more concerned
with manner than matter, but that is a very different thing. When he
sees Juliet and falls in love with her, his starting point may still be this

conventional way of thinking and talking about love, but what the play then shows is his progress away from these conventional attitudes to an understanding and an expression of what he really feels.

The introduction of Juliet, too, sees her placed in a thoroughly conventional setting. We first hear of her from her father's disclaimer to Paris of any desire to force her into a too-hasty marriage, or to make her choice of husband for her. From this encounter, and from Juliet's own acceptance of her place as a young girl, the only child of doting parents, watched over by a bawdily garrulous but kind-hearted nurse, there is little to indicate any inclination on her part, or need to go against her parents' wishes. But already attitudes very important for the play's later development are being suggested. It is clear that Paris is regarded as being a very good match by Juliet's parents, and that, in spite of old Capulet's disclaimers and Juliet's own youth, 'It is an honour that I dream not of' is her answer to her mother's question of what she thinks of the prospect of marriage—a man nevertheless is being chosen for her, and this in spite of her mother's own experience of what, on the available evidence, we must assume to have been a not very rewarding marriage made on the same sort of basis. Juliet is old Capulet's only surviving child and he sees her very much as a possession. His pun on earth speaks volumes, while her mother urges Paris' case with a rather more than disinterested force. More even than Romeo, Juliet is being urged to yield to age its traditional prerogative, that it knows better, and must therefore be allowed to choose a course of action for youth.

Her nurse, who would seem to be her natural ally against authority, is only partly that, even at this stage of the play. She does seem to show at first a warmth and genuine affection for Juliet, and an awareness that marriage is a more personal relationship than a mutually profitable merging of fortunes. But if her view of marriage seems less cold than that of Juliet's parents, it is soon shown to be as partial, and in its own way, as calculating. For her, what marriage offers is sexual pleasure: this is what every woman needs, and whether Juliet realises it or not, any man will do as a partner, provided he is virile enough, as her praise of Paris as 'a man of wax' shows. Because the nurse is so splendid a character part, and also because of the way in which she helps the young lovers to their marriage, and to their single night of love-making, there has been a tendency to treat her part in the play somewhat too sympathetically. It is important for the play as a whole to recognise that her philosophy is both simple and inadequate, and that it does not change. Here she is prepared to urge Juliet to marriage with Paris. When the situation changes, she will be as willing to help Romeo to Juliet's bed, and when it changes again, and Romeo is

banished, then without any sense of incongruity, she can return to her
advocacy of Paris.

Hers is a view of the sexual relationship that is set against the exclu-
siveness of the love claimed by Romeo and Juliet, but it is not one that
ultimately has an ironically deflating effect, because that relationship
includes in itself a more discriminating awareness of and respect for the
physical than the Nurse can ever imagine. At this, her first appearance,
the Nurse's dramatic function does not extend much beyond showing
by her earthy good humour that, like the Capulets, but with a different
emphasis, she sees love in strictly practical terms. Juliet's modesty and
meekness here, like Romeo's early immaturity, make her growth in
feeling and confidence during the play all the more remarkable.

Mercutio, Romeo's quick-witted and bawdy friend, has a similar
function to that of the Nurse as a tester of the quality of Romeo's and
Juliet's love. His is the cynicism of a wider vision than that of the
Nurse, because he sees a general principle where she sees only a particular human truth. His Queen Mab speech, so close in tone to much
of *A Midsummer Night's Dream*, assembles a number of examples on the
theme of man's ability to deceive himself into thinking that whatever he
happens to desire most is most valuable. His picture of the Fairy Queen
herself is a beautiful one, but he recognises that she is insubstantial,
fantastic; the dreams she sends deny the possibility of disinterested
love, or any disinterested action, for the Courtier, the Clergyman, the
Soldier, the Lover, all fabricate their own ideals and illusions out of
their own desires. When chided by Romeo for talking nonsense, his
answer seems to sum up his whole philosophy:

> True, I talk of dreams;
> Which are the children of an idle brain,
> Begot of nothing but vain fantasy,
> Which is as thin of substance as the air,
> And more inconstant than the wind, who woos
> Even now the frozen bosom of the North,
> And being anger'd, puffs away from thence
> Turning his face to the dew-dropping South.
>
> (I, iv, 96)

Mercutio's anti-romanticism brings him close to the Nurse, for like her,
he sees the romantic protestations of the lover as a rationalisation of a
simple urge to get his mistress into bed. But he is a much more complex
character than she, for there is something strange about an imaginative
power than can produce something as vivid as the Queen Mab speech,

and yet apparently can find no purpose in life worthy of occupying this quickness of intelligence. Odd too, is the way in which Romeo, in his foreboding, for all that he is still 'in love' with Rosaline, can see no clear purpose or direction as the end of his life.

> But he that hath the steerage of my course
> Direct my sail! On lusty gentlemen.
>
> (I, iv, 112)

Interestingly, in these early scenes of the play, neither Romeo nor Juliet is presented as at all isolated or distinctive in their respective societies. Romeo has his friends, and as is soon disclosed, another close companion in his confessor, Friar Lawrence. Juliet is firmly ensconced in what looks to be an ordinary family situation. But when they fall in love, we see that their conventional relationships become meaningless. This is, in Juliet's case at least, prepared for by the way in which she is gradually revealed as being in that most daunting of family situations, one where there is lip-service paid to the familial bonds of affection, but where her parents show a complete lack of imaginative understanding of her as an individual. Capulet's self-characterisation, in his tedious and embarrassingly jocular speeches at the masquerade, his dwelling on what a gay dog he used to be (his wife is not yet 30) shows an ageing man accustomed to having his own way, and one wholly satisfied with himself. As the play goes on to show, his pompousness, his unshakeable conviction that he always knows best, can quickly change to bad temper and to a sort of obtuse cruelty when he finds himself thwarted. Old Montague does not play much part until the play's ending, but if he is at all like old Capulet, it is easy to see how the feud has been perpetuated.

If we remember that almost a fifth of the play has elapsed before the lovers see one another for the first time, we may better appreciate how careful Shakespeare has been to establish the essential ordinariness of his hero and heroine. It is the unique strength of their feeling for each other that is to distinguish them from the world around them, but the play does not ask for that uniqueness to be taken on trust, for it has already been suggested how much such a feeling of uniqueness may stem from pure physical attraction. The Nurse and Mercutio both suggest criticisms against which the claims made for their love by Romeo and Juliet must be judged, and established, if we are to believe with them that their love is something out of the ordinary.

Seen from the point of view of the establishment of this special quality, the falling in love, and the subsequent balcony scene, are beautifully managed; the lovers are protected from the charge of

romanticising by the very fact that Romeo tends to do so and is cor-
rected in this by Juliet. Moreover, in spite of the shortness in represented time of the scene, there is a definite progression from the
charming formality of the first exchanges at the masquerade to the
simplicity and directness of Juliet's avowal of love, the whole being
given urgency and tension by the sense of danger, not now some vague
'consequence yet hanging in the stars' but defined and focused in
Tybalt's malice, which announces itself at the very moment Romeo
falls in love.

In falling in love Romeo speaks the only language that he so far
knows, but even from his first sight of Juliet, though the convention of
his speech is the same, it is very clearly being informed by a far stronger
feeling than Rosaline could ever inspire. There has been some critical
complaint about the artificiality of his first question to the servant:

> What lady's that, which doth enrich the hand
> Of yonder knight?
>
> (I, v, 40)

Spencer even suggests that the servant fails to understand because of
the extravagance of the phrasing! It seems to me though, that Romeo's
words have a raptness and seriousness of tone in spite of their extravagance, which is admirably sustained when Romeo goes on

> O, she doth teach the torches to burn bright!
> It seems she hangs upon the cheek of night
> Like a rich jewel in an Ethiop's ear . . .
>
> (I, v, 41)

The suggestion of enrichment, reinforced by the image of the rich jewel
standing out against a dark background, that even the unobtrusive
'knight'–'night' pun helps to intensify, of course looks forward to the
final scene, where Romeo finds the brightness of Juliet's beauty in the
darkness of the tomb, but much more directly than that, its movement
suggests the way in which he, who came only to confirm the superiority
of Rosaline, has been surprised into an awareness of Juliet's beauty.
His speech continues in rhymed couplets, but the spontaneity of his
first exclamation is not thereby diminished. It is a measure of how far
he has forgotten his former state that he himself uses the crow comparison that had drawn from him such an ornate rebuttal (I, ii, 87) when
Benvolio had used it to decry Rosaline's charms. The dramatic effect of
this, his first sight of Juliet, is very striking, the more so because
Tybalt's outburst makes the audience realise, even before Romeo
knows it himself, that he has put his life in jeopardy.

There is a strong and obvious element of formality in this first meeting of the lovers, as they speak alternately their conventional courtly compliments in the rhymed patterns of the sonnet. It is very difficult to comment adequately on the deftness with which Shakespeare manages the exchange, for a number of aspects of this first meeting are held in a delicate balance. The lovers are in public, and therefore on the first level are exchanging polite conversation, yet the vivacity of both emerges from the skill and quickness of wit with which, inside this formal situation, they explore one another's feelings, with each indicating an interest in the other without in any way overstepping the bounds of decorum. The ease with which they fit their conversation into the formal pattern indicates not only accomplishment, evoking Juliet's teasing accusation of practice—'You kiss by the book'—but also a natural harmony between them. The language of the exchange in its imagery of religious devotion fits squarely into the Petrarchan convention. Perfectly suitable for this sort of situation, it must nevertheless be abandoned in favour of some plainer speech, which Juliet teaches to Romeo, under the stress of the danger that accompanies each further step in the love affair. Here, though, the good humour and good manners of the exchange provide a most stable foundation for the rapid development of their love, for the decorum and restraint which they show here, for which there is no time later, in some measure protects them from the charge of being swept away by their passion, and blinded by the sheer force of the sexual attraction they feel for each other. Here the leisurely movement, fitting so well with the visual picture of the dance going on behind them, gives a poetic and dramatic illusion of the scope of time they might in other circumstances have been allowed.

Henceforth, urgency is never absent from their wooing, and though the intensity of their love sometimes gives them the illusion of an enclosed world, away from the operations of time and other men's affairs, it is more accurate to say that right up to the final unlucky mischance in the tomb, they are terribly aware of time's passage. At this moment of their meeting they cannot choose but love, though each recognises without yet fully appreciating the danger. Romeo's 'My life is my foe's debt' and Juliet's

> My only love, sprung from my only hate
> Too early seen unknown, and known too late
>
> (I v, 138)

simply accept without question the inevitability of their love, just as, later, each will accept the inevitability of suicide rather than life without the other. To say this, though, is not to suggest that they are carried away by the flood of their passions like mindless bubbles on a stream. What they learn is what the lovers in the other two tragedies are also forced to learn: that as they become more aware of its value, so they also become more aware of the cost that their love exacts. As I have already suggested, though the time depicted by the play is only of four days' duration, this growth to awareness is presented as a gradual one. Romeo, who such a short time ago was the sworn lover of a girl who barely seemed aware of his existence—the fact that she too is a Capulet did not then seem to threaten any danger, perhaps because there was no suggestion of a real relationship—is still inclined to strike attitudes and to indulge in verbal flourishes. The difference now is that a greater awareness both of what he himself feels, and of the mutuality of that love, keeps supporting and strengthening his language. He has become immune to the gross obscenities of Mercutio, witty though they are, which can now be shrugged aside with a simple statement that his friend does not know what he is talking about—'He jests at scars who never felt a wound'—an image that suggests at least some awareness of the danger and the pain of loving. This kind of new-found confidence seems to me to carry absolute conviction, and to provide the answer to those critics who argue that Mercutio has to be killed off by Shakespeare because his point of view is becoming too dangerous to the love affair. The reverse seems rather to be true: he has made with wit and an attractive liveliness his point that romantic love is, like every other human ideal, a rationalisation, in this case for the simple sexual urge. Romeo and Juliet, because they do not deny the physical but find more in each other than Mercutio's philosophy can dream of, are not damaged by the criticism that his bawdy talk suggests, nor are we made to feel that the Nurse's earthy commonsense points to something that is lacking in their attitude. If they indeed saw their love in the pure and abstract terms of Romeo's love for Rosaline, then the presence in the play of both Mercutio and the Nurse would be damaging to our view of the lovers; as it is, their understanding of what love is is more comprehensive than that of any of those who, by implication, criticise them.

The famous balcony scene provides a beautiful example of the way the two young lovers learn to acknowledge the integrity of their feeling for each other. Romeo's language, in particular, modulates from the conventional lover's mode—'But soft! What light through yonder window breaks?' (II, ii, 1)—which could well be the opening of an address to Rosaline's or anyone else's window, into something much stronger and freer. As the speech continues a fluency of movement asserts itself, which suggests a stronger current of feeling breaking through. The end-stopped lines, the contrived sound of the 'eyes'–'stars' comparison—'What if her eyes were there, they in her head?' (II, ii, 18)—gives way to a much more spontaneous image of brightness:

> Her eyes in heaven
> Would through the airy region stream so bright
> That birds would sing and think it were not night . . .
>
>   (II, ii, 20)

where the freshness of the figure of the birds at dawn regenerates the otherwise rather tired-sounding hyperbole. In the same sort of way in the following lines, the comparison with the angel is animated by the detail of its leisurely freshness and beauty,

> O speak again, bright angel! for thou art
> As glorious to this night, being o'er my head,
> As is a winged messenger of heaven
> Unto the white-upturned wondering eyes
> Of mortals, that fall back to gaze on him,
> When he bestrides the lazy-pacing clouds
> And sails upon the bosom of the air . . .
>
>   (II, ii, 26)

and in particular by the way it catches the rapt movement in the earth-bound onlookers as they raise their eyes to the graceful, leisurely-moving clouds. The cliche, 'my love is like an angel', is reanimated, and the liveliness of the emotions is made to stand out from the conventional figure. Romeo's feelings are the more credible because he so obviously is still the young man who was in love with the idea of being in love with Rosaline, just as Juliet in the rhetoric of her musing over her dilemma still shows as a very young girl. The starkness of her first acknowledgement of her plight—'My grave is like to be my marriage bed' (I, v, 133)—has given way to the indulgent and wishful thinking of ''Tis but a name that is my enemy' (II, ii, 37), but when she understands that it really is Romeo who stands before her, her sense of reality, of the danger he is in is much stronger than his. Her 'Art thou not Romeo, and a Montague' (II, ii, 60) denies her previous fantasy, though he is prepared to continue it with his 'Neither, fair maid, if either thee dislike.' (II, ii, 61). Through the exchange that follows, the contrast between her sense of reality and his exhilaration at this confirmation that she cares for him, at the exciting nature of the role he is playing, is very marked, with Juliet emerging as much the more mature. Her questions, from the first

> How cam'st thou hither, tell me, and wherefore?
> The orchard walls are high and hard to climb,
> And the place death, considering who thou art
> If any of my kinsmen find thee here . . .
>
> (II, ii, 62)

are concerned with practicalities; revealingly, her kinsmen are already 'they', her enemies because they are Romeo's enemies. Her clear awareness of the danger—'If they do see thee, they will murder thee' (II, ii, 70) and 'I would not for the world they saw thee here' (II, ii, 74)—must be set against the romantic silliness of Romeo's

> Alack, there lies more peril in thine eye
> Than twenty of their swords.
>
> (II, ii, 71)

Clearly it cannot be said that at this stage he is very conscious that he is risking death. The exhilaration of being in love is carrying him away; it is a measure of Shakespeare's skill that he is able to use both Juliet's directness and Romeo's verbal excitement as testimony to the strength of their feeling. All in all, the sheer dramatic skill of this scene is a strong warning against pushing too hard any charge of immaturity in the writing. The essential speed of development of the affair is made credible, without any loss of modesty for Juliet, by the fact that she has admitted her love without knowing Romeo could hear her. Their lack of familiarity with each other is brought out in the way they address each other: Juliet calls him 'fair Montague' and 'fair gentleman', as well as by his name. Her endearments become more confident towards the end of the scene, while he calls her first 'fair maid', 'saint' and 'lady', before, as they begin to feel secure in each other's love, he too becomes more intimate in his address.

   All this, together with the explicit statement by Juliet that things are happening too quickly, prevents us from feeling that we are being asked to accept too much too soon. If the happiness the lovers find themselves possessing were quite unclouded we might feel more reluctant about accepting it, but Juliet's own insistence on the danger, and the many reminders throughout the scene of the threat to this love that seems so vital and tender in its beginning, turn aside any suggestion of an over-romantic idyll. From Romeo's offer to swear,

> Lady, by yonder blessed moon I vow
> That tips with silver all these fruit-tree-tops
>
> (II, ii, 107)

itself a concealed frost image, to Juliet's quite explicit

> ... Although I joy in thee
> I have no joy of this contract tonight:
> It is too rash, too unadvised, too sudden,
> Too like the lightning, which doth cease to be
> Ere one can say 'It lightens.' Sweet, goodnight!
> This bud of love, by summer's ripening breath,
> May prove a beauteous flower when next we meet ...
>
> (II, ii, 116)

there is the insistence that love begun at this pitch of intensity cannot last long. The shortness of the time they will have is further emphasised in their reluctance to part from one another. Juliet for all her greater clarity of insight into the dangers that face them, loses no femininity or tenderness thereby, for the modest directness of her offer of marriage

> And all my fortunes at thy foot I'll lay
> And follow thee my lord throughout the world
>
> (II, ii, 147)

and her inability to allow Romeo to leave her—she calls him back twice, the last time for no reason other than to see him again— show what little doubt she has that her destiny lies with his, no matter how dangerous this may be. There is to be no doubting of their love for either of them, and in this they are different from, and perhaps luckier than, the lovers in the other two tragedies. The dangers and impediments that they face are all external: there is no time wasted doubting each other. Though they experience the grief of being parted, they are at least spared the possibility of the greater grief of fearing that the love each feels for the other is not returned.

This scene's extraordinary achievement is to advance the relationship from the stage of a meeting between virtual strangers to the intimacy of tone and the mutual trust of an established love. There is a tremendous sense of tenderness; the desire for possession that love always in part implies, the willingness of the lover to surrender something of his own identity to the person he loves, above all the trust that has blossomed between them, are all summed up in their parting.

> JULIET   'Tis almost morning. I would have thee gone,
> And yet no farther than a wanton's bird,
> That lets it hop a little from his hand,
> Like a poor prisoner in his twisted gyves,
> And with a silken thread plucks it back again,
> So loving-jealous of his liberty.
> ROMEO   I would I were thy bird.
> JULIET   Sweet, so would I.
> Yet I should kill thee with much cherishing ...
>
> (II, ii, 176)

The fact of their love has been firmly established, though the lovers have not so much as touched hands since their first meeting.

It is clear that one very good reason why Romeo and Juliet do not fulfil the Aristotelian requirement of being important, powerful people in their society is that the nature of their passion is dependent on their being young, and the young do not usually command power. Having no power of their own they must depend on the help of others, their friends, the Nurse, the Friar, on all those in fact who claim by their greater age and greater experience to know better than the lovers. One by one, as we shall see, their supporters prove either inadequate, or worse than that. Of these advisers the Friar, because he speaks with the authority of his office (though this is perhaps somewhat qualified), and because of the major part he plays in the action, is the most important. The stage history of the play shows that he has been played in a number of ways, the one extreme being that of a man who speaks with the full weight of orthodox sixteenth century Christianity, in such utterances as

> Two such opposed kings encamp them still
> In man as well as herbs—grace and rude will;
> And where the worser is predominant,
> Full soon the canker death eats up that plant . . .
>
> (II, iii, 27)

though this is difficult to reconcile with the futility and fulsomeness of some of his later speeches and actions, to say nothing of what has immediately preceded these lines in this speech. The other extreme is to see him as a self-interested and bumbling old man, who may mean well, but who in the end acts to protect himself and serves only to help in the destruction of the lovers, just as the self-interest of Capulet and the animosity of Tybalt also help to bring about their destruction. Clearly a fairer estimation of his role lies somewhere in between these two extremes, though one should beware, as Norman Rabkin has pointed out, of the danger of always feeling compelled to reduce possibly complementary views of a character to their mean. The Friar's first appearance, though, does help to prepare us for his function in the play. What he says is true, if somewhat sententious,

> Virtue itself turns vice, being misapplied
> And vice sometimes by action's dignified . . .
>
> (II, iii, 21)

and while this utterance can be interpreted to fit his religious station, it contains a fairly broad hint to the audience, in its obvious ambiguity, that the Friar's moral judgements are not the only way of viewing the situation. The burden of the Friar's advice throughout the play is a plea for control and moderation, and this is consistent with an orthodox position, as his little homily on the herbs makes clear:

> For this being smelt, with that part cheers each part
> Being tasted, stays all senses with the heart.
>
> (II, iii, 25)

It surely is not too fanciful to see this last phrase as quite distinctly applicable to the lovers' situation, as he will come to see it. On the other hand, the play does not at any time present the lovers with the opportunity for moderation, even if, in the nature of the emotion that Shakespeare is depicting, such restraint were possible. Donne's phrase sums up the mood of their love very neatly in one of the play's own images:

> Who would not laugh at mee, if I should say
> I saw a *flaske of powder burne a day*?[11]

It may be because of this intensity that the play conforms to W. B. Yeats's comment that tragedy requires a situation where no solution is possible. It does not seem to me, at any rate, that the play's authority is vested in Friar Lawrence's demands for caution and a more deliberate pace: 'wisely and slow' he counsels, 'they stumble that run fast', but his own scheme fails because neither the messenger nor he can reach Romeo in time to avert the tragedy. It would be a mistake, though, to draw the conclusion that the Friar is quite out of touch with reality. His archness with Romeo may be a little jarring to modern ears, but his chiding of his young friend for the quick change in the object of his affections performs the very useful dramatic function of dismissing Rosaline from the play. Romeo's present purposefulness—'I stand on sudden haste'—contrasts so markedly with the Friar's description of his artificial agonies over Rosaline, where the brine, the sallow cheeks, the salt water sighs, the groans are finally explicitly dismissed as something 'read by rote'. There is, moreover, a good deal to be said for the Friar's suggestion that the marriage may heal the feud between the houses. Both are rich heirs, and old Capulet has already shown himself to be not unkindly disposed towards Romeo, and in favour of an advantageous match. Up to this point in the play, if we ignore for the purpose of my argument the constant foreshadowing of the final scene in the tomb, which runs through even the Friar's conversation with Romeo, there is nothing shown to be inherently disastrous in the speed and force of the way in which Romeo and Juliet have fallen in love. It takes the intervention of Tybalt, with his opposed quality of almost pure hatred, to set the seal of impossibility upon the affair.

Love and death have so often been recognised as being vitally connected in this play that perhaps not enough attention has been given to the fact that hatred and death too are closely linked, and in the person of Tybalt give the impetus to the tragedy. T. J. B. Spencer points out that the feud, in the opening scene, is made to appear tawdry and ridiculous, and this comment can surely be extended to include Tybalt's participation in it. Because the play is a study of love and not of hatred—there are enough examples of hatred elsewhere in Shakespeare to refute any charge that such a thing lies outside his early power—Tybalt is not allowed to compete for a larger share of audience attention. He is little more than a bully-boy, providing an unpleasant equivalent in hatred for Romeo's 'love' for Rosaline, for he is someone who devotes himself to a hatred which has no reasonable cause other than his enjoyment of the role he has adopted. The terms of old Capulet's scolding of him at the masquerade seem wholly appropriate, as does the way Mercutio describes his affectations. He devotes all his attention to the business of fighting and quarrelling. Even his name, on which Mercutio gleefully seizes to mock him as the rat-catcher, the prince of cats, seems to reduce his stature, but not of course the danger he represents. Very adroitly, the play builds up our awareness of how easy it is to continue the feud, to quarrel, to kill a man, which requires no more than a sudden burst of animal energy, as opposed to the resources the lovers have to call on to develop and defend their love.

Tybalt's reappearance in the play, and the triangular quarrel he develops with Romeo and Mercutio, is another most useful point of reference in charting the development of Romeo as a man. Mercutio has just been seen in his most witty and engaging mood; his pun on Romeo 'without his roe' is funny at a number of levels—including the one that Romeo without the 'Ro' leaves a half man, whose truncated name is a repeated lover's complaint—but this should not obscure our recognition that Mercutio is quite happy to play Tybalt's game, and expects Romeo to do so as well. It would be too much to suggest that Mercutio takes up Romeo's quarrel for no other reason than to pass the time (he clearly feels that his friend is behaving dishonourably) but since he cannot seem to see any great purpose in anything, one sort of action to him is much the same as another. And both he and Tybalt, though for different reasons, share an indifference to the consequences of their actions.

In this scene, both before and after Tybalt's entrance, Romeo shows himself to have matured beyond the level of his companions. It is most noticeable that Mercutio's jibes no longer really touch him, which is understandable enough, for they are directed at the old Romeo, in love with love. The calmness, and if it is not stretching the word too far, the dignity of Romeo's reply when charged with having abandoned his friends

> Pardon, good Mercutio. My business was great, and in such a case as mine a man may strain courtesy . . .
>
> (II, iv, 45)

makes a very good impression. What Romeo feels for Juliet is simply removed from the area in which he is prepared to bandy words with Mercutio. He can thus turn the conversation aside in a way which leads Mercutio to believe that he is 'cured', and so he is, of his silliness about Rosaline.

That the lovers are hurried by circumstances which will never allow a pause for consideration, or, more importantly, allow any attempt to realise the Friar's desire to win over the contending families to the match, emerges most clearly in the arranging of their marriage. The Nurse makes the agreement with Romeo, and carries the message back, not without some rather unfeeling enjoyment of her teasing role, to Juliet. The breaking of the news to Juliet provides an amusing scene, and one not without a certain tenderness, but there is nevertheless in it a hint of the Nurse's imaginative inability to understand in more than a very limited way what Juliet is feeling, which is important for the play's development. As far as the Nurse is concerned, the essential thing is to bring Romeo to Juliet's bed. This is all that matters, and to her the marriage ceremony and the rope ladder are equally means to that end; Mercutio's teasing of her as a bawd is not so far removed from the truth.

Urgency and haste are stressed again and again as Juliet waits impatiently for the Nurse's news, as Romeo and the Friar wait for her arrival at the cell, even affecting that advocate of prudence, the Friar himself:

> Come, come with me, and we will make short work
> For, by your leaves, you shall not stay alone
> Till Holy Church incorporate two in one.
>
> (II, vi, 35)

This brief scene of their meeting is heavy with foreboding. Romeo's reference to 'love-devouring death' is immediately followed by the Friar's famous speech

> These violent delights have violent ends
> And in their triumph die, like fire and powder,
> Which, as they kiss, consume.
>
> (II, vi, 9)

When Juliet approaches, his

> Here comes the lady. O, so light a foot
> Will ne'er wear out the everlasting flint . . .
>
> (II, vi, 16)

with its two-edged tribute to Juliet's beauty, merges into an almost Mercutio-like perception of the possibility of all this passion being an illusion. Yet for all the force of his caution, the speech carries its own in-built reasons why Romeo and Juliet must reject his advice. Romeo, somewhat extravagantly perhaps, has just indicated that for him the intensity of the feeling sweeps aside any consideration of duration. By their very natures, power and fire die in their triumph, and if this is so then they can hardly 'confound the appetite'. There is something inherently ridiculous in the conjunction of words in 'love moderately' as if it lay in anyone's power to do so, and this note is further strengthened by the reminder that Juliet is, like all lovers, mortal. Their 'long love' must be set against the lightness that 'will ne'er wear out the everlasting flint'. If the lovers feel that they neither can, nor wish to quantify their love, the effect is not of their rashly ignoring Friar Lawrence's advice to proceed carefully, but rather that his advice is not relevant to their situation, which will ultimately allow the Friar no more time for care and reflection than it will allow the lovers.

Romeo and Juliet then, and to some extent Friar Lawrence himself, are victims of circumstance, but both Mercutio and Tybalt seem to go out of their way to encounter their deaths. Again, the triviality of the circumstances is stressed. It is hot, Mercutio feels quarrelsome, so does Tybalt. Both may share the illusion of personal invulnerability common to the young, though Mercutio's sceptical intelligence perhaps suggests a different reason for his indifference to danger. Both are vain, confident in themselves to the point of blindness, and quite reckless of any consequence. Against this, Romeo, who has a newfound awareness of a relationship to the rest of the world, particularly to the Capulets, stands out very clearly and admirably. Although the point is made with much more force in *Othello* or *Antony and Cleopatra*, one of the first things that love demands here is an acknowledgement that its claims are superior to those of any personal concern of honour, whether measured as mere fame or reputation, or as something more serious. Of course,

Romeo is never asked to make the choices of an Othello or an Antony: in this sense, as I have already suggested, the price his love exacts is a less agonising one, though it costs him his life, as their loves cost them theirs. Here, his reply to Tybalt's challenge, itself ridiculous in the sense that it is a mere form of words that bears no relation to anything but Tybalt's animosity, is controlled, reasonable and manly, very far from Mercutio's description of it as 'calm, dishonourable, vile submission'.

It is one of the puzzles of the play, not really settled by any recourse to the theory of humours, that Shakespeare should have chosen to give to Mercutio, largely his own invention, a quickness of intelligence, coupled with a quickness of temper expressing itself in trivialities, that produces his own death. We may argue that Mercutio is attempting to expunge the insult to his friend's honour, but to do so we must conveniently forget that he has already with great alacrity offered himself for a duel with Tybalt for no real reason at all, since he does not even own a share of the feud except by adoption of what he thinks his friend's attitudes should be. It is enough for him that it is hot, and that he dislikes Tybalt's affectations. It does not seem to me too far-fetched to see in him a similarity to Enobarbus, and even, though of course in a strictly limited way that precludes any suggestion of a share in villainy, to Iago. Each of these characters operates by a sort of cynical intelligence, each priding himself on his ability to see through the romantic illusions that may deceive other men, yet neither seems to find in this operation of the intelligence an attitude to life that will reveal a rewarding purpose. Iago can only destroy, with a lack of satisfactory motive that is almost proverbial; in the end he destroys himself, while the love whose reality he denies is proved real. Enobarbus too, thinks he can see Antony's infatuation for what it is, and by contrast sees reason as indicating that his own most profitable course of action lies in deserting to Caesar. He finds that his cynical assessment of Antony has missed the quality of the man, and that his betrayal has left him with no reason to live. Mercutio, seeing everything from which men fashion a purpose as illusion, perhaps sees no reason for living at all and so, appropriately, makes his exit in a fashion that his satirical intelligence can relish, hurt under the arm of his friend, who is trying to stop the fight.

The argument is a delicately balanced one, for if I am claiming that Mercutio's death is in a sense a dramatisation of a lack of comprehensiveness in his philosophy, it must be admitted that Romeo and Juliet die very soon after: the purpose that their love confers on their existence cannot be seen as any kind of a protection against disaster. But at least the possibility of fulfilment, the discovery of the potentiality of their

...re, though from the moment they fall in love, when love
...ll their world, they put themselves in jeopardy, for the loss of
...ew-found centre, as Othello and Antony also discover, reduces
chaos. But the vision that acknowledges the possibility of chaos
...sequent on loss is radically different from that which sees no pattern
or value anywhere. Much of the sympathy that Mercutio's death
evokes seems to me to come from our awareness of the futility of a life so
snuffed out. He dies as he has lived, wittily, bravely, almost gaily, but
we are very conscious of a sense of waste that is not really commensurate with the strict content of anything that Mercutio has said or
done in the play. In one sense, as we have noted, he dies because his
function in the play is complete; in another, he, like Martin Decoud in
Conrad's *Nostromo*, dies because he can find no saving illusion in which
he can believe. If the lovers run the risk of losing in death the sense of
commitment, which while it lasts engrosses all their lives, Mercutio's
cynicism runs the greater risk of finding no commitment at all. To
argue as I have done is obviously to extend Mercutio's function out of
the proportioned place it occupies in the play, but I have done so
consciously, for the sake of demonstration, for he has so often been seen
as a sort of sport of the Shakespearean imagination, so brilliantly done
that he distracts attention from what ought to be the central theme,
that it is as well to make clear the precision of his relation to that
central theme.

Mercutio and Tybalt, then, find the deaths that they did not imagine
could come to them. Romeo returns to avenge his friend, bringing
about his own banishment before he has spent even one night with
Juliet. As any happy outcome moves now out of the bounds of possibility, and the lovers are forced out of a situation where they need only
attend to each other, they and their love are subjected to the severest of
tests. How immature they both still are emerges clearly now that they
are faced with adversity. Romeo, though presumably he could not do
other than avenge Mercutio and so prove his courage, is in another
sense less impressive as a man when he storms back, with all the fury of
the stock Revenger

>Alive in triumph, and Mercutio slain!
>Away to heaven respective lenity
>And fire-eyed fury be my conduct now! . . .

(III, i, 123)

if only because we know, as he almost immediately realises, that there
is something more important in his life than this taking of vengeance.

After all, the possibility of justice in the play, though not stressed, is nevertheless not negligible. Tybalt could have been left to the law, the more so since Mercutio is the Prince's kinsman. The tragedy that is brought down on the lovers, we ought to notice, comes about not because of their surrender to their passion for each other, but more directly because of Romeo's surrender to hatred, and his participation, admittedly under very great provocation, in the feud.

Act III, scenes ii and iii, see the lovers exposed to the most stringent criticism that the play offers of them, and many critics see also the most marked signs of the play's immaturity in these scenes. Particularly noticed have been the ornateness of Juliet's language when she hears the news, as she thinks, of Romeo's death, and the equal extravagance of Romeo's surrender to despair in Friar Lawrence's cell. In spite of such criticism though, I maintain that the placing of these scenes is most important for the play's subsequent development. What we, the audience, must be made most aware of at this point is the youth and inexperience of the lovers, of how desperately unfair it is that they should be asked to deal with so terrible a situation. What is surprising is not that they should momentarily surrender to despair, but that they should so soon find the strength and control to rise above it. Moreover, their love is still so very new, their meetings have been so brief, that as Juliet intimates in her great epithalamion 'Gallop apace, you fiery-footed steeds' she has

> . . . bought the mansion of a love
> But not possessed it.
>
> (III, ii, 26)

This speech itself has been generally admitted to be one of the great passages of poetry of the play, one that is sufficiently well known to make detailed elaboration unnecessary, so I shall content myself with the observation that Juliet's modesty is in no way lessened by the ardour of her love. Her longing for the night that will bring Romeo to her is given a double poignancy by the audience's knowledge of the fatal duel and of his banishment, as well as by the way that the images of ill omen, the darkness of night, the ominous associations of the raven, look onward to the death and darkness of the final scene. But despite this tragic undercurrent, the central effect of the speech is to communicate in the most touching way the joy and excitement of Juliet, her clear knowledge of her own worth, her glad surrender of herself to Romeo. Even the fanciful image of Romeo's beauty, the 'Take him and cut him out in little stars' is informed by a youthful charm and vigour that

depend in part on the audience's growing realisation that it is the
daylight world that is harsh and violent, that it is only in the dark of the
orchard, of Juliet's room, that the lovers can experience any real happiness, when the world can for a while be excluded. The dual association of darkness with joy as well as with death returns more and more
forcefully, more and more insistently as the play progresses, culminating in the brilliant and moving complexities of the final scene in the
tomb.

   But now there is an almost farcical element in the way that the Nurse
so mangles her news once again, even though it is of so serious a nature,
that Juliet for the moment believes it is Romeo who has been killed.
Criticism has been made of the inappropriateness of her series of puns
on 'I', 'ay', and 'eye', in her incredulous reception of this news, but we
should remember T. J. B. Spencer's apt remark that 'though the verbal
complexity pervades much of the expression, it does not determine its
quality'.[12] The effect of hearing this repeated pattern of sound need not
be that of attracting attention to a purely verbal facility. As Grierson
has observed of a well-known passage from Donne's third Holy Sonnet,[13] the repeated chiming of the vowel sound may intensify rather
than diminish the feeling of distress

> O *might* those *sighes* and teares returne againe
> Into *my* breast and *eyes*, which *I* have spent,
> That *I* might in this holy discontent
> Mourne with some fruit, as *I* have mourn'd in vaine;
> In *mine I*dolatry what showres of raine
> *Mine eyes* did waste? What griefs *my* heart did rent?
> That sufferance was *my* sinne; now *I* repent;
> 'Cause *I* did suffer *I* must suffer paine.

and give the feeling of a mind working at high pressure. On the other
hand, the very contrived antitheses, 'beautiful tyrant', 'fiend-angelical'
and so on, as Juliet wrestles with the conflict between what she feels for
Romeo and what she knows she ought to feel about the murderer of her
kinsman, do suggest that she is not really getting to grips with the
reality. It is only when the Nurse, seizing what she thinks is her cue,
starts to blame Romeo, that Juliet realises that there is no actual
conflict in her heart at all. She rounds on her Nurse with surprising
force

> Blistered be thy tongue,
> For such a wish! He was not born to shame . . .
>   (III, ii, 90)

and proceeds clearly and directly to announce her allegiance to Romeo and to him alone. It is this sort of singleness of devotion which, when the crisis comes, both Romeo and Juliet can show, that leads me to argue that in this play, unlike the other two love tragedies, love has no serious rival in the consciousness of the lovers.

The approaching separation from her husband occupies all Juliet's attention at this point, but she has no notion of what to do about it. Romeo seems equally helpless. Both show the instinctive reaction of the young, when faced with a difficulty beyond which they cannot see; they turn to their elders, Juliet to the Nurse, even for the moment seeming to consider confiding in her mother and father (III, ii, 127). Romeo turns to Friar Lawrence; both he and Juliet give way to a despair in which they seem very little more than children, and foolish children at that. Both defiantly announce their readiness to die rather than endure separation; by a master-stroke, Shakespeare risks the staginess of these self-dramatising declarations in order to make their later choice of the same course of action the more impressive. Why these declarations seem so self-consciously dramatic is because at this point in the play, at the level of common sense, there seems to be no call for such heroics. Banishment for Romeo is not death; at the worst, it would seem, an elopement could be arranged. Ironically, the lovers are right, and the commonsense view is wrong, but at this point they certainly seem vulnerable to its criticisms: the reports of Romeo rolling about 'on the ground, with his own tears made drunk' and of Juliet 'Blubbering and weeping, weeping and blubbering' seem to deny them all dignity and nobility. They are wholly dependent on the good offices of the Nurse and the Friar to be together at all. Romeo apparently even has to be dissuaded from offering to kill himself, though he manages, when scolded, to control himself sufficiently to hear the Friar's plan to get Juliet to him in Mantua, and is reassured by the Nurse that there is no impediment to his going to Juliet that night as they have arranged.

It seems to me extraordinarily daring for Shakespeare to have risked reducing his lovers at this point to something so close to the level of ridiculousness. How silly these children are, we seem asked to feel, and how easily a little adult commonsense can put things right. But from this point on, the inadequacies of the adult world are relentlessly exposed, and immediately, by the sort of ironic juxtaposition of scenes that this play shares with the problem comedies, we are offered gross examples of adult stupidity and insensitivity.

The impossibility of Juliet's situation and the urgency of her plight is brought out by the little scene in which her marriage with Paris is decided upon. Old Capulet is tired, for a death in the family is a

wearying business, and so eager to be in bed that he can hardly bring
himself to be polite to Paris. Anxious to be rid of him, he makes little
attempt to conceal his feelings:

> I promise you but for your company
> I would have been abed an hour ago.
>
> (III, iv, 6)

But when Paris takes the hint, and with the deadly appropriate politeness of which he is the play's acknowledged master—'These times of
woe afford no time to woo'—offers to leave, Capulet decides to get the
whole thing over and done with. Tybalt has been killed that morning,
Monday; Wednesday is too soon, but on Thursday, Juliet must at once
be informed, she is to be married to Paris. Even the prospective bridegroom is almost stunned by this callous haste, though he does manage
to find the right thing to say, and allow Capulet at last to go to bed.
This almost incredible perfunctoriness is made believable by the bril-
liance of the characterisation by which, brief though Capulet's appear-
ances have been, we have been prepared. Capulet, as we have seen, is
accustomed to getting what he wants; now he wants to go to bed, and
moreover, he can manage to settle Juliet's future with a quiet wedding,
which will be a relief after all the fuss Tybalt's death has caused. An
appointment with his tailor could hardly be arranged with more indifference to anything but his own convenience.

I have already indicated that the lovers' progress in the understanding of themselves and their feelings for each other is not presented as a
continuous one. They are allowed so bitterly little time together it is
hardly surprising that they progress not by stages, but with great leaps
forward. When we see them again, with Romeo taking his leave after
their one night of love-making, they are hardly recognisable as the boy
and girl who lay 'blubbering and weeping' on the previous day. Each
now belongs wholly to the other, and has gained a new strength and
understanding from that relationship. Their parting is managed with
great tact by Shakespeare, for, after the explicitness of Mercutio and
the Nurse on the physical nature of the love relationship, it would be
easy to allow the situation to slip into a reminder of that bawdiness
which could spoil the mood of tenderness and restraint of the parting.
The joy of their love-making is suggested only indirectly in the imagery,
but in their tender reluctance to let each other go there is no hint of a
prudishness that might suggest any embarrassment at their sexual
union: both accept it as part of their total feeling for one another.

Day comes as the enemy of the lovers, with a reversal of all the normal associations of the dawn as a thing of beauty, freshness and new beginning that the image usually carries. Finality, separation and loss are conveyed in every aspect of the poetry, in the plain sense, the imagery, the movement of the verse. Consider, as typical of the whole, Romeo's

> It was the lark, the herald of the morn,
> No nightingale. Look love, what envious streaks
> Do lace the severing clouds in yonder East.
> Night's candles are burnt out, and jocund day
> Stands tiptoe on the misty mountain tops.
> I must be gone and live, or stay and die.
>
> (III, v, 6)

It is perhaps only a modern sensibility that would give great emphasis to the sexual undertones of the images of penetration, possibly of tumescence, but they are there nevertheless, although the primary sense is of the pain of parting and of a dreadful feeling of finality that depresses the lovers even as they try to shake it off. Romeo's opening lines

> It was the lark, the herald of the morn,
> No nightingale . . .

come to a dead stop, and are then followed by a new sort of imagery, suggesting the active hositility and envy, the malice of the world, which in the phrase 'jocund day'—surprising in this context—is seen as at best cheerfully uncomprehending of the sorrow it produces, and at worst as a kind of destructive maliciousness which delights in the suffering it causes. The irony of the lovers' situation comes out strongly in the forced unnaturalness of choice Romeo must make. They are young, at the start of a new day, literally and symbolically, and yet he must 'be gone and live, or stay and die'.

Again it is interesting to see how the stock props of a romantic scene, the nightingale for instance, are given new life by Shakespeare's use of them. Without my wanting to seem too Holmesian, the most remarkable thing about the nightingale is that it is not there, so that to the customary associations of its suffering for love, (it sings in the thorny pomegranate tree) is added the suffering of the lovers, called to the parting by a harsh and jangling quality Juliet now recognises in the song of the lark. It is very striking how much divisive power is invested in the bird

> . . . whose notes do beat
> The vaulty heaven so high above our heads

and how skilfully this is accomplished in a scene whose tone is through-out suggestive of a very strong control of the emotions. The need for secrecy and quietness imposes this hushed tone on the lovers, but it also gives them a dignity and a strength in adversity which is a new measure of their maturity. For all their reluctance to accept the inevitability of their parting, there is no serious confusion of reality; each knows that the time has come for parting and each reveals concern and tenderness for the other. However attractive the dream may be, it cannot be yielded to. The quickness of wit of Juliet's 'It is the lark that sings so out of tune . . . ' speech seems to spring from great emotional tension, and to be a successful attempt to impose a net of language on a feeling that is on the verge of escaping out of control. The cost at which this restraint and control are achieved emerges in the power of the image—'Dry sorrow drinks our blood'—with which Romeo responds to Juliet's premonition of disaster as she sees his pale face looking up at her. Elizabethans believed that sighing made one pale, but the effect of the image goes far beyond that piece of contemporary physiology. Their sorrow is dry because they cannot risk the luxury of tears; in another much more frightening way it looks forward to the dryness and deadness of the Apothecary's shop, for what the grief of this parting is to exact in the end, is in fact the life's blood of the lovers. The whole notion of some malignant force operating against them concentrates itself in this vampire-like 'dry sorrow', in much the same way that Donne suggests a similar loss of all of life's vitality in his

> The world's whole sap is sunk
> The general balm the hydroptic earth hath drunk . . . [14]

The restraint they must show here is to be characteristic of their behaviour to the end of the play, for the only hope of renewing the brief happiness they have experienced (all that they are allowed) lies in secrecy. Juliet has the more difficult part to play, for she can only gain any sort of relief from her feelings by presenting them to the audience of her mother and the Nurse as something very different. In rather the way that Hamlet's assumed madness gives him licence to speak in a way that others cannot wholly comprehend of what most torments him, so Juliet in one sense welcomes the opportunity to talk about Romeo in ambiguous phrases, whose contortions again reveal a mind working at very high pressure indeed. She is, moreover, pitilessly assailed, for she is on public show at this, the moment of her most intense grief, and to make matters worse she is being treated with a quite frightening lack of understanding and sympathy by her parents.

Juliet's defiant reception of the news of the arranged marriage to Paris succeeds in winning only her parents' anger. All Capulet's familiar characteristics are now shown in a situation which strips him bare of any semblance of generosity, kindness or affection. If Juliet's refusal were due to nothing more than the reasons she advances to her parents, his lack of consideration and his insensitivity to anything other than his own convenience and his own self-satisfaction would still be shocking. As Coleridge has noticed,[15] he has before threatened to cut Tybalt out of his will; now he does the same to Juliet, and goes much further in his rage. When Juliet directs her pitiful appeal to her mother, she gets no more sympathetic reply:

> Talk not to me, for I'll not speak a word.
> Do as thou wilt, for I have done with thee.
>
> (III, v, 202)

Even the Nurse, who has seemed an ally up to now, and who at least has supplied some of the affection that the relationship with her parents so clearly lacks, now proves quite useless. It is a considerable dramatic shock to the audience, as well as a shock to Juliet, when the Nurse produces what is now revealed as the fatuity of her worldly-wise advice: all her previous praises of Romeo now ring hollow as she showers similar praises on Paris:

> I think it best you married with the County
> O, he's a lovely gentleman! . . .
>
> (III, v, 219)

After this, Juliet's description of her as 'Ancient damnation' does not seem too strong. For everyone in the play but the lovers (with the possible exception of Paris, who is not given much chance to reveal what he really thinks), marriage is seen as a means to an end. For the Nurse it is a licence to go to bed with a man, for the Capulets an alliance that they hope will be profitable. Even Friar Lawrence, the only person left to whom Juliet can now turn, sees this marriage primarily as a possible path to the reconciliation of the two houses. Only for Romeo and Juliet does it mean something sacred in the terms of their relationship with each other.

The play, always so rapid in its succession of events, now gathers even more momentum as it rushes to its final catastrophe. The Friar's scheme to have Juliet take a drug that will counterfeit death—again a

scene heavy with foreboding—and Capulet's seizing on Juliet's apparently more cheerful mood to try to advance the marriage yet another
day, rush us on to Juliet's great speech before she swallows the potion,
but we ought to spare a moment to notice how well the exchange with
Paris outside Friar Lawrence's cell is managed. If we compare this
courtly exchange of compliments with the first encounter of Romeo and
Juliet at the masquerade, we can see how here Juliet indeed makes her
responses 'by the book', but how empty and dreary the whole tone is,
not enlivened by anything more than conventional gallantry on Paris'
side, and evoking only a forced politeness from Juliet, as her mind
never wavers from the fact of her separation from Romeo.

From the moment the Friar's plan has been decided upon, the lovers
are hurried to their deaths. The play does not dwell on the causes; it is
as if the doom that has been gathering around them ever since its
beginning now simply takes over their lives. Juliet is, in a dramatic
sense, dead from the moment she takes the potion, for from this point
everyone in the play except the ineffectual Friar sees her as being in
death's power. Her true death speech is the speech before she takes the
drug, in which she sees herself as giving herself to death. It is a speech
that sums up the values of her life and is worthy of the most careful
attention. In all three plays, it should be noticed with what dramatic
tact Shakespeare manages the problem of the dual death scenes. If we
take as a comparison, for this limited purpose only, a play like *Julius
Caesar*, and look at the deaths of Cassius and Brutus, it is difficult not to
feel some slight sense of disappointment at the juxtaposition of these
two tragic statements, so close together, and so similar in their effect.

In the love tragedies, where the bond between the two individuals is
the cause of death, the danger of a similar kind of anti-climax is clearly
present, but without in any way distorting the shape of the action,
Shakespeare achieves a separation which maintains the complementary nature of the actions without allowing them to compete with one
another. Thus Desdemona makes it clear why she is prepared to die in
the Willow Song scene, and is therefore free to fulfil her intensely
pathetic role as the victim in Act V, without the need for speeches
which might complicate the simplicity of her dramatic function here.
Othello's recognition of his own culpability comes only after her death.
In *Antony and Cleopatra* the feigned death of Cleopatra allows Antony to
make his final testimony to love, to die because he believes she is dead,
without this interfering with her right to choose in turn to die because
he is no longer alive. Cleopatra has Act V to herself, though it is filled
with echoes of Antony in her memories of him. In *Romeo and Juliet*, too,
the misreported death allows both the lovers to choose to die rather

than live without each other, and yet not to have to be involved in any suggestion of a suicide pact, or of the simple desire to leave the world together. It is vital for the understanding of these plays to recognise that the lovers would rather live, no matter what the difficulties, because only in life can they experience their love. It is only when the death, actual or assumed, of one of them makes it clear that no possible happiness can continue to exist that life becomes intolerable. Leaving aside Othello, whose situation is clearly somewhat different, it is necessary to recognise that the lovers would continue to live wholly for each other, if circumstances would allow them the chance. Any suggestion of cowardice, or of irresponsibility and delusion, any feeling that they are choosing to die rather than continue to fight for what they have claimed is the supreme value in their lives, is carefully avoided by the device of the misreported death.

Juliet is fully prepared to risk death and its almost unimaginable terrors, in order to be with Romeo. That is the plain sense of her speech, but on another level she is also indicating her acceptance of death itself, rather than a life without Romeo. It is because she makes this clear now that her quick decision to kill herself when she wakes and finds Romeo's body in the tomb can be accepted as a natural conclusion to her life, rather than as a sudden and panic-stricken action. The play does not allow the courage Juliet needs to embark on Friar Lawrence's scheme to be underestimated. Her first words

> Farewell! God knows when we shall meet again,
> I have a faint cold fear thrills through my veins.
> That almost freezes up the heat of life . . .
>
> (IV, iii, 15)

show a surprising strength in what might be a conventional contrast between the warmth of life and the chill of death, which perhaps comes from the paradoxical use of an adjective like 'faint' to describe so strong a feeling. It is because she now knows she has so much to live for that death seems so terrible, and the thought of oblivion, of loss of the senses, so fearful to contemplate. Throughout the speech we are reminded of her youth: practical considerations such as the integrity of the Friar, who may be trying to get rid of her to avoid being exposed, the possibility that Romeo will not arrive in time to rescue her, contend in her mind with nightmare-like terrors which have an almost comic sound. She is afraid of the dark, of bad smells, of noises, of losing her wits:

> . . . in this rage, with some great kinsman's bone
> As with a club dash out my desperate brains?
>
> (IV, iii, 53)

But what emerges most strongly from her imaginings, and what therefore makes her resolve to run the risks the more admirable, is the
intensity of the horror with which the physical presence of death is
evoked by her imagination

> Or, if I live, is it not very like
> The horrible conceit of death and night,
> Together with the terror of the place—
> As in a vault, an ancient receptacle
> Where for this many hundred years the bones
> Of all my buried ancestors are packed;
> Where bloody Tybalt, yet but green in earth,
> Lies festering in his shroud . . .
>
> (IV, iii, 36)

The unnaturalness of her willing her youth and beauty to go, as the
phrase is, to join her ancestors, is made sufficiently striking by the
image of this place of death 'packed' with bones, but the real horror
comes from the immediacy of the realisation of the death of somebody
young like herself, 'bloody Tybalt, yet but green in earth', where the
word green, with its macabre reversal of the normal association of
young growing things, evokes the very sight and smell of corruption so
vividly that it becomes almost a living presence, a continuing process
whose horror the active phrase 'festering in his shroud' strikingly reinforces. Juliet must hope that the potion is the way to a happy life with
Romeo, but she is prepared to risk, even to welcome a death whose
terrors she can so vividly imagine, rather than face a life without him:
she drinks, as she says, 'to Romeo'.

The scene which follows, the discovery of Juliet's apparent death,
serves both to reinforce the idea of her now being a possession of
Death's—repeatedly personified from now until the play's end as
Juliet's bridegroom—and to distance her still further from any claim
her family may seem to have on her. The plan, after all, involves a cruel
deception of them, or would do so if the play allowed them to show any
real sense of loss. Of this scene too, we have to say that either Shakespeare intended it to strike an almost unbearably false note or else he
mismanaged it to an astonishing degree. The wordy and repetitive
bewailings of their loss by old Capulet, Lady Capulet and the Nurse, to
which Paris in turn joins his voice, do not carry much conviction either
in their own right or when judged by the family's treatment of Juliet.
The Nurse may perhaps be partly excused on the grounds that she is
taking her lead from her betters, but of the others, Capulet, true to
form, bewails the loss of his heir—'Death is my son-in-law. Death is my

heir'—and even rebukes Death for coming at such an inconvenient time, while Lady Capulet claims a special affection for Juliet—'But one thing to rejoice and solace in'—for which the earlier scenes have offered little or no confirming evidence. Paris, too, expresses his disappointment and joins the chorus with something of the air of an eager anthropologist taking his part in a tribal rite.

The dramatic effect is a complex one, for while the audience knows Juliet is not in fact dead, thus adding an element of the ridiculous to the artificiality of the protestations, there is nevertheless the strong suggestion that her death has only been for a little while delayed. The Friar, though author of the plot and therefore aware that Juliet is still alive, can thus rebuke the mourners without himself seeming hypocritical. His charge that all they care about is Juliet's 'advancement' is so obviously true that any awkwardness which might be aroused if we were allowed to feel that Juliet's participation in the plot were causing real grief and suffering to her parents, is avoided. The odd little scene with the servants and musicians that follows seems to show a more genuine feeling of sorrow, impersonal though it is, than family, Nurse and prospective bridegroom can manage between them.

Of course, as the whole play has from its Prologue implied, the Friar's plan cannot work. It cannot be allowed to work, as the limits in time placed on the love affair are essential for the creation of its intensity. Act V is essentially concerned, not with any real hope of escape for the lovers, but with the demonstration of the change in Romeo, and with his making of his choice to die a meaningful one. Before he gets the news of Juliet's supposed death he is composed and confident; when the blow falls there is an absolute contrast with the sort of wordy panic he has previously shown in adversity. His 'Is it e'en so? Then I defy you, stars!' (V, i, 24) shows an instant resolution, as impressive in its stark simplicity as was Juliet's triumphing over her fear of death and near-hysteria at the thought of waking in the tomb. Since the central dramatic point of Romeo's reception of the news is to show the change from helpless boy to decisive man, it is impossible subsequently to allow him a discursive speech on what life without Juliet means to him, but this difficulty is surmounted by giving him instead the famous description of the Apothecary's shop, into which his feelings are projected. The grim quibble 'Well, Juliet, I will lie with thee tonight . . .' (V, i, 35) leads into a description of the Apothecary himself, 'Sharp misery had worn him to the bones' and of his 'needy shop' bedecked with its sparse and dusty images of death, including the 'green earthen pots' that echo back to Tybalt's corpse, and connects Romeo's indirect acknowledgement of his awareness of what death means firmly to Juliet's. The contrast between the clinging to life of the miserable Apothecary, who is prepared to risk that life by selling poison to Romeo in order to try to preserve it a little longer, and Romeo, who wants a poison so potent

> That the life-weary taker may fall dead
> And that the trunk may be discharged of breath
> As violently as hasty powder fired
> Doth hurry from the fatal cannon's mouth . . .
>
> (V, i, 63)

is strong indeed.

It is at this point, if an adverse moral judgement on the lovers is being elicited, that we ought to feel that Romeo should stop to reflect, that it is his rashness and despair here which not only lead him into the mortal sin of suicide, destroying any chance of his own and Juliet's happiness, but that by so doing he directly causes her death as well. Clearly the action can be made to sustain such an interpretation, but it seems to me most unlikely that it is actually doing so. By putting the argument for going on living in the person of the Apothecary, a figure like death itself, Shakespeare effectively shields Romeo from a moral or religious criticism that is clearly irrelevant to the play at this point. Romeo's whole being is concerned with his love for Juliet; without her, life appears to be worthless, empty, barren, parsimonious, something to be eked out until death comes. Rather than sustain this mockery of the fullness he has experienced, Romeo prefers to die. It seems to be pointless to evoke everyday experience here, and to argue that even if Juliet is dead, Romeo, if he were to go on living, would get over his grief in time. Because of the way the situation has been presented, that choice, the only one which might prolong their lives, is not available to him. The only choice he can make that will bear out the violence and strength of his love is to die rather than live without Juliet, and in making this choice he attracts sympathy and admiration for the courage and decisive qualities which earlier he has been shown to lack, but which he can now, if only in death, demonstrate. In other words, the all-important testimony of the integrity of his love can only be his willingness to die rather than live without Juliet.

Just as in *Othello* and *Antony and Cleopatra*, where the lovers make claims for the strength of their love which seem extravagant to other characters (and to some critics, too) the proof of those claims lies ultimately in their refusal to continue to live without each other. Of course we must recognise that this action is a self-defeating one, that there is no unequivocal triumph possible over time or death, no real suggestion, that I can see, of some reunion in happiness beyond the grave, but equally I can see no trace of any suggestion here that Romeo and Juliet ought to have been 'sensible' and acted otherwise.

It is Romeo's determination not to have a separate existence from Juliet, his recognition that to do so would be a betrayal of her and of their love, that drives him to his death; in his final scenes, though his actions are desperate and their disastrous consequences not minimised in any way whatsoever, what emerges most poignantly and strongly is not his folly, but the strength of his and Juliet's mutual love. For both the lovers, their maturity is measured in the end by their capacity to love, to care about each other, in the midst of a brawling and selfish world, and that capacity, in the circumstances of the play, is finally measured by their readiness to die. As John Lawlor remarks on the subject of their maturity, it is different from the so-called experience and wisdom of those about them.

> The 'ripeness' or readiness, especially as it is manifest between fellow sufferers in the bond of love, is all. If that tie holds, Death is robbed of the greater glory, the ending is triumph, a transcending of the limits of mortality by holding fast, in a union of suffering, to what is best in the mortal condition.[16]

Lawlor's contention that such love is 'what is best in the mortal condition' is borne out by the way in which the very considerable poetic force of this play is concentrated in showing the intense awareness that being in love confers. In comprehensiveness, and in acuteness of feeling, in capacity to experience joy and grief, the lovers simply exist at a far higher level of consciousness than anyone else in the play, even than Mercutio, for all his intelligence. As in all the plays which deal with the theme of love, this heightened consciousness is presented as a value in itself, even though by definition, it makes its holders as susceptible to suffering as to joy. *Romeo and Juliet* shows almost the extreme limiting case, where the joy, the actual time they are allowed to enjoy their love, is quantitatively very small, but for all that a balance is struck, and what they experience in these brief moments is made to seem worth dying for.

I have already suggested one of the dangers inherent in the situation of young lovers is that they may be seen as weakly refusing to struggle against the world's adversities, as taking an easy way out by choosing rather to die, and I have also suggested that one insurance against the play's being read in this way lies in the fullness of imagination with which the idea of death is accepted, directly by Juliet, indirectly by Romeo. Death is not for a moment seen as something desirable in itself, even when in Act V, it becomes a goal, the winning of which costs

Romeo a great effort of physical and emotional courage. For the audience, death is seen as inevitable as the action surges on, making the
Friar's acquisition of the news that his message has not been delivered
and his plans to rectify the omission seem almost irrelevant. The suspense of the ending is not of that kind. In the scene at the tomb, we feel
very strongly that Romeo must not be prevented from getting to Juliet's
side; the possibility of rescue for both the lovers always seems to be
remote. Yet Romeo's intention to die with Juliet has literally to be
fought for. Paris is killed because he gets in the way, but even so the
effect of this is not to make us see Romeo as a half-crazed murderer.
This is, I think, partly because Paris has had fair warning, and partly
because there is no element of delusion in Romeo's quest; death is not
seen as the means to some happy end achieved at the expense of Paris'
life. Life for Romeo is intolerable without Juliet, and death is therefore
preferable, but it is still an ugly thing. The play is tragic precisely
because this is the only way left in which Romeo, and later Juliet, can
prove the value of their love. To choose not to be, in other words, is the
only meaningful choice left for them in a world that does not allow their
love to exist.

Paris is certainly unlucky, but his death seems of no great importance. At no point in the play is he allowed an individuality that lifts
him beyond the exercise of politeness and civility, and even here, at the
tomb, in contrast to the directness and strength of Romeo, he cuts a
poor figure. His devotional exercises 'nightly . . . to strew thy grave and
weep' seem a very long way from the unbearable sense of loss that
Romeo feels, and his politely rhymed sentimentalities are cut across by
the brutal practicality of Romeo's opening words, 'Give me that mat-
tock and the wrenching iron' (V, iii, 22) by his sense of revulsion at the
idea of Juliet dead, and by the tremendous physical effort he makes as
he starts to prise open the tomb

> Thou detestable maw, thou womb of death,
> Gorged with the dearest morsel of the earth
> Thus I enforce thy rotten jaws to open
> And in despite I'll cram thee with more food.
>
> (V, iii, 45)

There is little suggestion of being in love with death here, as the
repeated heavy stresses starkly emphasise the greed and corruption of
the tomb. I feel indeed of Paris' intervention that Shakespeare comes
close to over-playing his hand, so affected is the movement of his speech
and so completely out of touch with reality is its matter.

> Condemned villain, I do apprehend thee
> Obey, and go with me, for thou must die.
>
> (V, iii, 56)

Even if Romeo were what Paris believes him to be, this invitation to come and be killed would hardly be likely to be accepted. Set against this fatuity, the sense of power in Romeo's holding himself back is tremendously strong; threats of death do not frighten him because he is already given to death. It is the quietness of his reply that carries this menace, with its suggestion of his complete identification with the world of the dead.

> I must indeed; and therefore came I hither.
> Good gentle youth, tempt not a desperate man
> Fly hence and leave me. Think upon these gone.
> Let them affright thee.
>
> (V, iii, 58)

It is very noticeable that in this exchange, Romeo proves his right to call himself a man, while Paris remains the youth, the 'boy' that Romeo used to be. It is only in death, and then only by Romeo's tribute to him, that Paris attains any kind of real dignity. As always he finds the appropriate thing to say, but even his dying request to be buried in Juliet's tomb does not testify to any devotion comparable with that of Romeo. 'One writ with me in sour misfortune's book', Romeo calls him, and really his death does seem to be quite fortuitous, for he has shown none of the rashness of ungovernable passion that we are sometimes told causes the ruin that the lovers bring upon themselves. To be sure, he may be an innocent victim caught up in that ruin, but the prudence and decorum he has shown have not protected him; moreover, in his part in the play there is little to suggest that he has lived before he dies. Nor is there any stress laid on Romeo's guilt, for with this one dismissive reference he returns to his goal: the tomb, and Juliet.

His first words begin the final clustering together of those paradoxical images of light and darkness, love and death that have throughout stressed the inexorable direction of the play. He first saw Juliet as a jewel's brightness against a dark background, now the darkness of the tomb becomes a lantern

> For here lies Juliet, and her beauty makes
> This vault a feasting presence full of light
>
> (V, iii, 86)

It has been suggested by Spencer, among others, that Romeo's response to the lifelike quality of Juliet's beauty almost gives hope that he will stumble on the truth, thus adding to the suspense of these final moments, but while this element may be present, Romeo's dwelling on the image of Death and the Maiden seems to me to have another more direct bearing on the central paradox of the play's ending, which is presented both as a triumph and as a defeat. There is a sustained ambiguity that runs through Romeo's speech, through all his tributes to Juliet's beauty. Even the opening image of the vault as a 'feasting presence' (which the new Cambridge edition of the play glosses as 'a room in a palace set out for a feast') carries a sinister undertone, made more explicit by Romeo's later

> Here, here will I remain
> With worms that are thy chambermaids.
>
> (V, iii, 108)

The images of life and death seem to melt and merge into one another. Romeo knows that Juliet is dead, but her beauty seems still alive:

> Death, that hath sucked the honey of thy breath,
> Hath had no power yet upon thy beauty.
> Thou are not conquered. Beauty's ensign yet
> Is crimson in thy lips and in thy cheeks,
> And death's pale flag is not advanced there . . .
>
> (V, iii, 92)

but when he turns to Tybalt—'liest thou there in thy bloody sheet'—the crimson of life becomes only a stain on death's pale flag, the shroud. All the previous suggestions of Juliet's belonging to death are now concentrated in the one great image

> Shall I believe
> That unsubstantial death is amorous,
> And that the lean abhorred monster keeps
> Thee here in dark to be his paramour.
>
> (V, iii, 102)

The macabre effect of this, the vision of what we know is the still living Juliet kept in her state of suspended animation for the sensual satisfaction of 'insubstantial death' seems to me to forbid any easy romanticising of the ending, of the order of Stauffer's 'the quick bright things remain shiningly alive.'[17] The finality and horror of these images of death surely make us realise that of the physical being of the lovers nothing will remain. Romeo does not even claim that by dying he will save Juliet from the monster's embraces or reclaim her for his own. All that he can do is to stay with her in death, give up the life that is to him, to borrow Hermione's words, 'no commodity'. He has said that he has to 'shake the yoke of inauspicious stars / From this world-wearied flesh'; now he decides his course for himself, no longer trusting as he did earlier, to him 'who has the steerage of my course', but becoming at the last his own pilot, choosing to 'run on / The dashing rocks thy seasick weary bark!' Yet for all the bitter despair that he feels at the contemplation of a world that does not contain Juliet, what is most noticeable about the tone of his last speech, until the violence of its ending, is its gentleness. The tenderness he feels for Juliet, the generosity of his salute to Tybalt—'Forgive me, Cousin'—the lack of reproach against anyone or anything for his own sake, this is what confers the final value on his love, his conviction that though it is about to cost him his life he finds it a fair price. The wry irony of his words

> O true Apothecary
> Thy drugs are quick . . .
>
> (IV, iii, 119)

where the death-dealing poison has more life than he, is worthy of Mercutio, but they are not his last words. 'Thus with a kiss I die' is his final tribute to a love that has cost him all he has.

Juliet's death soon follows. We are very aware of the need for a swiftness that the wise Friar cannot manage

> St Francis be my speed! How oft tonight
> Have my old feet stumbled at graves!
>
> (V, iii, 122)

and of the poignantly bad luck of her awakening, so little too late, with her recognition as she kisses his lips that Romeo has only just died. There is only time for the Friar to show his panic (some blame surely must attach to his flight from the watch and his abandonment of Juliet, even though we know that she has to die) before Juliet too chooses death rather than life without Romeo. She has made her choice before, so there is no need for a lengthy speech of renunciation and resolution from her. What must appear to her, at least partially, as Romeo's needless death draws no reproach; she shows only tenderness for her love, and resolution and courage in snatching her own way out of a life that has now become for her, too, intolerable. Neither Romeo nor Juliet has needed any time to deliberate in following the action their love demands; for neither of them has there been the slightest sign of anything of even faintly comparable value in their lives.

The tidying up which follows the catastrophe occupies more space, I think I am right in saying, than it does in any other of Shakespeare's tragedies. I cannot really account satisfactorily for this length, and must conclude that it is simply a lapse on Shakespeare's part or perhaps more probably, that it is an attempt, not sufficiently dramatic in itself, to hold our attention, to cast a further light on the events that have been witnessed, even though Friar Lawrence's recapitulation of these events seems to have no particular emphasis. That in itself may be remarkable, for though a priest, he does not point out the sin that the lovers have committed by their suicides. Certainly there is no strong censure of their action coming from any authority within the play; the Prince blames their deaths on the quarrel, and Friar Lawrence regards this as the workings of the will of heaven, without in any way illuminating this belief. If, as some critics have contended, the focus of interest and the play's true end is the ending of the feud between the Montagues and the Capulets, then we must conclude that this too is at best perfunctorily dramatised. The golden statue that is to be raised over the grave, in token of atonement, seems poor substitute indeed for the youth and ardour that have been lost, and emphasises the permanence of that loss by its unchanging metal. But if throughout my account of these final scenes, I have come down heavily against a reading that sees death as an unequivocal triumph for the lovers it is only because I want to redress a critical imbalance that seems to me to have inclined too far towards a comfortably romantic view of this play, either in order to praise it or to dismiss it. The play is the stronger because it does not flinch from showing the physical extinction of the love by the same act that supremely testifies to its unique value. There is no human victory to be won in death, not for Romeo and Juliet, or Othello and Desdemona, or Antony and Cleopatra. Even if we recognise, as I believe we are meant to recognise throughout the play, that love of this intensity cannot endure, there is still a sharp sense of loss. The love cannot exist without the lovers; the 'quick bright things' have come to confusion, because it is in the nature of such things that they should. In a way reminiscent of the theme of Keats's *Grecian Urn*, the unnaturalness of a Juliet eternally young and beautiful in death points to the need for acceptance of both change and destruction as a part of existence. The value that is established for the love lies in the quality of the feeling that is demonstrated, and in our conviction that, given knowledge of all that is to happen between them because of their love, Romeo and Juliet would choose to love again.

CHAPTER FOUR

OTHELLO

If *Romeo and Juliet* is a tragedy of love's intensity, *Othello* is a tragedy of love's vulnerability. Othello's love for Desdemona, like Romeo's for Juliet, is sudden, unforeseen by Othello or anyone else, and like Romeo's love, it becomes the central value in his life, replacing all that has gone before. While it is obviously true to say that Romeo's past experience holds little of real importance, that he in fact begins to live when he first sees Juliet, it may seem surprising to claim that Othello is in much the same case. His past, as we know from his own account, is full of vivid and varied experiences, but it is nevertheless clear that he begins life anew when he falls in love. What has happened before can provide him with no guide to his present conduct, though it has made him the man that he is. He is less emotionally experienced even than Romeo, who has at least played with the idea of being in love. When he does commit himself to love he commits himself utterly, so that the all-engrossing importance of this new emotion becomes its greatest danger:

> . . . perdition catch my soul
> But I do love thee, and when I love thee not,
> Chaos is come again.
>
> (III, iii, 91)

As he himself realises, the fact that Desdemona's love has replaced all other values at the centre of his universe makes him terribly vulnerable. If anything should happen to her, or to his faith in her, he knows he could not go back to being what he was before, and he is right, for when he is led to believe that this sure and stable point of reference is an illusion, he can find no form or order anywhere in his existence, though he labours desperately to create some such order in an ideal of abstract justice that will at least allow some place for Desdemona's infidelity in

its scheme of things. The audience is, of course, aware all the while that
Othello is being deceived, but I believe that a good deal of the play's
agonising force derives from an underlying awareness, based on common experience, of the precariousness of the happiness of anyone who
loves as completely as does Othello, or Desdemona too. We are made
aware of the wreck that can follow the loss through death or through
alteration of feeling of one of the partners in so intense a love, but even
more painful is the realisation that Iago's story, untrue of Desdemona,
could be true of many other women. And if it had been true, Othello
would have been utterly in Iago's power and would have been
destroyed body and soul.

It is, I hope, clear from even these brief introductory remarks that I
see *Othello* as very much concerned with the nature of love, with the
emphasis falling on its dangers. Professor Dickey,[1] although he uses the
famous 'Not wisely but too well' as the title of his book on the love
theme in some of Shakespeare's plays, does not deal with this play in
detail, since he sees it as centrally concerned with jealousy, and not
love. I cannot agree, for it seems to me that Shakespeare makes everything depend on the quality of Othello's love for Desdemona. What
some critics try to see as a different subject, the jealousy, is integrally
related to this central theme. It all depends on what we make of Othello
himself, for in a way unlike Romeo or Juliet, he dominates the action
in which, in the classic pattern, he moves from the attainment of his
greatest happiness to misery and death. Although Iago, as the practical
cause of Othello's destruction, has come in for his share of attention,
which varies from the perhaps undue emphasis given to him by Bradley,[2] to Leavis's dismissal of him as a piece of plot mechanism,[3] most
critics agree that what is made of the presentation of Othello himself is
crucial to any reading of the play. There, however, agreement effectively ends. The main critical attitudes to the central character are
sufficiently well known to need no lengthy recapitulation here. Othello
is seen either as a noble hero, baffled and destroyed, through no fault of
his own, by the motiveless malignity of Iago, or as a man so flawed by
self-conceit that he reacts to Iago's suggestions, as Leavis suggests,
with 'a promptness that could hardly be improved upon'.[4] He dies
either with this vanity still largely undamaged, 'cheering himself up'[5]
as T. S. Eliot has it, with a wistful speech about his own worth, or as a
man who by this execution of justice upon himself acknowledges, in the
only way possible for one so great of heart, his own guilt, and the
supreme worth of the love his folly has destroyed.

Othello's fluctuating critical fortunes in this century are ably discussed by Professor Helen Gardner in her essay '*Othello:* a retrospect,

1900–67'.[6] Herself a staunch supporter of the 'Noble Moor' side of the argument (which she forcefully states in her address of that title[7] to the British Academy), she discusses the reasons for many critics of our century seeing a very different Othello from that of Johnson or Coleridge, and identifies some of the main causes of difficulty in the contemporary response to the play's situation. The first and perhaps major difficulty is not of course unique to our time; it is the power of the play itself, and the particularly agonising effect that the temptation and destruction of Othello, the murder of Desdemona, have upon us. It is undoubtedly less painful to create an Othello who is disqualified from our sympathy and respect by reason of his stupidity or his vanity: the very human desire to make the tragedy, and therefore the view of human existence that it embodies, more tolerable, is itself a potent reason for misreading. Professor Gardner notices, as related to this desire to make the play easier to accept, contemporary attitudes to war and soldiership generally and also to sexual jealousy. Since the First World War and particularly in view of what is now known of the incompetence of some of the General Staff, it is very difficult to accept a General as someone entitled by rank to our respect. Somehow a General sounds like a semi-comic Establishment figure, and any plea for his nobility, or any attempt at understanding for the strength of the passion aroused by his wife's infidelity, is likely to be regarded in our age of scepticism and fashionable sexual permissiveness as either distortion or inflation of the proper emotional content of the situation, and is therefore dismissed as sentimentality in the reader, in Othello himself, or possibly even in Shakespeare. I shall return to many of these points in my discussion of the play. However, since a good deal of twentieth-century criticism has tended to chip away at the notion of a noble Othello, it is perhaps as well to remind ourselves of what both Dr Johnson and Coleridge felt. In his *General Observation* on the play in the 1765 edition of Shakespeare's plays Dr Johnson writes of

> the fiery openness of Othello, magnanimous, artless, and credulous, boundless in his confidence, ardent in his affection, inflexible in his resolution, and obdurate in his revenge: the cold malignity of Iago, silent in his resentment, subtle in his designs, and studious at once of his interest and his vengeance; the soft simplicity of Desdemona, confident of merit and conscious of innocence, her artless perseverance in her suit and her slowness to suspect that she can be suspected, are such proofs of Shakespeare's skill in human nature as I suppose, it is vain to seek in any modern writer. The gradual progress which Iago makes in the Moor's conviction and the circumstances which he employs to influence him are so artfully natural that, though it will perhaps not be said of him, as he says of himself, that he is a man *not easily jealous*, yet we cannot but pity him when at last we find him *perplexed in the extreme*.[8]

Coleridge, too, makes the point that we must credit Iago's skill:

> Othello's *belief* is not caused by jealousy; it is forced upon him by Iago,
> and is such as any man would and must feel who had believed in Iago as
> Othello did. His great mistake is that *we* know Iago is a villain from the
> first moment . . . Othello does not kill Desdemona in jealousy but in a
> conviction forced upon him by the almost superhuman art of Iago, such
> a conviction as any man would and must have entertained who had
> believed in Iago's honesty as Othello did. We, the audience, know that
> Iago is a villain from the beginning; but in considering the essence of
> Shakespeare's Othello, we must perseveringly place ourselves in his situ-
> ation and under his circumstances. Then we shall immediately feel the
> fundamental difference between the solemn agony of the Noble Moor,
> and the wretched fishing jealousies of Leontes, and the morbid sus-
> piciousness of Leonatus, who is, in other respects, a fine character.
> Othello had no life but in Desdemona:— the belief that she, his angel,
> had fallen from the heaven of her native innocence, wrought a civil war
> in his heart . . .[9]

My own feeling is that Coleridge is pushing things too far when he
suggests that Othello did not kill Desdemona 'in jealousy' for there
surely can be no gainsaying that he does credit Iago, falls under his
influence, and savagely murders his wife. The real question is whether
there is something uniquely corrupt in Othello himself, which Iago
exposes, or whether Othello reacts to the situation in the only way that
he can, and that our understanding of this and our response to his
discovery of his error, convince us of the tragedy of his fate rather than
of his culpability as a man. In the discussion of the play that follows, I
shall try to concentrate my attention on the way Othello himself is
presented, his situation, his feelings, his actions, in an attempt to
resolve, for my own satisfaction at least, this central issue.

Written in 1604, at about the same time as *Measure for Measure* and
perhaps *Troilus and Cressida*, with both of which plays it shares the
explicit sexuality of its theme, and between *Hamlet* and *King Lear*, which
also share some of its concentration on the bitterness of sexual disillusionment that is such a feature of the fallen Othello's mind, this is a
play of Shakespeare's maturity and is usually acknowledged to be one
of his undoubted dramatic successes. What the play is really about,
then, is the central critical issue, for most critics, however they interpret
it, feel that its intentions are finely realised.

　　As with *Romeo and Juliet* and *Antony and Cleopatra*, a comparison with
the obvious source (in this case Cinthio's tale of the Moor, his wicked
Ensign and his wife Desdemona, in the *Hecatommithi*) is instructive in

pointing to a different emphasis in Shakespeare's handling of the plot. The original is what Kenneth Muir, in his *Shakespeare's Sources*,[10] quite fairly regards as a sordid tale of sexual jealousy and murder: what is vastly different is the treatment of the central figure of the Moor, who, in the Italian, almost completely lacks the dignity and the respect that Othello can command. It is surely this conviction that Othello, in spite of his succumbing to Iago's corruption, is a man of value and nobility, which produces the feeling that so many critics have noticed, an almost intolerable feeling of helplessness as we watch the destruction of the lovers, and it is this feeling that causes some critics to construct a less admirable Othello, so that his fall may seem less painful.

It seems to me that Shakespeare has written a play which allows of no escape either for its central figures or for the audience. If we read it with due attention we are denied the comfort of 'making trifles of terrors, consoling ourselves with seeming knowledge when we should commit ourselves to an uncommon fear'[11] or, as John Bayley has it, 'Like all great works of art, *Othello* deprives us of the confident sense of ourselves *vis-à-vis* the rest of the world'.[12] G. K. Hunter, in his 1967 lecture to the British Academy, '*Othello* and colour prejudice',[13] argues that there is a deliberate intention to shock us by using this story, with its central figure of the Moor, in this particular way. Shakespeare's audience would be only too ready to make the easy and customary equation of the colour black with things evil, ugly and damned. They would expect that a black man must be a wicked man, and they would be shocked to be confronted in the opening scenes with the black Othello's nobility, and with the white Iago's villainy. If we can agree with this argument, and Professor Hunter makes out a strong case, then we should see how from the play's beginning, there is an over-turning of expectation that ought to make us uneasy about accepting simple and stereotyped moral judgements on Othello and his situation.

Certainly the situation of the play, with the isolation of Othello as its central characteristic, depends to a very large extent on the fact that he is a Moor, a black alien in a white society. For his sake Desdemona becomes isolated too, for when she leaves the security of her father's home she places herself outside the protection of her society and is symbolically as well as literally cut off from its ordinary social contacts by her commitment to the alien. The closeness, the almost claustro-phobic nature of the whole situation, the lack of powerful outside intervention which give the tragedy what has sometimes been called its domestic flavour, have often been remarked upon. the despatch of Othello and Desdemona to Cyprus not only symbolically serves to isolate them further, it makes them wholly dependent on each other and on themselves if they are to resist Iago's attack on their love. They are, it is true, surrounded by people who admire and respect them and who wish them well (though with the exception of Cassio and Emilia, these people are virtually anonymous) but who are powerless to help or protect them. In this isolation, both Othello and Desdemona behave as their characters lead them to behave; they can do nothing else, and the full, terrible effect of their tragedy, I believe, depends on our recognition of this. In saying this I am not suggesting that Desdemona's actions bear a share of the responsibility for the catastrophe which is even remotely comparable with those of Othello, but I shall argue that just as in the particular situation in which she is placed she is trapped by her own innocence, her meekness and by her great love for Othello, so he too is trapped by his innocence, by his passion, and by his great love for Desdemona. Let me make it quite clear that I do not propose to try to 'excuse' Othello: what he becomes, in the full passion of his jealousy, and what he does, are terrible indeed, but we, the audience, are given an understanding of his predicament, and consequently a sympathy for him, which can never be a part of his own consciousness, or that of any other character in the play.

If we are to achieve this imaginative understanding of Othello's tragedy, then it is important that we should recognise the care with which his isolation, and the new factor in his life, his love for and acceptance by Desdemona, are presented, before the brawl on the battlements starts the workings of Iago's plot. I think it is now sufficiently generally accepted that the nineteenth-century desire to see Othello as an Arab rather than a Negro has little foundation in the text. On the contrary, the repeated references to his blackness, his sootiness and, in particular, Roderigo's contemptuous epithet 'the thick-lips' (I, i, 66) all make very clear the huge dramatic fact of his difference from all those around him. Not only is he different in appearance, he is different in temperament, different in experience and in achievement. He is a stranger; even his birth, we later learn, is a mystery, for Othello has never revealed his royal origins. His position in Venice he owes to his success as a soldier; it seems likely that he senses that underneath all the respect that is paid to him lies the fact that he is valued for the use he is to the state, and not for what he, as a man, is. How wide the gulf is between his official and his personal acceptance emerges quite clearly from the opening scenes. His worth to the state is undoubtedly great. He is needed, particularly now that the Turks threaten Cyprus and consequently Venice, but Iago with his skilful eye for seeing human weakness knows that Brabantio will feel very differently about having his friend, the great General, who also happens to be black, for a son-in-law. And so it proves: Brabantio's first reaction to the obscene jestings of Iago is incredulity: no daughter of his could ever make such a grotesque mis-match. When he discovers that she has indeed gone, he has only one thought, revenge. His first words on meeting Othello in the street are 'Down with him, thief' (I, ii, 583), and his subsequent attack

> O thou foul thief, where hast thou stow'd my daughter?
> Damn'd as thou art . . .
>
> (I, ii, 62)

is based on his firm conviction that his daughter must have been drugged or enchanted, for how could she otherwise

> . . . (to incur a general mock)
> Run from her guardage to the sooty bosom
> Of such a thing as thou?
>
> (I, ii, 69)

He is confident that the rest of Venice will share his view of things. When Othello appears before the Senate, to be confronted at once by Brabantio's accusation, the two modes of his life, the public life which has hitherto been his whole life, and his new-found private life, are brought into conflict; it is difficult to avoid the implication that as far as the Senators are concerned it is the public aspect of their General that is the more important. The overriding need is for Othello to be sent to Cyprus, so that when Desdemona herself makes her declaration of unforced love, while the Senators are glad for Othello's sake, they are even more glad for their own, and their relief is obvious.

It is, I think worth looking in some detail at Othello's account of his wooing, in particular at the way in which he speaks in these early scenes, since Dr Leavis and to some extent Professor Wilson Knight[14] claim to have detected a sort of emptiness or rhetorical flourish which they see as a sign of some basic flaw in Othello's character, a self-regarding quality which makes him unable to resist Iago's attacks. Leavis feels indeed that these attacks are directed against his vanity and not his love,[15] or rather perhaps that what Othello claims as his love is only an extension of his vanity. We may best begin by calling attention to a quality of formality in Othello's utterance, which disappears only when he is at his most incoherent, under the goading of Iago's insinuations. Appropriate to a man of some standing in a community, who is speaking a language not his own, this formality also serves to distance Othello somewhat from his fellows, and shows his

own consciousness of his public role in society. Even before the famous
'Keep up your bright swords, for the dew will rust them' (I, ii, 58) he
has said

> Let him do his spite,
> My service which I have done the Signiory
> Shall out-tongue his complaints . . .
>
> (I, ii, 17)

and in response to Iago's suggestion that he should avoid the confrontation with Brabantio he replies

> Not I, I must be found.
> My parts, my title, and my perfect soul
> Shall manifest me rightly . . .
>
> (I, ii, 30)

We should notice too, his avowal that this marriage is made for love,
not for any social advancement, and his declaration of the value he
places upon his independence. It is unnecessary to look for clues to
conceit here. He is accustomed to being a public figure, and knows his
importance to the State; he is being publicly accused, and must make a
public answer. 'Not I, I must be found' should be taken in the sense of
'Not I, the Commanding General' rather than 'Not I, the valiant
Othello', for when he goes on, it is clear that he is referring specifically
to that with which Iago tells him he is being charged, the abduction or
seduction of Desdemona. He refers to his qualities as a man, ('parts')
and his title as husband, as opposed to ravisher or seducer, and to his
clear conscience, telling Iago he has nothing to fear. But interestingly,
in view of the doubts that Iago will be able to inspire in him later, he
does not appear to be surprised by his father-in-law's reaction to the
marriage, nor by the fact that his private life must go on public trial. He
retains his dignity and his self-control, but it is as if he does so by the
exercise of a control that circumstances have made habitual. I am
arguing here that Othello, by the very fact of his difference from the
men in the society in which he occupies a respected place, is constantly
subjected to the conflicting pulls of an awareness of his own worth and
of his alienness. The way out of this conflict seems to have been discovered by Desdemona's love for him, unsolicited, unhoped for. His
speeches before the Senate are reminders to himself and to others of his
worth, not just as a soldier, but as a man, a worth that only Desdemona
has recognised. And yet, even in the moving

> She lov'd me for the dangers I had pass'd
> And I lov'd her that she did pity them . . .
>
> (I, iii, 167)

there is a hint of the same insecurity. Desdemona loves him because he
is the man who has so nobly endured the dangers, because his story has
revealed the kind of man he is, but Othello can hardly credit that at last
he is being valued for what he is. Later, when Iago suggests that it is
Othello's strangeness, the exotic quality of his person and of his story
that have briefly attracted the interest of a jaded appetite, the insecurity that he has clearly lived with in all his time in Venice comes
rushing back. Consider the outcome of the scene before the Senate:
Brabantio, hearing how Desdemona's love has been won, casts her off
as depraved, yet this is the same man who was proud to call Othello his
friend. He is advised by the Senate to make the best of what they
acknowledge to be a bad job

> When remedies are past, the griefs are ended
> By seeing the worst, which late on hopes depended.
>
> (I, iii, 202)

Othello must plead for permission for his wife to join him in Cyprus,
and is despatched in haste with Desdemona to follow. Brabantio is
offered the consolation that while Othello may be ugly to look at, there
are his virtues to be considered, and the scene ends in an ominous
exchange, spoken in malice by Brabantio, and stored in his mind in
malice by Iago, as the absolute importance of Othello's faith in
Desdemona's fidelity is stated.

> DUKE Let it be so.
> Goodnight to everyone. And, noble signior,
> If virtue no delighted beauty lack,
> Your son-in-law is far more fair than black.
>
> 1st SENATOR Adieu brave Moor; use Desdemona well.
>
> BRABANTIO Look to her, Moor, if thou hast eyes to see;
> She has deceived her father, and may thee.
>
> OTHELLO My life upon her faith!
>
> (I, iii, 287)

Even Desdemona, in her avowal of love 'That I did love the Moor to
live with him . . . ' has referred to Othello by his racial type, as do the
Senator and Brabantio here, and the scene is followed by Iago's sneer-
ing references to 'These Moors'. I hope that it will not be thought that I

am trying to turn this play into a twentieth-century polemic on the dangers of colour prejudice, but it does seem to me remarkable how little attention many critics who find a gross moral culpability in Othello's surrender to Iago's temptations pay to the overwhelming dramatic fact of Othello's blackness and his consequent occupation of only a public place in his society. Until Desdemona has given him her love, his own private life has been something that has never been allowed to show: it is quite remarkable how little we know of what Othello has felt, as opposed to what he has done, beyond that he has endured. When his self-control does crack, those who think they know him best are amazed: can this be the man who has never lost his composure in the face of mortal danger? But to say that he has not exhibited his private feelings before is not to suggest that he has not had them; he knows, as the others do not, at what a cost his self-control has been maintained, and indeed says so when he is aroused by the drunken brawling of Cassio and Roderigo.

Desdemona's love for him and his for her have therefore a double significance. Not only has she accepted him as a man in the most intimate of human relationships, but by their marriage and her father's opposition to it, what has been private to Othello and unshared with the world at large is brought into the open. It is significant that the first time even Iago learns of the nobility of Othello's birth is after the marriage. Desdemona's acceptance of him as an individual is more important to him than any of the respect that his usefulness as an efficient defender of the State can buy. I think it is not too much to say that his faith in her is absolute, that he means exactly what he says when he declares 'My life upon her faith . . .' (I, iii, 294). That declaration marks his emergence from his public *persona*, from the ability as a soldier that has been his protective shield against an alien and potentially hostile society. As he himself seems to realise, he has put himself in jeopardy, put his free condition into circumspection and confine, but he has no choice, because he cannot help but love Desdemona. It is his tragic fate that his emergence as a full man, trusted and trusting, happy in his love, should also be the action by which he exposes himself to his enemies' attacks, but this is love's nature. As Professor Gardner has remarked, 'It is perilous to garner up one's heart in the heart of another human being, and whoever does so loses control of his destiny'.[16]

For what is to follow, much depends on how strongly the play succeeds in establishing the state of happiness that Othello and Desdemona briefly attain before Iago's plot starts to work. As in *Romeo and Juliet*, time seems by its very nature the enemy of the lovers; though it has brought them together, in the action of the play its only operation

is to bring them to destruction. Any happiness that can be won has to
be snatched out of time, enshrined in what seems a timeless moment.
Such a moment is the meeting in Cyprus, which has a numinous quality of perfection about it, and yet is suffused with an awareness that the
perfection cannot be preserved. First Cassio's ship, then Desdemona's
and Iago's and finally Othello's (who had set out first) emerge from the
hazards of the storm and make safe landing. The news comes too, that
the threatening Turkish fleet has been scattered by the same storm; the
dangers from outside have been dispelled, the perils of separation
endured, all have come safely to harbour. The rapt quality of the
speeches, the awe with which Othello accepts love as a gift for which he
feels himself quite unworthy, the way in which the whole experience of
being in love, after what he has endured and experienced before in his
life, seems almost too good to be true, is admirably captured in the
movement of the verse:

> OTHELLO O my fair warrior!
>
> DESDEMONA My dear Othello!
>
> OTHELLO It gives me wonder great as my content
> To see you here before me. O my soul's joy!
> If after every tempest come such calms,
> May the winds blow till they have waken'd death!
> And let the labouring bark climb hills of seas
> Olympus high and duck again as low
> As hell's from heaven! If it were now to die,
> 'Twere now to be most happy; for I fear
> My soul hath her content so absolute
> That not another comfort like to this
> Succeeds in unknown fate.
>
> (II, i, 181)

Obviously, the verse carries its undertones of foreboding; it is so clearly
true that this first achievement is also the peak of their happiness that it
hardly needs Iago's

> O, you are well tun'd now!
> But I'll set down the pegs that make this music,
> As honest as I am . . .
>
> (II, i, 199)

to make the threat clear. The description of the storm, the confusion
between hell and heaven, the narrow margin that is implied between
safety and disaster, all point to the risk that so absolute a love entails.
Othello's declaration

> . . . If it were now to die
> 'Twere now to be most happy . . .

takes the play to the point reached by Romeo and Juliet, who have to endure a physical separation, but even in death find no shadowing of their love for each other. I have already suggested that one of the points Shakespeare repeatedly makes about the nature of love is that of its vulnerability to the forces of time, though he also sees it as being in a different sense, time's conqueror. I have suggested too, that the first intense love of Romeo and Juliet cannot by its nature endure, must be cut off or altered to some other feeling, so that in one sense death preserves them from change. Unlike *Romeo and Juliet, Othello* is a play that investigates one possible aspect of such a change. Othello, though a much older man, and one who can justly express his love for Desdemona in the image of having come to safe harbour after the storms of his life, is also experiencing first love, with all its thrilling intensity, and its illusion of inhabiting a different planet from other mortals, and with the added feeling, because of his customary relationship with society, that for him to experience all this joy is almost incredible. 'My soul hath her content so absolute', with its pun on content, suggests both the idea of having found all that his soul requires, and the bewildering sense of joy and security that Desdemona's love gives him. The exchange between the lovers is brief; it is also formal and public, but I believe that for all that it does create for us, in the hushed movement and the simplicity of the language, the charmed world which the lovers momentarily inhabit. It is a world which is absolute in itself, for neither in this life or a life to come, can Othello imagine as great a happiness. This moment of stillness, the eye of the storm in Othello's life, is a fixed point of reference to which he returns again and again in his expression of the worth which he is made to believe has been lost.

I do not want to seem needlessly paradoxical by seeing in Othello's feelings both a new-found security and a new-found fear. The new experience of a happiness so great, as love poetry often testifies, can bring its own bewilderment, its own fear that this is all a dream or an illusion, and it is when Othello is in this state of hovering between belief and doubt, not in Desdemona, but in his own good fortune, that Iago steps in and demonstrates, with the air of one who is only trying to be helpful, the precise nature of what he presents as a common illusion. A man not so newly in love, or a man more confident in himself would have been better able to resist.

So far I have considered the central situation of the play in terms of Othello's prior isolation, and of the nature of the love he shares with Desdemona. The third major element in the situation is the intervention of Iago.

As the cause of Othello's destruction, Iago has sometimes been written up to almost the status of the play's villain-hero, and sometimes written down to a mere plot device to allow Othello to expose his own corruption. It may be useful at this stage to make a comparison between Othello's situation and the situations of Leontes and Posthumus Leonatus in their respective plays. Leontes' jealous outburst is very different, for it is clearly unfounded, having its origin only in his own brain. Moreover, there is a good deal in that play[17] to suggest that it is Leontes' attitude to his wife, his treatment of her and their son as mere extensions of his own personality, that allow the jealousy that threatens to destroy them all to take root. He can plead no outside cause to excuse his lack of faith and his resulting cruelty. Posthumus, by contrast, does have to endure the plottings of Iachimo, who as his name suggests is an Iago-like character, but nothing like as important in the play, or as formidable in resource and resolution. Posthumus, too, before his jealous outburst, shows some obvious inadequacy in his feelings for Imogen. He too thinks of her as a possession, and like Leontes when he believes Hermione unfaithful, Posthumus wants Imogen destroyed because he feels she has humiliated him in the world's eyes. Both feel that they have been disgraced and that they want revenge, but neither feels, as Othello comes to feel, that life itself has become intolerable. Personal vanity is wounded, but there even seems to be some perverse satisfaction in this. The evidence against Imogen that Iachimo presents is very flimsy, as Posthumus' friends are quick to point out, but Posthumus seems almost determined to believe himself wronged. Leontes, too, brushes aside the reassurance of his courtiers, seeming to enjoy the importance of his role as the wronged husband. Othello, I believe, resists for as long as he can.

It is almost too obvious to be stated that the amount of time Shakespeare devotes to Iago's temptation of Othello means that this temptation must be taken seriously; indeed Iago shares prominence with Othello from the play's opening, so that we are made very fully aware of the sort of man he is, and even more important, of the sort of man that others think him to be. It is easy to forget that we, the audience, are in possession of knowledge which characters in the play cannot share. Many critics have implied by the whole direction of their accounts of the play that because we know from the beginning that Iago is a villain, Othello ought to know it too, as if the only reason for letting us into the secret were to heighten our sense of Othello's stupidity. A much more powerful dramatic reason for doing so, and one that agrees very much better with most people's impression of the play in performance or even in reading—where it is sometimes easier to ignore a dramatic emphasis—is the intensification of the agony (I think it not too strong a word) that Iago's deception produces. The point apparently needs to be made repeatedly, that nobody in the play, not Othello, who has known him for years; not his wife Emilia; not his comrades in arms; not Roderigo, whom he dupes so outrageously and who knows of the plot against Othello, but seems convinced that at least Iago is honest with him; not even the gentle and sensitive Desdemona suspect for a moment that Iago is anything other than a bluntly spoken soldier, practical, reliable, *honest*. The only time before his final exposure when, accurately, he is called a villain, is when he is taunting Brabantio, but Brabantio does not then know to whom he is talking.

It may perhaps be objected that it is not reasonable to believe Iago could either have kept up the pretence of truthfulness for so long, or have changed his whole nature so suddenly after being disappointed in his expectation of promotion, but such an argument seeks to extend the play beyond its legitimate terms. Shakespeare, particularly in the tragedies, is much more concerned with the consequences of passion than with its causes, though in any account of its nature its causes must play some part. In any case this fuller account of cause and effect is generally provided only for a central character. There may be hints about minor characters, who always, when it is dramatically necessary that they should do so, exhibit with absolute credibility the quality that most affects the central situation. We are not told, for instance, why Lady Macbeth is fiercely ambitious, or why Goneril and Regan are evil, as they undoubtedly are; their qualities are part of the given situation and we accept that they are so. In the Romances Shakespeare daringly pushes this concept of dramatic construction to its very limits, and by sheer poetic power persuades us to accept whatever is needful to illuminate what is of central interest.

In *Othello* we simply have to accept that Iago is as he is, both absolutely trusted, and wilfully destructive. As has often been observed, he offers a variety of reasons for his attack on Othello: disappointment in his career, professional and sexual jealousy of Cassio, lust for Desdemona, the suspicion that Othello has cuckolded him, are all advanced by him, without any one of these motives seeming to carry more than a passing conviction. Ever since Coleridge characterised this as the 'motive hunting of motiveless malignity'[18] critics seemed to have been impelled either to find a convincing motive for Iago, or feel that he is unconvincing without one. I suppose that I fall into the first category, though I believe that we look in vain to find any satisfactory single specific motive for his actions. In the most general terms, his actions depend upon his opinion of himself. He believes that he is intelligent, rational, cynical, in absolute command of himself and therefore able to manipulate others. He believes that he himself is the only judge of his true worth; he also believes that he can see through and exploit for his own satisfaction the illusions of others. Moreover, he believes that his destiny is to do what he wants to do, and that any devotion to any less selfish ideal is a romantic delusion. All of this is suggested in the opening speeches of Iago and Roderigo in Act I, scene i, and is made clear in their later exchanges at the end of the Act. For Iago, the 'Power and corrigible authority . . . lies in our wills' and he puts the exercise of reason at no greater value than to achieve the desires of the will. Because he finds it impossible to acknowledge a love that can contradict his assertion that all a man needs in life is to know how to love himself, all other love must then be reduced to appetite, to 'carnal stings and unbitted lusts'. If others cannot control themselves as well as he, and Roderigo is the obvious case in point, then he, the cool man who keeps his head, may profitably take advantage of them. It is because Othello cares about something other than himself that Iago can strike at him, but this does not make Iago superior to his victim.

It is clear that Iago, in order to sustain this view of the world, has to remodel reality just as much as those whom he accuses of deluding themselves. For him to sustain the good opinion of himself that is central to his character he must either ignore or destroy anything that threatens to prove his philosophy false. In Act V he says of Cassio

> He has a daily beauty in his life
> That makes me ugly . . .
>
> (V, i, 19)

and all his actions against others seem to me ultimately explicable in the light of this remark. In Iago's immediate world, Othello, by his action in failing to prefer Iago to Cassio, by the example of his love for Desdemona, by his very existence, is the living refutation of Iago's cynicism. Above all, the mutual interdependence of the lovers, living for each other rather than for themselves, is an affront to his whole picture of the world. For a while he seems to toy with the idea that Othello and Desdemona are acting out a sham, that the Moor *will* prove changeable, and she unfaithful, but soon he sees that if they are to be destroyed it will have to be by deception. Then if their perfect love can be brought down, there will be one thing less in his immediate world to refute the supreme value he places on himself. It is likely moreover, that Iago embarks on his scheme for a variety of practical reasons: Roderigo, who has proved profitable to him, is threatening to despair and give up the whole enterprise of the wooing of Desdemona. His interest must be maintained, and in order to do this some breach must be manufactured between Othello and Desdemona. If this can be done there will be revenge for his own slighting as well, and if his supplanter Michael Cassio can be involved, then so much the better. It is a complex plot, but Dr Leavis has rightly pointed out the fallacy of regarding Iago as possessing a diabolical intellect.[19] Nobody having the superhuman powers of evil with which he is sometimes credited could possibly proceed so clumsily, depend so much on chance, and in the end so badly miscalculate the character of his own wife, so that he is caught and destroyed by his own plottings. But even before Emilia's disclosure, it is clear that Iago is very far from being the cool controller of the whole situation that he would like to think himself. Once the germ of the idea presents itself to him, at the end of Act I

> . . . Let me see
> To get his place, and to plume up my will
> In double knavery—How, how?—Let's see:—
> After some time, to abuse Othello's ear
> That he is too familiar with his wife.
> He hath a person and a smooth dispose
> To be suspected, framed to make women false.
> The Moor is of a free and open nature,
> That thinks men honest that but seem to be so,
> And will as tenderly be led by the nose
> As asses are.
> I have't. It is engender'd. Hell and night
> Must bring this monstrous birth to the world's light . . .
>
> (I, iii, 390)

he functions as a splendid opportunist, but one who inevitably becomes more and more entangled himself. Othello's frenzied threat 'Villain, be sure thou prove my wife a whore' (III, iii, 356) reminds him how precarious a path he is treading, and involves him in the virtual impossibility of attempting to arrange the double murder of Cassio and Desdemona, so that his plots may remain undiscovered. But that goes wrong too, for the very simple and practical reason that Cassio wears a shirt of mail. Then Roderigo must be silenced; then, in a flurry of desperation, Emilia, and so inevitably he is trapped.

All this is true, but the conclusion sometimes drawn from it, that if Iago is a bungling plotter, we ought to infer that Othello should not have been deceived, by no means follows. The way Iago destroys Othello's faith is extremely clever, clever enough to make Othello want to believe, if he could do so, that Iago *is* the devil, though he knows he cannot be allowed that comfort—'But that's a fable.' Clear-sighted enough about the weaknesses of others, Iago cannot recognise his own, so that his moment of triumph is also his defeat. He can rejoice at Othello's suffering, but he must also acknowledge Desdemona's fidelity, and therefore must be aware that the re-establishment of Othello's faith is likewise a fact that cannot be denied. He can claim no triumph, for the qualities which his plot was created to deny still exist; it is appropriate that the master of words should go to his torture and death with no words left.

Finally, in this consideration of the particular circumstances of Othello's temptation and fall, we ought to remember the part played by sheer bad luck. The operation of chance attracts a good deal of comment in *Romeo and Juliet*; in *Othello* it is often overlooked, but it plays its part, most obviously in the dropping of the handkerchief, which provides the one piece of 'circumstantial' evidence to support the whole fabric of Iago's deception. We should not forget, though, the headlong rush of events (I shall try to deal with the question of 'double time' later) which separates Othello and Desdemona on the night of their marriage day, which, by the drunken brawl in Cyprus, disturbs their first night together, and which allows Iago to take advantage of their strangeness to each other to work so on Othello that he becomes incapable of communicating with Desdemona, whose meekness and submissiveness do not allow her even to question the growing strangeness of her husband's behaviour until it is too late. There is the final, fatal ambiguity of Desdemona's response to the news of Cassio's death, which, uttered in all innocence, is taken by Othello as final confirmation, from her own lips, of her unchastity, and arouses in him the resolution and fury he needs to kill her. And, of course, running through it all, is the seemingly overwhelming probability that a chance word, an idle question, will blow away the whole flimsy net of words that Iago is weaving around Othello, and yet it does not. Much of the almost intolerable tension that the play produces comes from the hopes of the audience that something will bring Othello to his senses, expose Iago for what he is, before it is too late. Nothing does.

What has often been seen as the central critical issue of the play, whether or not Othello too easily becomes jealous, must be judged against the carefully presented elements of the situation that I have been trying to analyse, but obviously, the temptation scenes themselves, the methods and underlying assumptions of Iago's attacks, and Othello's reactions to them, are of crucial importance.

The whole question of sexual jealousy is a difficult one to discuss. There is no reason to suppose that it was not, in Elizabethan times as now, one of the most intensely felt of emotions, irrational, violent, terrifying both to the person experiencing it, and to the onlooker. It is also a degrading passion, which is one of the reasons why the spectacle of Othello completely in its sway is so painful, and why this affords such pleasure to Iago. However, in our present climate of sexual permissiveness, we are perhaps predisposed to feel there is something profoundly barbaric, uncivilised, about someone who cannot keep this jealousy under control, though it is perhaps truer to recognise that the only way in which this apparently desirable state of indifference can be achieved, whereby sexual partners can be lost or changed without heartache, is to accept that all such relationships are as valuable, or as valueless, as each other. To do so is in fact to deny, as Iago denies, the possibility of a uniquely valuable relationship between two people, to reduce all love to the level of pleasure, appetite, will. Few people, I believe, who care intensely about each other can contemplate with any detachment the sexual infidelity of their partners. Something must break: either they must cease to care, or they must suffer in proportion to the strength of their feelings of attachment. This is indeed the choice that Othello sees as open to him as he begins to contemplate, still fairly impersonally, the implications of what Iago is suggesting:

> Why, why is this?
> Think'st thou I'ld make a life of jealousy?
> To follow still the changes of the moon
> With fresh suspicions? No, to be once in doubt
> Is once to be resolved: exchange me for a goat,
> When I shall turn the business of my soul
> To such exsufflicate and blown surmises,
> Matching thy inference. 'Tis not to make me jealous
> To say my wife is fair, feeds well, loves company,
> Is free of speech, sings, plays and dances well;
> Where virtue is, these are more virtuous:
> Nor from mine own weak merits will I draw
> The smallest fear or doubt of her revolt;
> For she had eyes, and chose me. No, Iago;
> I'll see before I doubt; when I doubt, prove;
> And on the proof, there is no more but this,—
> Away at once with love or jealousy!
>
> (III, iii, 180)

His reply is the reply of any reasonable man who is considering the question with as much detachment as the topic allows, and does not yet feel himself directly threatened. The choice seems so easy: 'Away at once with love or jealousy'. Some eighty lines later, when he is being faced with the possibility that Desdemona may be betraying him, the choice has become much more agonising:

> . . . if I do prove her haggard,
> Though that her jesses were my dear heartstrings,
> I'd whistle her off, and let her down the wind,
> To prey at fortune . . .

(III, iii, 264)

but he still thinks of it as a choice he can make; significantly, there is no thought of revenge upon Desdemona yet; she is a wild thing of beauty, dangerous, untameable, destructive, but she will be given her freedom. It is only when he finds that he cannot stop caring about her, that he still finds her intensely attractive sexually, that his whole consciousness is thrown into chaos and incoherence.

There can be little doubt that the general Elizabethan attitude, if one may legitimately speak of such an abstract concept, was to take the business of being cuckolded very seriously indeed. And a general, of course, would lose all authority if cuckolded by one of his own officers. We need only to remember the seemingly inevitable jokes on horns that stud the plays of the period to recognise how deep a preoccupation it must have been, how frightening a depth of feeling must have been covered by the cynical avoidance of real thought on the subject that the jokes allowed. Othello, under the remorseless goadings of Iago, is not allowed to turn aside from anything, and is forced to contemplate the degradation of sexual rejection to the full. The pain this causes him ought not to be underestimated. In fact, Iago's technique depends for its success to a large extent on the confusion engendered in Othello's mind by the grossness of the sexual images Iago presents. It is a technique that has had a trial run, as it were, in the baiting of Brabantio, where Iago has supplied the emotive detail to confuse and infuriate the old man;

> Even now, very now, an old black ram
> Is tupping your white ewe;

(I, i, 88)

> You'll have your daughter covered with a Barbary horse; you'll have your nephews neigh to you . . .

(I, i, 110)

and

> . . . your daughter, and the Moor, are now making the beast with two backs.

(I, i, 115)

The visualisations that Iago's words seek to induce are of the crudest kind, they are charged with the contempt that Iago feels for the act of love, for the gratification of an appetite is all that he can ever allow love to be. We ought to remember, for instance, his comments to himself during the exchange of courtesies between Desdemona and Cassio in Act II, scene i. Because of their very grossness, Iago's images tend to defeat any rational reaction. Brabantio is roused to almost hysterical fury by Iago's account of what has occurred, without being able to consider how little it may correspond to the realities of the situation. The same technique is used on Othello, at two crucial points in the temptation scene, but before Iago has won sufficient ground to be able to do this, he mounts his first attack against Othello's own insecurity. The drunken brawl he engineers gives him the first stage of his revenge, the dismissal of Cassio, which is then in its turn put to work against the lovers by his encouraging Cassio to persuade Desdemona to plead for his reinstatement with her husband. Once Desdemona makes the initial approach to Othello on the subject, Iago is free to proceed, which he does with a great deal of skill and assurance.

He utilises to the full his reputation for bluff honesty, by seeming to allow himself to be drawn only with reluctance to utter his thoughts. This ploy, obvious enough to need no illustrative quotation here, I think, has the double merit, for Iago's purpose, of seeming to allow Othello to arrive at the truth for himself, and also of keeping open an avenue of escape for Iago himself should things go wrong. It is interesting to notice that at this point Iago seems anxious to provide himself with a line of retreat: as he progresses further in his conquest of Othello's mind he becomes himself more and more involved, more and more vulnerable, until even the accomplishment of what becomes the aim of this plan, the killing of Cassio and Desdemona, can hardly be held to offer much hope of his plot remaining undiscovered.

From the cover of his seeming reluctance, Iago concentrates first on Othello's sense of alienation. He reminds him, with the air of a local inhabitant imparting to a stranger something that is common knowledge, of how little Othello knows of Venetian women, of how notorious they are for their sexual whims and infidelities. Othello, by his own admission 'for since these arms of mine had seven years pith . . . ' (I, ii, 83) knows little of peaceful society, let alone of the sophistication of Venice. Iago suggests to him that he knows equally little of Desdemona. The reminder that she has deceived her father puts Othello back into the painful situation of Brabantio's emotional accusation of him before the Senate, and, perhaps, brings back to him many of his old insecurities. In these early stages, Iago is shrewd enough to base his insinuations on known facts, the truth of which cannot be in dispute, but also to claim a wordly wisdom which interprets these facts in a way which, he suggests, is obvious to anyone of any experience. This is an interpretation completely different from the construction Othello has put on these facts. Othello's own modesty has made Desdemona take the initiative in the wooing; at the time, Othello ascribes this openness to the simplicity of her love and to her innocence, as indeed is the case. Now Iago skilfully suggests that it is Othello's vanity, his own desire to be loved, that makes him interpret it so, that perhaps Desdemona has always been too ready to make the running, to encourage men to make love to her. He even goes so far in daring as to use Othello's feeling, natural to someone in love, of not deserving so great a treasure as Desdemona's love, by suggesting that the match is inexplicable on any grounds other than sexual whim. His 'come, we are men of the world' tone in the following passage

> IAGO Ay, there's the point: as—to be bold with you—
> Not to affect many proposed matches
> Of her own clime, complexion, and degree,
> Whereto we see in all things nature tends—
> Foh! one may smell in such a will most rank,
> Foul disproportion, thoughts unnatural.
> But pardon me; I do not in position
> Distinctly speak of her; though I may fear
> Her will, recoiling to her better judgement,
> May fall to match you with her country forms
> As happily repent . . .
>
> (III, iii, 232)

plays upon Othello's doubts, uses Brabantio's astonishment that Desdemona should have rejected so many eligible young Venetians 'of her own clime, complexion and degree'. Iago is guarded in his terms, but the thrusts nevertheless get home. After he has left, we find Othello with his sense of wonder at his good fortune beginning to be changed into something very much more disturbing. Othello knows that Brabantio, for one, thinks of him as old and black and ugly, as a grotesquely unfit match for Desdemona. Now Iago, who ostensibly wishes him well and seems anxious to help, is saying very much the same thing in a more roundabout way. Othello's musings

> Haply, for I am black,
> And have not those soft parts of conversation
> That chamberers have, or for I am declin'd
> Into the vale of years—yet that's not much—
> She's gone, I am abus'd and my relief
> Must be to loathe her: . . .
>
> (III, iii, 267)

show how much he is disturbed, as much by the whip-flicks of Iago's contemptuous pity— 'I see that this hath a little dash'd your spirits' (III, iii, 218) and 'Long live she so, and long live you to think so' (III, iii, 230) as by any clear realisation of what he is being led to believe.

It is perhaps appropriate at this point to begin our consideration of whether or not there is something in Othello's responses here that reveals some radical flaw in the nature of his love for Desdemona, or in the man himself. Is he so conceited that any suggestion of being in a position that invites ridicule at once makes him lose all control, or is there something so inordinately possessive in his feeling for Desdemona that makes him see her, not as she is, but as a chattel who is only a projection of his own desires, in rather the way that Troilus sees Cressida? Is he responding to Iago's suggestion too promptly, and are we asked to blame him for this? I think the first point to be noticed here is the pace of this temptation scene. I have earlier remarked that the workings of the plot rush the lovers along to destruction at a headlong pace, but I do not mean to imply that the pace throughout the play is uniformly fast. A common enough experience is that Act III, scene iii, particularly in performance, gives the impression of a considerable length of time passing. Iago leaves the stage and comes back twice, Othello himself leaves and comes back, and this coming and going, together with the sustained intensity of the emotion, produces the impression of a man being kept under pressure for an intolerably long time.

There has been a recent, closely-argued essay[20] which sets out to show that far from the so-called double-time scheme in *Othello* being evidence of consummate dramatic skill, it in fact provides some strong evidence for seeing the play as having been composed in two parts, probably with the second part written first, and the first part, written on a different plan, botched on later. The author tends rather to ridicule the critics who have elevated such an obvious blunder into a dramatic strength, but whatever the mode of composition of this play may have been, even if Shakespeare perhaps forgot what detailed use he had made of part of his source when he was working on another section of the play (which seems to me to be very improbable, to say the least) my own impression of the finished work is more in line with those critics from Dr Johnson onwards who have seen this play as one of the most tightly-knit of Shakespeare's dramatic constructions. Fortuitously or by design, the play's two different time-schemes, one requiring some length of time since Othello's marriage for Iago's stories of Cassio's attentions to Desdemona to be even possible, the other hurrying things to their fatal conclusion two nights after the arrival in Cyprus, so that there is no time for chance to reveal the falsity of Iago's witness, each works with perfect dramatic credibility when required to do so. Thus the audience does not feel that Othello is reacting to Iago's suggestions with undue haste, but rather that the racking of his sensibilities is stretched out almost beyond the limits of human endurance. We know, in retrospect, that there has not been time for Cassio's dream, as Iago recounts it, but we can appreciate that the confusion induced in Othello's brain is so great that he can believe of his wife that she has repeatedly been unfaithful to him. In a strange way, this jealous fury actually protects him from a loss of too much sympathy, for if he could keep a cool head, weigh the flimsy evidence that Iago produces, and then believe the story, his credulity would indeed be monstrous. Patently, he hardly knows where or who he is, once the possibility of belief takes hold of him, and it is worth reiterating that it gains its first foothold, not through his conceit, but because he is too ready to accept that he cannot really be worthy of winning Desdemona's love.

It is easy, from our superior position as critics or audience, to say that Othello ought not to have listened to Iago for a moment, that his faith in the woman he loves ought to have made him dismiss instantly the slightest breath of suspicion against her. This, after all, is the reaction of Cassio, even of Roderigo, when Iago suggests to them that Desdemona is 'full of game'. Anyone else to whom Othello suggests that Desdemona is unchaste is openly incredulous. Why cannot the man who loves her most see what outsiders can see?

I think the answer lies in the honesty with which Shakespeare investigates the dualities of love. Those critics who see a radically flawed Othello, and who claim that any reading that allows him to regain his nobility is a romanticising one, are perhaps themselves guilty of basing their arguments on a highly romantic supposition, that intense love will admit of no doubt, and conversely that if doubt arises, then the love is not worthy of the name. It would be reassuring if this were so; common experience tends to show that it is not. The more precious the love, in one sense, the more we fear to lose it.[21] J. I. M. Stewart's interesting account of this aspect of the play,[22] in which he argues that what Shakespeare has done has been to split the two parts of the lover's nature, love's trust and happiness on the one hand, and its subconscious fears on the other, and embody the conflict between them in the persons of Othello and Iago, though perhaps too neatly symbolic, has a great deal to commend it, particularly as it makes it unnecessàry to see in Othello's response something uniquely corrupt and culpable. What Othello fears is in part what any lover fears, just as Romeo's and Juliet's fear of losing each other to death is part of the experience of any love affair. (Robert Graves's poem 'Pure death'[23] makes this point neatly.) In this aspect, at least, the play seems to combine easily the worlds of symbol and reality: the danger that Iago represents is a danger that any love that is to endure must face, but Othello does not surrender to that doubt simply because he does not love Desdemona well enough. On the natural level, he does so because an old friend in whose honesty he has absolute trust informs him, with every appearance of doing so for the best motives, of the *fact* that his wife *is* unfaithful. Then, as Stewart again very shrewdly suggests, there is something of an affinity with the operation of time in Iago's temptings: time seems to be on Iago's side, as he manipulates to his advantage the discrepancy in age between Othello and Desdemona, the shortness of time they have known each other, and stretches time to manufacture credibility for the affair he conjures up with Cassio. The arbitrariness of the relative duration of time, most marked when we are in the grip of strong emotion, seems to ally itself with Iago and operate to the destruction of Othello. Whereas in the comedies, time is finally on the side of the lovers, unravelling the complications in which they seem hopelessly entangled

VIOLA   O Time, thou must untangle this, not I;
               It is too hard a knot for me t' untie!

                                        (*Twelfth Night*, II,, ii, 38)

in the tragedies time has become the destroyer which alters or corrupts all that is of most value.

Iago, then, exploits the fears that are a part of Othello's intense caring: he also exploits those other elements, impurities, if some critics are to be believed, which Shakespeare's honesty leads him to acknowledge as part of the nature of love. I have elsewhere[24] quoted Blake's lines from 'The clod and pebble', evoking love's mingled nature, its compound of selfishness and selflessness, of giving and receiving, of possessiveness and the acknowledgement of the individuality of both the self and the beloved. Vanity plays a part too: we like to be proud of the people we love, for our own sake as well as theirs. Any critical attack on the integrity of Othello's love which points to this line or to that as evidence of possessiveness, or of pride, or of humiliation at the notion of what other people will think of him, is not conclusively damning simply because it shows that these qualities are part of what he feels. Only in an absurdly romantic picture of a lover would they not be present: the question is rather whether their disproportion can be demonstrated, whether they outweigh the other qualities. Thus the lines

> I had rather be a toad,
> And live upon the vapour in a dungeon
> Than keep a corner in the thing I love
> For others' uses . . .
>
> (III, iii, 274)

are often seized on as an example of Othello's possessiveness, and of his insensitivity to Desdemona as a person. It seems to me rather that what he is saying is that if she *is* promiscuous, then she is indeed an object, with the depersonalising words 'thing' and 'corner' attempting to push away from him the pain of the sexual hurt, of the disappointment of his conviction of her uniquely individual value. Leontes and Troilus, as we have already noticed, provide a comparison with Othello's attitude here, and at this point in the play, when he is first falling into the trap Iago has set, his initial response comes close to theirs. He feels injured in his pride, in his self-respect; above all he feels unjustly treated, for as he quite reasonably implies, he has given Desdemona no cause so to injure him. He has remained what he was: if she has changed, her fault must be common to all women, for she had seemed perfection. Leontes and Troilus too, in order to ease their personal hurt, claim that their betrayal (real in the case of Troilus, wholly imagined, without the slightest provocation, in the case of Leontes) is man's universal destiny. But Othello, unlike the others, cannot long take any sort of comfort in this: his agonised cry

> . . . Desdemona comes,
> If she be false, O, then heaven mocks itself,
> I'll not believe it . . .
>
> (III, iii, 280)

is a highly complex dramatic statement, and again, its complexity may best appear by comparison with *Troilus and Cressida*, where Troilus, confronted with the sight of Cressida and Diomede together, cries,

> Let it not be believed for womanhood!
> Think, we had mothers; do not give advantage
> To stubborn critics, apt, without a theme,
> For depravation, to square the general sex
> By Cressid's rule: rather think this not Cressid.
>
> (V, ii, 125)

Troilus attempts at first to deny what he, and the audience, know to be true; his pain is great, but his refuge, broadly speaking, is in the vision

of a wholly corrupt world, in which his mistake about Cressida's nature
need not therefore be his fault. He moves from the particular to the
general. Othello, though he too tries to derive consolation from a general vision of corruption, is brought back to the particular with
Desdemona's entry. His cry of 'I'll not believe it' is an affirmation of
faith against what he can see as strong evidence to the contrary, and it
gains strength and poignancy from our knowledge that his instinct is
right. We cannot expect betrayed lovers to say with Malcolm that
'Angels are bright still, though the brightest fell', yet there is a difference between those who because of their betrayal see the whole world
as futile and fit to be given to destruction, like Troilus, and those like
Othello, who, while his own life may be reduced to chaos, still does not
seek refuge in the vision of a chaotic world, simply because it does not
run his way. Troilus cannot accept that he has made a mistake: Othello
cannot initially believe that Desdemona is false, but when he is
deceived into thinking that she is, he can admit the possibility that he
may have been wrong. The irony is that he was right, that he should
have trusted his instincts.

It is, I think, psychologically accurate and not indicative of some
peculiar conceit in Othello, that when we next see him a few minutes
later in actual time, but dramatically distanced by Iago's

> Dangerous conceits are in their natures poisons,
> Which at first are scarce found to distaste,
> But with a little act upon the blood,
> Burn like the mines of sulphur. I did say so:
> Look where he comes!
>   Not poppy, nor mandragora,
> Nor all the drowsy syrups of the world,
> Shall ever medicine thee to that sweet sleep
> Which thou owedst yesterday . . .
>
>   (III, iii, 331)

he is brooding on a sense of his own injury. The full realisation of what
he has lost dawns on him only slowly. His big speech

> I had been happy, if the general camp,
> Pioneers and all, had tasted her sweet body,
> So I had nothing known. O, now, for ever
> Farewell the tranquil mind! farewell content!
> Farewell the plumed troop, and the big wars,
> That make ambition virtue! O, farewell!
> Farewell the neighing steed, and the shrill trump,
> The spirit-stirring drum, the ear-piercing fife,
> The royal banner, and all quality,
> Pride, pomp and circumstance of glorious war!

> And, O you mortal engines, whose rude throats
> The immortal Jove's dread clamours counterfeit,.
> Farewell! Othello's occupation's gone! . . .
>
> (III, iii, 351)

is more interesting in its revelation of his state of mind at this stage than has sometimes been acknowledged. In our intellectual, anti-militaristic age, many critics have been only too apt to agree with Iago's diagnosis of this as militaristic bombast. I have already said that, in a play on this subject, the painful nature of the material, the pressure of the emotion it engenders is such that it is most difficult to read with the necessary attention, to avoid snatching a general impression and hurrying on. When Othello says

> Pioneers and all, had tasted her sweet body,
> So I had nothing known . . .

He is *not* degrading Desdemona and elevating his own monstrous conceit, though he has sometimes been accused of doing so. The emphasis falls almost unendurably on ' . . . so had I nothing known'. Obviously, there is bitterness against Desdemona, and mortification at the thought of being that figure of scorn, the betrayed husband, made the more painful because of his position as commanding general, but there is also a sort of inconsolable longing back to an earlier state of happiness which Othello now feels is lost for ever. His previous words have made the point: if Desdemona, unchaste, could yet bring him the joyful security of their love, then his enemy is not so much her unchastity as his knowledge of it. This is a rueful sort of praise of ignorance which could only be uttered in retrospect, for he knows that the ignorance could not have lasted. Thus a man might look back at his actions and feelings before the news had arrived of the sudden death of someone he loves: he had continued to be happy, even after the person was dead, because he had not known. But implicit in this desire to go back, is the recognition of the fact that nothing can be changed: it is a desire for any release from the present turmoil, even a second-best release, not a sober statement of what is seen as an ultimately desirable state.

It is because Othello has become aware of what he can only see as an enormous gap between appearance and reality that he returns to the imaginings of that chaos which he had unthinkingly prophesied earlier. His farewell to war is prefaced by 'Farewell the tranquil mind, farewell content . . . ', the qualities so beautifully shown at the arrival in Cyprus. These have become central in his life, and there is no possibility of going back to what he was before. He has nothing now to be ambitious for, he can see only a life that lacks all purpose. I do not find it surprising that in a speech whose central point is the denying of any purpose in the pursuits which have previously filled his whole life, that he should concentrate on the trappings of that life, and suggest that they no longer have the power to move him. As we shall see later when we consider *Antony and Cleopatra*, Antony also feels a close link between his integrity as a man, which depends on the acceptance of his love, and his ability to be a great soldier. Othello too is saying that he cannot be a soldier if he is not a man, and it is significant that he cannot again act like a soldier, until, with the tragically belated recognition of Desdemona's fidelity, his integrity is restored.

His admission here, that, far from being able to act out his resolve of 'away at once with love or jealousy', his whole life is devastated by the destruction of what has become its central value, his faith in Desdemona's love, makes this the most dangerous moment for Iago, for Othello, torn between his belief in Desdemona, and his vision of the abyss if she is false, makes the demand for proof that could have proved fatal to Iago's scheme. Ironically, the effect of this is to make it clear to Iago that his life depends on being able to manufacture that proof:

> Villain, be sure thou prove my love a whore,
> Be sure of it; give me the ocular proof:
> Or, by the worth of man's eternal soul,
> Thou hadst been better have been born a dog
> Than answer my waked wrath!
>
> (III, iii, 365)

Those who argue that this shows in Othello a desire to be convinced seem to me simply to prove their own disqualification as readers of this play. Othello is losing his self control as he sees the possibility of the whirlpool opening, but he demands what we want him to demand, 'ocular proof'. It seems to me a central element in the tragic irony of the play, in the tragic situation that, as W. B. Yeats suggests, does not admit of solutions, that this demand for proof should seal his fate, for Iago is now aware that he has gone either too far or not far enough. He cannot extricate himself without bringing about the deaths of all the others enmeshed in his plot, which proves to be beyond his capability; Cassio survives, and as for Desdemona and Othello, Iago's own death is bound up with theirs.

The present danger, of a maddened Othello directing at least part of his violence against him, calls up all the resources of Iago's opportunism, and typically, he snatches his safety from a purely verbal source. Once again, it is tragically ironical that Othello, a man accustomed to quick decisions in the field of battle, not given to introspection, provides the means, as he struggles, as honestly as he can, for clarity in a situation that frightens and confuses him.

> By the world,
> I think my wife be honest and think she is not;
> I think thou art just and think thou art not.
> I'll have some proof. Her name, that was as fresh
> As Dian's visage, is now begrimed and black
> As mine own face. If there be cords, or knives,
> Poison, or fire, or suffocating streams,
> I'll not endure it. Would I were satisfied!
>
> (III, iii, 389)

His knowledge of Iago's honesty, his faith in Desdemona, his hurt pride, his sense of the futility of everything if what he now fears is proved true, all tangle up together in his confused awareness of his blackness, his lost reputation, his desire for suicide or revenge. Nothing is clear, and for such a man particularly, such confusion is unendurable. He must be 'satisfied', and Iago immediately seizes on the word, snatching his safety out of his apparently greatest danger. His mastery of tone in dealing with Othello is nowhere more apparent than here, where he uses the demand for 'ocular proof' as another goad to madden Othello.

Taking up first the sexual overtones of 'satisfied' (see *Romeo and Juliet*, II, ii, 126: 'What satisfaction canst thou have tonight') he manages to suggest a sort of perversion in Othello's attitude

> And may: but, how? how satisfied, my lord?
> Would you, the supervisor, grossly gape on—
> Behold her topp'd?
>
> (III, iii, 400)

He seems to suggest that Othello, supplanted in Desdemona's embraces by Cassio, may yet find it sexually stimulating to watch the act by which he is betrayed. The contempt he feigns for such a perverse conniving at one's own injury spills over to Othello's attempts to retain his faith in Desdemona's innocence, and the one contaminates the other in a sort of guilt by association. Then comes the dryly experienced tone of

> It were a tedious difficulty, I think,
> To bring them to that prospect: damn them then,
> If ever mortal eyes do see them bolster
> More than their own! What then? How then?

What shall I say? Where's satisfaction?
It is impossible you should see this,
Were they as prime as goats, as hot as monkeys,
As salt as wolves in pride, and fools as gross
As ignorance made drunk. But yet, I say,
If imputation and strong circumstance,
Which lead directly to the floor of truth,
Will give you satisfaction, you may have't . . .

                                             (III, iii, 403)

with its air of humouring a madman, as if he were asking whether
Othello really expects to be shown the spectacle of their coupling, and
suggesting that Othello is as foolish to expect it as Cassio and
Desdemona would be to allow it. The whole speech is couched in such
contemptuous terms as vividly to suggest the unbridled lust of the
participants, 'prime as goats', 'hot as monkeys', 'salt as wolves', even as
the primary sense of the speech denies that they are so. As with the
confusing of Brabantio, the grossness of the sexual detail that Othello is
asked to visualise is made intensely painful: his mere asking for proof is
made to seem something shameful, some perverted sexuality of his
own. And when he persists in asking for proof, the 'living reason, that
she's disloyal', the revolting fiction of Cassio's dream, made the more
distasteful by its homosexual overtones, is produced, with the crowning
ironic ambiguity of 'Nay, this was but his dream' (III, iii, 433). Iago
still affects the tone of the reasonable man, suggesting that Othello
ought not to take this as proof (though he has produced it at Othello's
insistence) but also conveying the suggestion that if this is truly
Cassio's dream, then how much worse the reality must be.

   It is at this point that Othello's last resistance breaks down: in his
pain and rage he believes that he has been shown proof. That an
outsider's imagination should fabricate such gross physical details is
simply unthinkable to him. At this crucial stage, Iago throws in his one
'objective' piece of evidence, his possession of the handkerchief, though
he does not yet know how he will be able to use it, investing it too, with
the sexually painful detail (to Othello) of Cassio's using it to wipe his
beard. There is a sort of concentrated lasciviousness about every detail
of this stage of Iago's ensnaring of Othello that can only make us
marvel at the intensity of Shakespeare's shaping imagination. At no
stage is Othello given a chance to regain his balance: the intensity of his
rage, lately directed at Iago, has been if anything heightened, but its
direction is changed. After the profound emotional experience Othello
has been through, he feels as if so great a trauma could only have been
produced by his having been shown proof of Desdemona's infidelity:
seeing Cassio with Bianca does later provide apparent confirmation,

but effectively, from the end of Act III, scene iii, Othello's faith in Desdemona has been destroyed, and the vows, Othello's a pitiful struggle to regain some measure of stability and self-control, Iago's a mocking parody of his, underline the point.

﹒The question that next presents itself is how, with Othello at least until Act V completely in Iago's control, Shakespeare nevertheless manages to compel enough sympathy for him to make the reassertion of his nobility at the end of the play successful. The technique by which this is done is, I believe, recognisable even in the 'Like to the Pontic sea . . . ' speech, which marks the completeness of Iago's victory. If Othello could do as he once said he would do, and as he claims to do now, simply dismiss his love for Desdemona

> . . . look here Iago
> All my fond love thus do I blow to heaven, . . .
> 'Tis gone,
> Arise black vengeance . . .
>
> (III, iii, 450)

then he would indeed become a monster of jealousy, but he cannot. The formality of the speech, and the way in which it strains onwards with its run-on lines, suggests to me not so much an uncontrollable lust for revenge, or an incurable talent for self-dramatisation, as the forcing of the will into a course which is not its natural one, one which requires all Othello's resolution, and all Iago's prompting, to be sustained. He can never for long think of Desdemona without remembering what she seemed to be, and, of course what the audience knows she indeed is, no matter how much Iago reminds him of the fury he ought to feel.

Andrew Bradley, by his virtual insistence that Othello does not really become jealous, or that if he does, this does not in any way diminish his nobility, has done later readers of the play some disservice, particularly because other critics anxious to refute this obvious overstatement have gone to the other extreme, feeling called upon to argue that far from retaining his nobility, Othello never has truly possessed that quality. Either extreme seems to me to distort the play radically; both seem to seek to make the tragedy easier to bear. The truly tragic spectacle the play presents is that of a man, shown to be great and good, reduced by Iago's conquest of him to something like a jealous savage, incapable of rational thought and emotion, shockingly cruel in his treatment of his wife. Yet Othello is never degraded quite to the level of an animal: in some ways it would be easier to bear if he were. Because he still retains so acute a sense of the happiness that has been lost, he still swings sickeningly between the instincts which, correctly, seek to persuade him of Desdemona's worth, and a sense of outrage at her falsity, and at a world in which appearance is so far divorced from reality. The torment of his situation is that at no point can he give himself wholly up to revenge, for revenge alone cannot satisfy the sense of loss that he feels. If he is seized by a madness, it is a madness with lucid intervals, which elicit the further goadings of Iago whenever they seem to be becoming too persistent.

From the beginning of the fourth scene of the third act, Othello begins to reveal his feelings directly to Desdemona, and it is here that the element of bad luck begins to make itself strongly felt. No critic as far as I know, has mounted much of an attack on Desdemona's conceit and self-interest, though I would have thought that if she received the same unsympathetic treatment as Othello something might be made of her obstinate refusal to believe that *she* could be suspected of infidelity. But Desdemona is so clearly a victim that she has quite rightly escaped censure; the pathos of her plight is so strong as to disarm criticism. The feeling of inevitability, that the lovers are caught in the trap of their natures and their circumstances, becomes increasingly strong through Act IV. Desdemona cannot credit that she is the cause of Othello's obvious disturbance; some strange distraction has seized him, and she can only humour him and hope for his recovery. Her innocence, which will hardly allow her to be aware of his feelings, her anxiety to do what she can to get Cassio reinstated, an intention of which she makes no secret, all act most unfortunately to convince Othello that she is not only corrupt, but quite brazen about it. Even her unhappy choice of the word 'committed' with its Elizabethan sense of 'committed adultery', serves to madden Othello, and make him quite unable to take in her denial.

It is their joint fate, and another of the play's great tragic ironies, that by the time she understands the nature of his accusation (and we should remember that at this time she still does not even know with whom she is supposed to have committed adultery) he is so convinced of her guilt that her denials only confirm his conviction that she is also a liar, dishonest in every way. The one unfortunate lie that she does tell, so trivial in itself but so terrible in its implications for Othello, that she still has the handkerchief she knows she has lost, predisposes him to disbelieve whatever she says. She, aware that for some cause she does not understand she has lost his love, can find nothing in her life to live for. Like Hermione in *The Winter's Tale*, she may well say that the loss of her life holds no terrors for her, since she has lost what gives it its value, her husband's love. And like Othello, her sense of shock and confusion at having to admit the loss of this supreme value throws her into a bewilderment, not violent like Othello's, but a vague, dazed state, in which she cannot comprehend, much less deal with this terribly altered world.

Meanwhile, Othello believes that the conditions of *his* terribly altered world are all too apparent. Desdemona's childlike insistence, after denying that she has lost the handerchief, on returning to the subject of Cassio's reinstatement, seems to him a calculated mocking of his cuckolding, and he is quite incapable, from the beginning of Act IV, of examining rationally any further piece of evidence that Iago offers. Iago now very shrewdly concentrates, though without abandoning his flow of obscene sexual suggestions, on Desdemona's duplicity: she will deny it, none of her protestations can be trusted. Oddly, as some critics have noticed, his explicit conjunction of the two dishonesties, the lies, and the adultery, brings with its pun the possibility of Othello's recognition that Desdemona is being belied, but his hurt and fury are by now so great as to be physically intolerable, and mouthing incoherently he falls in a swoon. When he recovers, he too is in something of a daze, and can be led to watch Cassio with Iago and Bianca, told what to think of the meeting, and obediently think it. Even the final apparently conclusive appearance of the handkerchief is hardly necessary: there is even perhaps the implication in Othello's two references to it, 'By heaven, that should be my handkerchief ' (IV, i, 155) and 'Was that mine . . . ?' (IV, i, 170), that he is too disturbed to recognise it, and simply takes Iago's word that it is his. The final insult Iago has devised, the suggestion that Desdemona is only one of Cassio's conquests, passes almost unnoticed in the total collapse of Othello's world that comes with his total belief in Desdemona's infidelity.

When Iago returns after his carefully staged piece of mime with Cassio, I have the feeling that Othello is so shocked by his own surrender, that Iago has to work hard to urge him to what he sees as the only hope for his own safety, the murder of both Cassio and Desdemona. It is difficult to sort out the movements of Othello's mind from the incoherence of his speech here, as he moves in a bewildered and bewildering fashion between his rage at Cassio (whom he sees as Desdemona's seducer, if 'a fine woman, a fair woman, a sweet woman!' is to be taken unironically, which his later words suggest is the case) and his sense of loss. He demonstrates that he cannot simply turn his heart into a stone: the savagery of 'I will chop her into messes . . . Cuckold me!' (IV, i, 196) is itself testimony of that, but there is, as well, the pitiful alternation between the desire for revenge that Iago works so hard to foster, and the much gentler awareness of what, as he believes now,

Desdemona used to be, but as his confused use of the present tense
reminds us, still is in fact:

> O the world has not a sweeter creature, she might lie by an emperor's
> side, and command him tasks . . . so delicate with her needle, an admira-
> ble musician, O she will sing the savageness out of a bear; of so high and
> plenteous wit and invention!
>
> (IV, i, 185)

Othello has been very harshly treated over his feelings here: if it is felt
that he ought not to show some sense of personal injury, the standards
by which his moral conduct is being judged are high indeed, though I
suppose I need, in so contentious a matter, to make it quite clear that in
saying this I in no way intend to excuse the extreme savagery of 'I will
chop her into messes'. I think it needs to be recognised, though, how
insistently Iago works to push Othello towards Desdemona's murder,
and how difficult Othello finds it to see her solely as an object for
revenge. Even his desperate

> Get me some poison Iago, this night; I'll not expostulate with her, lest
> her body and beauty unprovide my mind again, this night Iago . . .
>
> (IV, i, 200)

has been severely censured by F. R. Leavis[25] as conclusive evidence of a
'voluptous sexuality', of 'the association of strong sensuality with ugly
vindictive jealousy', and of what Leavis has earlier called 'an angry
sensuality' in Othello's acceptance of the possibility of Desdemona's
infidelity. This seems to me to be more than a trifle unfair. Othello may
have been able to say, before the marriage was consummated, that he
wanted Desdemona in Cyprus with him

> . . . not
> To please the palate of my appetite
> Nor to comply with heat, . . .
>
> (I, iii, 261)

but it is abundantly clear, I think, that he loves her body and soul, her
body and her soul; with his body and his soul. If he has come to believe,
in the way that I have attempted to trace, that he has been deceived in
his opinion of her, he is at least not so inexperienced in the world that
he does not know that men, particularly older men, can be strongly
attracted sexually to young women, and under the influence of that
sexual attraction, may make utter fools of themselves. After all, he
thinks it has happened to him: he knows that even though he can no

longer love Desdemona, he cannot simply stop wanting her. The cruelty of his revenge, the violence of his emotions, surely spring quite directly from the combination of the sexual attraction he cannot help but feel and his belief in her utter worthlessness. The alternation is still between his sorrow for Desdemona herself, for the fact that so much goodness has been corrupted

> Ay that's certain, but yet the pity of it, Iago:
> O Iago, the pity of it, Iago!
>
> (IV, i, 191)

and his own torment, and if we miss this point, that throughout the utmost violence of his jealousy, Othello always retains his sense of the tremendous worth that his love and Desdemona's held for them both, then it is only too easy to see him as a figure who invites our harshest moral censure.

If we should set out to answer the question, 'Is Othello sorry for himself?' then the answer would certainly be yes. How can he avoid self-pity, believing that he has been betrayed, that he has been deceived or mistaken in what he has thought the most wonderful thing to have happened in all his life? Some critics write as if any trace of this feeling were evidence of a general corruption in the man, without, apparently, being willing or able to make the imaginative effort to put themselves in Othello's place: what is remarkable is the way he strives to retain some dignity, and achieves it, in my opinion, even while the audience recognises that he is hideously wrong about Desdemona. The question of Othello's retention of tragic stature, it seems to me, now resolves itself into a judgement on how far, in the final scenes before and after Desdemona's murder, he deceives himself, and how far he is still the victim of Iago's deception. It is a delicate judgement to make, for obviously, neither of the absolute answers, that he is completely or not at all self-deluded, is right. His attempt to shore up the ruins of his life by setting up some abstract ideal of justice, which will allow him to believe that he is killing Desdemona not because of what she has made him suffer, but because her death will weld the rift between appearance and reality, is pitifully weak, and cannot be sustained. On the other hand the crucial speeches, one before her murder, 'Had it pleased Heaven to try me with affliction . . . '(IV, ii, 48), and his final judgement on himself, 'Behold, I have a weapon . . . '(V, ii, 260), and 'Soft you, a word or two . . . ' (V, ii, 339), cannot simply be dismissed, as T. S. Eliot dismisses the latter speeches at least, as Othello 'cheering himself up'.[26]

It is important to notice that the first of these three speeches occurs in an immediate context that could quite easily make it utterly damaging to our impression of Othello. Emilia's indignant avowals of her mistress's innocence have been dismissed as the lies to be expected from a bawd, and even the pitiful pleading of Desdemona herself, her protestations on her knees, are brushed away as still further signs of her dishonesty, while Othello turns to a consideration of his own situation. If the scene is considered in this sort of isolation, it would seem to lend support to the view of a grossly egotistic Othello, wholly wrapped up in his own sense of hurt, and unable, as we are sometimes told he has always been unable, to conceive of his wife as a person in her own right. But such a view, even on a close reading of only this scene, must be seen to be superficial, and one which fails completely to take into consideration the effect of the dramatic development that has preceded it.

I have already suggested that the unendurable point of Othello's agony has been reached in Act IV, scene i, when he falls in a swoon. Thereafter, he shows something of the strained or dazed reaction of somebody who has suffered a tremendous shock: what he is left with is the absolute belief that Desdemona's guilt has been proved beyond all possible doubt, and the determination that he must not allow her disturbing beauty, and his memory of what she has meant to him, to distract him from his revenge. The scene in which he strikes her in public is his public repudiation of her; thereafter, to ease the pain, he tries to give himself over to the role of public executor of justice, but his sense of personal loss keeps obtruding itself. Desdemona's true innocence appears as acting of consummate skill, but he cannot avoid feeling a kind of horror when she, as he thinks, falls into his trap, and damns herself utterly by her false swearing. His terrible dilemma, and hers, is that since he believes her false, any protestations of innocence can only seem to make her falser. If she *were* false she would behave so; but being innocent she has no other way to behave. That he is still touched by her youth and beauty, and saddened by what he sees as her falling off, surely appears here:

OTHELLO	Why, what art thou?
DESDEMONA	Your wife, my lord; your true And loyal wife.
OTHELLO	Come swear it, damn thyself; Lest being like one of heaven, the devils themselves Should fear to seize thee: therefore be double damn'd: Swear thou art honest.
DESDEMONA	Heaven doth truly know it.
OTHELLO	Heaven truly knows that thou art false as hell.

DESDEMONA	To whom, my lord? with whom? how am I false?
OTHELLO	O Desdemona! away! away! away!
DESDEMONA	Alas the heavy day! Why do you weep?
	Am I the motive of these tears, my Lord?

(IV, ii, 34)

The line 'O Desdemona, away! away! away!' I cannot see as showing anything other than a concern still for her, that she should not damn herself eternally, that makes the start of his next speech impossible to see as being merely self-centred. That Desdemona should prove false is the worst thing imaginable, and impossible to bear, and why he finds it impossible is, I think, honestly and movingly set out.

> . . . Had it pleased heaven
> To try me with affliction; had they rain'd
> All kind of sores and shames on my bare head
> Steep'd me in poverty to the very lips,
> Given to captivity me and my utmost hopes,
> I should have found in some place of my soul
> A drop of patience: but, alas, to make me
> A fixed figure for the time of scorn
> To point his slow unmoving fingers at . . . oh, oh.
> Yet could I bear that too, well, very well:
> But there, where I have garner'd up my heart,
> Where either I must live, or bear no life,
> The fountain from the which my current runs
> Or else dries up; to be discarded thence!
> Or keep it as a cistern, for foul toads
> To knot and gender in!

(IV, ii, 48)

What makes this so impressive is that it carries the feeling throughout that Othello knows what he is talking about. This is no idle imagining to bolster his own sense of worth, or even, though it is despairing, the despairing feeling that any imagined hardship would be more bearable than the present one. If we read the speech in conjunction with Othello's own account of his life, we see that he has in fact borne, not easily, but has borne, the sores and the shames, the defeat and the selling into slavery. There is also the element of rage at the futility of his life, to have borne so much, to have achieved so much, only to be wrecked in this way, but it is not dwelt on. It, too, is a component of the highly complex feeling of a man who has lost the love that is central to his life. Physical hardship could be borne again, and even the terrible sense of having been publicly betrayed, which Desdemona's unlucky advocacy of Cassio's cause before Ludovico and the others has convinced him is a fact. (Iago has worked hard at this too, skilfully suggesting that the affair is so well known that if Othello does nothing about it he will be scorned as a wittold as well as a cuckold.)

Even this can be borne, though he feels the pain of it, as who would not. The density of the verse here, with its compressed images, the 'fixed figure' suggesting both the way his life seems to have no meaningful movement (time will pass, but he will remain forever fixed in lifelessness) and underlying it, the idea of himself as a target, or the bear at the stake, shows how deeply he feels his disgrace, but even more strikingly, how deeply he feels that his life has been drained of all meaning and value. Again the feeling of being made a public mockery, the many pointing fingers (if we accept the First Quarto reading) is confused with a painful sense of the slow passage of time now that the current of his life is failing. If it were only this sense of being a notorious gull and fool, he says, he could bear that too, despite what this would mean to a man of Othello's stature and temperament. The question is, can we believe him, or must this be dismissed as empty rhetoric? I think we can, not only because once he realises how wrong he has been, his main concern is not with the figure he cuts (though I realise that this is still to be argued) but more importantly, because here his sense of what has been lost, implied in these images of flow and stagnation, outweighs his sense of hurt pride. We should remember, by the way, that if Desdemona really had treated him as he believes she has, hurt pride would seem a very inadequate description for the wound her scorning of him would have inflicted. It is to the images of running water and stagnation that the speech finally turns, with their archetypal associations of life, purity and freshness on the one hand, and foulness, monstrous efflorescence, and ultimately death, on the other. The very moving phrase 'Where I have garner'd up my heart' tells much of the story, for the harvest image, with its religious overtones, carries very strongly the implication of fullness, peace and contentment, and catches in one phrase what the play as a whole has shown, how completely Othello has risked his whole life in his love for Desdemona, in this acknowledgement that their love has replaced all other values in his life. The life-giving imagery maintains its religious resonances

> Where either I must live, or bear no life,
> The fountain, from the which my current runs
> Or else dries up . . .

There is a finality implied in the greatness of such a love, because it will admit of no subsequent choices: all hope of fulfilment, happiness, peace for Othello now depends on being loved by Desdemona. The sexual relationship between them, life-creating in its literal sense, becomes also the symbol for Othello's source of life, either pure, free and self-renewing like the fountain or spring, or contained, limited and because not flowing, breeding more foulness from its initial contamination. If he has been discarded, then there is no choice either, life cannot be renewed, and the way he takes over a characteristically Iago-like view of the sexual relationship

> A cistern, for foul toads
> To knot and gender in!

shows how bitter is the sense of the life that is left to him.

But unless we carry our examination of the speech further, we are certainly concentrating only on what is most favourable to Othello. It cannot be denied that at the words 'Turn thy complexion there . . . an increasing violence invades the speech. His own echoing of Iago's foul imaginings awakes his rage again; the fury that must find some outlet bursts out with

> O, ay, as summer's flies are in the shambles
> That quicken even with blowing . . .
>
> (IV, ii, 67)

with its horrible image of a fecund corruption nurtured on death itself, but even as he sees Desdemona as this monster of corruption, he is brought back, as he thinks, to the gap between appearance and reality (I follow the Folio reading):

> O thou weed, who art so lovely fair
> And smell'st so sweet, that the sense aches at thee . . .
>
> (IV, ii, 69)

Here again is the pain which almost literally racks him apart, as he allows himself to feel once more the irresistible pull of her beauty, 'so lovely fair . . . that the sense aches at thee', and at the same time imagines the rankness of her fault, a rankness which her 'Alas, what ignorant sin have I committed?' (IV, ii, 72) makes him feel he is being taunted with. His grim pretence that Emilia is a brothel keeper, an example of the way in which his only protection from the pain is by a deliberate blunting of his sensibilities, sadly makes him quite unable to respond to Desdemona's innocence, and she, herself meek and inexperienced, knows no other way than by simple protestation. Like

Othello himself after his swoon, Desdemona after Othello's brutal
accusation seems dazed and hardly able to defend herself. She
approaches her own death with something of the same sort of lack of
volition, coming from the destruction of the central value of her life,
that Hermione, at her indictment and trial, shows. Yet Desdemona,
too, has enough spirit to feel that she does not deserve this, and in the
scene with Emilia and Iago, attracts our sympathy all the more because
of the irony produced by Emilia's blundering onto the truth. This touch
is interesting for a number of reasons. Obviously, it raises our hopes
again that Desdemona will see the truth and defend herself with it, for
who so close to Othello that his tale, of such a kind, would be believed,
but Iago? Desdemona, though, is in no condition to think coherently,
and Emilia, who is later given the task of so pitilessly stripping Othello's delusions away

> . . . O gull, O dolt
> As ignorant as dirt . . .
>
> (V, ii, 164)

is herself here in the same position of ignorance, even though her
common sense has suggested to her the true solution. Iago is still to
everyone, his victims, his wife, the 'honest Iago' he has always been
thought of as being, though he himself realises the danger, and tries to
turn the conversation to another subject, or at least get his wife to keep
her voice down. This incomprehension of Desdemona and Emilia must
in some measure provide a shield for Othello against our too-fierce
censure, for he is not alone in being deceived.

It would, I think, make the pain and pathos of Act IV, scene iii easier
to bear if we could apportion blame to Othello in measure with our
sympathy for Desdemona, for that would at least provide some outlet
for our feelings of anger at the injustice of her fate. Her innocence could
not be more touchingly presented than it is, as she goes obediently to
the bed made up with her wedding sheets, to wait for the death she feels
is coming, bewildered at the change in her lord, but incapable of ceas-
ing to love him, incredulous, as a child might be, at Emilia's demonstration of worldly wisdom. Her fidelity to her love is absolute, no less
absolute than Othello's love for her demands that it should be. From
their opposed points in the tragic situation, neither of them in their love
is able to make any kind of concession to the demands of the world, to
accommodate themselves by accepting something less than the absolute ideal. Both are prepared to die, and do die, rather than accept
anything less, and both die, in one sense, needlessly.

Yet here too, we are up against something not easy to express in any convenient abstraction, for there is something about the absoluteness of such love that makes it destructive. In the last plays, the lovers have to learn to accept something less exclusive, accommodate themselves a little to the demands and weaknesses of human existence, if they are to go on living: by that accommodation, they do win the chance to go on which is denied the lovers in the tragedies. Othello cannot accept a flawed world, Desdemona cannot attempt to save herself, and the tragedy creates the feeling that it is inevitable that this should be so, because they cannot change the way in which they love. Yet if their love is to continue, it must continue through time, and time must bring inevitable changes. It is in this particular sense that I agree with J. I. M. Stewart, when he argues that the challenge that Othello faces from his *alter ego* Iago, has something fundamentally to do with the nature of time and the nature of love.[27]

In loving the way they do, which completely excludes all other considerations, Othello and Desdemona, Romeo and Juliet, Antony and Cleopatra, all in a sense invite their own destruction: they try to dismiss the world, but the world refuses to be dismissed. Precisely as Othello claims, and as any of the other lovers could with equal justice claim, he has loved, 'not wisely, but too well'. Provided that we recognise that the greatness of such a love may be presented as an experience of greater value than that which the exercise of any wisdom could afford, there is no reason why we should not accept his claim. Two aspects of love, creative and destructive, coexist in the plays, and therefore in our minds. Had the lovers been other than they are, they might have behaved differently, 'adjusted better' to their situation, and avoided the rocks of passion and circumstance on which their lives are wrecked. But in order to do that they would have had to love at lower rate, and we admire rather than criticise them because they refuse to do that. The plays are love tragedies precisely because it is the force and splendour of their love that destroys the lovers; we respond as we do because this is so, and even if we grieve because of it, we would not want them to achieve safety at the cost of living less fully.

To return to Desdemona: she inhabits a world in which what Othello suspects is impossible, incomprehensible even to her imagination, and so she cannot defend herself effectively against what remains to the end an unimaginable charge. As the tragic ironies cluster thickly in the closing scenes, it becomes poignantly clear that her great love is in perfect accord with his deepest demands. Emilia's practicality, her readiness to adjust her notions of fidelity to the circumstances of profit and loss

E

> The world is a huge thing, it is a great price
> For a small vice . . .
>
> (IV, iii, 67)

are answered by Desdemona's

> Beshrew me, if I would do such a wrong,
> for the whole world . . .
>
> (IV, iii, 77)

which matches Othello's later

> . . . nay, had she been true
> If heaven would make me such another world
> Of one entire and perfect chrysolite
> I'd not have sold her for it.
>
> (V, ii, 145)

If there is any one image that sums up Desdemona's worth to Othello, it is surely this of the single, unflawed gem, more valuable than all the world, containing all that is valuable in the world.

Dover Wilson's observation, that Iago occupies less and less of the important part our consciousness in these closing scenes, is a very apt one. His scurrying about in the dark, as his plot begins to go wrong, the bungled killing of Cassio and the silencing of Roderigo in his frantic attempt to save himself, prove clearly that he is no superhuman force in the play: what ultimately happens to him, too, is unimportant; his function has been to break down Othello's faith in Desdemona, and once that has been accomplished, his role is virtually over. When Othello enters Desdemona's bedchamber in Act V, scene ii with his 'It is the cause, it is the cause, my soul', interest is wholly centred on the tragic end to their love; we are hardly distracted by any feeling that the partial miscarriage of Iago's plot may bring a last-minute rescue for Desdemona.

The pitiful futility of Othello's attempt to construct some notion of justice to replace, as some mark of reference in his life, his lost love for Desdemona, is nowhere more apparent than in the opening speeches of this scene, yet even here there are other matters to be noticed besides the lack of conviction that such lines as the opening ones, and 'Yet she must die, else she'll betray more men' carry. Othello is trying to convince himself of the justice of what he is about to do, trying to act the part of the impersonal executioner, trying to minimise his own hurt by seeing her sins as directed not against him, but against the world at large, but the part is unsustainable, and it is as well for him that it is. It hardly seems paradoxical to me, in the context, that his strength of passion should be his surest defence against forfeiting his nobility; if he were able so to deceive himself as to feel no qualms at his actions, then surely he would lose all our respect. There is a tremendous effort at self-control, a quality we know he prizes, which we can respect because we know of the fury that lies beneath it. We ought not to forget, too, that his insistence in giving her the opportunity of confession and saving her soul is not merely, as it might easily appear to be to an audience today, the turning of the screws to get her to confess her fault for his own emotional satisfaction. Othello and Desdemona take heaven and hell seriously, which is not to say that this is a play centrally concerned with the losing and saving of souls. As Helen Gardner says in 'The noble Moor': 'Damnation and Salvation are outside the field of reference of a play in which the last day is conceived as the confrontation of two human beings.'[28] Because the play is set in a Christian context, it is natural that Othello should feel he must control his rage, so that he does not kill body and soul; it is only when she appears to him to be quite unregenerate and unrepentant that he abandons this control. Her final fatally ambiguous cry, on hearing of Cassio's death, 'Alas, he is betray'd and I undone . . .' (V, ii, 76), gives him the impetus he needs to commit the murder.

Othello is confident that he knows what he is doing, and indeed, in a truer sense than he consciously realises, he does. This appears not merely in those images which show that her beauty can still move his senses; it is his underlying realisation that in killing her it is the source of his own life that he is destroying, that makes us see the murder as more than a brutal act of revenge. For a fuller appreciation of the complexities of tone in this murder scene, we ought to look again at the corresponding scene in Cinthio: there the glee the Moor and his Ensign display at the battering to death of Desdemona, and the callous attempt at concealing the crime by pulling the ceiling down on the bed, make it quite clear how far Shakespeare is here from seeking a simple effect of cruelty and revenge. Even without the subsequent revelation of his mistake, I think Othello's own death is shown to be the inevitable consequence of Desdemona's by the Promethean image, his sober awareness of what the extinguishing of the warmth of her life will mean to him. Her death is one of the most harrowing of stage experiences, for her natural terror overweighs her resignation and makes her struggle at the last, leaving Othello with no sense of achievement of revenge, satisfied vanity, not even a modicum of peace of mind. On the contrary, he is almost frantic: his

> My wife, my wife, my wife; I ha' no wife;
> O, insupportable! O heavy hour!
> Methinks it should be now a huge eclipse
> Of sun and moon, and that the affrighted globe
> Should yawn at alteration . . .
>
> (V, ii, 98)

is indication of his consciousness of some huge catastrophe, which gradually takes exact shape in his mind, as he frantically tries to stave off the dawning knowledge of his fatal deception. The first shock is presumably that of Desdemona's dying words, shielding him from the consequences of his action:

> Nobody, I myself, farewell
> Commend me to my kind lord, O farewell!
>
> (V, ii, 125)

Such evidence of love is almost unbearable, even if he still believes her guilty, and the force of his denial

> She's like a liar gone to burning hell,
> 'Twas I that kill'd her . . .
>
> (V, ii, 130)

shows how far he is from attempting to conceal what he has done, and what little concern he has for his own safety, unless we feel that he believes his deed is likely to be applauded and approved once the reason for it is known. Othello certainly feels that he must offer his justification for the murder, but it is hard to tell whether he thinks this will exonerate his action, or whether, as seems to me more probable, in the light of all that has gone before, that he has no interest in life continuing beyond Desdemona's loss.

His last agony is to be made aware that he himself has destroyed all that he holds dear, and as Emilia bitterly curses his ignorance and shows him, against his conviction, the truth he can only accept by acknowledging that he has been wrong, we must remember that this is the acknowledgement that Troilus could never make. For him the whole world was dislocated, not he at fault: Othello makes the acknowledgement gladly, and pays for his mistake in the only way that he can, with his life.

Terrible as the murder of Desdemona has been, the forcing of Othello to an awareness of the truth is, I think, even more so, and brings this play closest of all tragedies in English to the agony of that moment when Oedipus learns who he is and what he has done. Emilia has to learn too, that it is her husband who has proved to be the arch-villain her common sense had told her had belied Desdemona. It is interesting that she too, finds it almost incredible that it should have been Iago who has done this. Her three times repeated 'My husband?' shows her resistance to the terrible truth which, she now sees more quickly than does Othello, will destroy them all. His impatience at what he interprets as her slowness of understanding is bitterly ironic, as his last moments of confidence reveal instead to the audience the depths of his incomprehension, and to Emilia, the foreknowledge of her own tragedy.

> I say thy husband: dost understand the word?
> My friend, thy husband, honest, honest Iago.
>
> (V, ii, 154)

As Iago's villainy is swiftly realised and confirmed, as his attempts at bluster collapse into savage vituperation, culminating in the vicious stabbing of his wife, to silence her, or perhaps simply to repay her for having given him away, Othello at first says nothing. Then, as his terrible cry suggests, comes the dawning realisation of the horror of what he has done. He offers his account perhaps to push away for a little longer that horror, as much as to convince the bystanders. His words

> Are there no stones in heaven
> But what serves for thunder? Precious villain!
>
> (V, ii, 235)

as he dashes at Iago, seem equally an appeal for justice to strike him down. This is his moment of greatest weakness, for Iago escapes his attack, and he is disarmed. Everything that makes him a man seems to be gone; confronted with the knowledge of his loss of integrity, it is noticeable that he cares little or nothing for his reputation:

> I am not valiant neither
> But every puny whipster gets my sword;
> But why should honour outlive honesty?
> Let it go all.
>
> (V, ii, 245)

This is surely Othello at his lowest ebb, for in a very real sense he was not himself when he was reduced to a swooning confused fury by Iago's tauntings. But now, even the temporary stay against confusion, the notion of a just action, that he had constructed to allow himself to try to

continue to live after the loss of Desdemona's love, is swept away, and
he is confronted with a world made utterly desolate by his own gullibility.

Just as Antony feels his honour as a soldier cannot survive the loss of
essential manhood that his deception by Cleopatra would mean (see
Act IV, scene xiv), so Othello here, feeling that his credulity has
destroyed his integrity, cannot see any meaningful action left in his life.
Without his sword, he is nothing; as John Holloway remarks, his collapse and his pulling himself together are dramatised by the loss of one
sword and the finding of another.[29] Ironically again (this play seems to
me to be the most ironic of all the tragedies, suitably so, for a play
whose central plot mechanism is deception) it is Emilia's dying indictment of him, bitter, savagely aimed to hurt, almost taunting him with
his colour and his race, that makes him a man again: 'Moor, she was
chaste, she lov'd thee, cruel Moor' (V, ii, 250). Her words remind him
that the central value he has found in all his life, Desdemona's love, was
real, and not a sham. He has wilfully killed her and destroyed their
great happiness, but their love was real: in the most vital area of his life,
there is no gap between the appearance and the reality. The fact that
Iago was not what he seemed loses its significance before the realisation
that Desdemona was. In that realisation, Othello's life can find a meaning again; he recovers reason, faith and will, and though the only
direction he can take is towards death, it is not meaningless, a mere
apathetic sinking into oblivion. He recovers authority, dignity, control,
and reasserts himself as a man. His

> Behold, I have a weapon;
> A better never did itself sustain
> Upon a soldier's thigh: I have seen the day,
> That, with this little arm and this good sword,
> I have made my way through more impediments
> Than twenty times your stop: but, O vain boast!
> Who can control his fate? 'tis not so now.
> Be not afraid, though you do see me weapon'd;
> Here is my journey's end, here is my butt,
> And very sea-mark of my utmost sail.
> Do you go back dismay'd? 'tis a lost fear;
> Man but a rush against Othello's breast,
> And he retires. Where should Othello go?
> Now, how dost thou look now? O ill-starr'd wench!
> Pale as thy smock! When we shall meet at compt,
> This look of thine will hurl my soul from heaven,
> And fiends will snatch at it. Cold, cold, my girl!
> Even like thy chastity. O cursed slave!
> Whip me, ye devils,

From the possession of this heavenly sight!
Blow me about in winds! roast me in sulphur!
Wash me in steep-down gulfs of liquid fire!
O Desdemona! Desdemona! dead!
Oh! Oh! Oh! . . .

(V, ii, 260)

is a speech which ought to prepare us for his final judgement upon himself, though it has been criticised as an attempt to cheer himself up by harking back to happier days. It does not seem to me odd that his favourite 'sword of Spain, the brook's temper' should remind him of his exploits as a soldier, but it should be noticed that, to be more precise, what it makes him think of is how little a man can control his destiny, of how ill-founded all his confidence in himself has been. He does not now defend his valour; he denies that he has any, or that his life has any purpose save death. There is no hint of any belief that he will be reunited with his wife after death; in fact he thinks he has barred himself from her presence for ever, that he is not worthy to see her again. To argue that he is inclined to excuse himself for what he has done seems to me to ignore completely the force of his

. . . O cursed slave!
Whip me, ye devils,
From the possession of this heavenly sight!
Blow me about in winds! roast me in sulphur!
Wash me in steep-down gulfs of liquid fire!

(V, ii, 277)

It is impossible to be certain, but it seems to me likely that it is himself, rather than Iago, whom he apostrophises as 'O cursed slave!' for he is overwhelmed by a sense of his own unworthiness, by a knowledge of how thoroughly he deserves the misery he has brought upon himself. There is almost a wistfulness about the way he says, as Iago is brought back, 'I look down towards his feet, but that's a fable . . .' (V, ii, 287) for if he could believe that he had been led astray by the devil himself that would offer at least some excuse for judging himself less harshly, but he knows it is a human malice, and a human weakness in himself, that has wrecked his life. His final speech which, as Holloway claims,[30] has the conventional authority of a death speech, as well as the dramatic emphasis of a revitalised Othello, is itself the best proof of his regained nobility and honesty. It will be remembered that this is the speech that T. S. Eliot believes shows Othello 'cheering himself up'; F. R. Leavis[31] comments that it especially shows Othello's tendency to sentimentalise, to dramatise himself. Othello, he goes on to argue, has learned nothing through suffering, and dies essentially the same man as the one who slew Desdemona, persuading himself that he was acting morally. Dr Leavis's famous essay is well known, and other critics have tried to meet its admittedly forceful arguments in a detailed way. I shall only say here that I cannot agree that the effect that Othello's final speech and his suicide make can be dismissed as a *coup-de-theatre*, or as a self-exonerating attempt by a character who remains deluded about himself and what he has done. The last words he speaks before his death speech are 'O Fool, fool, fool!' as he learns the true explanation of Cassio's possession of the handkerchief. Then he begins his judgement upon himself, starting by explicitly setting aside any plea or desire for special treatment: he wants the truth to be told, and the truth, as he sees it, is completely damning to himself. With the hindsight he now possesses (knowledge which we, the audience, have had all along) he realises that he should have known that Desdemona loved him, that she was incapable of infidelity. That he was led to believe otherwise was his tragic error, and for that error he is completely willing to pay with his life. His thoughts are quite away from any notion of revenge on Iago, or even the possibility of any external punishment to be imposed on himself which could in any way compare with the suffering he himself has caused. I can see no reason to believe that he is in any way falsifying the picture of himself that the play as a whole has presented when he refers to himself as

> . . . one that loved not wisely, but too well;
> Of one not easily jealous, but being wrought,
> Perplexed in the extreme . . .

(V, ii, 345)

The Arden editor[32] comments on 'easily', that if Othello had said 'naturally' he would have been speaking the exact truth. I would not want to make even that qualification, for, as I have tried to show, I do not think any appeal to elapsed time on the stage, or even an accurate line count in Act III, scene iii can demonstrate that Othello 'easily' becomes jealous. Bradley's contention[33] that ' . . . it would have been quite unnatural in him to be unmoved by the warnings of so honest a friend, warnings offered with an extreme reluctance, and manifestly from a sense of a friend's duty', though it has attracted some ridicule, has more than a grain of truth. Neither by quickness of response, nor by an acquiescence without a struggle is Othello shown as easily jealous, but he certainly is 'perplexed', in the sense of being driven to distraction by the conflict between two apparently irreconcilable truths, his faith in his wife, and his belief in the honesty of his friend. It is inexcusable, from his point of view, that he should have resolved the clash as he did, and he does not attempt to excuse himself for it. For the man of action, whose life has depended on instant decisions, the state of being in an unresolvable situation is itself hard to bear; common sense has told him that the only possible solution must lie in the fact that one of the constituents is not what it appears to be, and we should not forget, that in his perplexity, the only voice he has been allowed to hear has been that of Iago, claiming to resolve the problem by his greater knowledge of the world. Othello made the wrong choice, but we must recall, as he does not do in this last speech, except very much in passing ('being wrought'), how strongly he was urged to it.

It seems to me that uppermost in his mind is not the cause of his delusion, but its consequence, and it is on the consequence, his killing of Desdemona, that the emphasis falls. It does not make much difference whether one reads 'base Indian', or 'base Judean' in the simile by which he condemns himself, though 'Indian' would, I think, fit better with the sort of crass ignorance which he sees himself as having exhibited, while 'Judean' would carry a stronger sense of betrayal. The general sense of having discarded something beyond price is clear. Othello weeps as he acknowledges this, though he is tartly condemned by Dr Leavis for his tears:

> Othello really is, we cannot doubt, the stoic-captain whose few words know their full sufficing up to this point, we cannot say he dramatizes himself, he simply is. But then, in a marvellous way (if we consider Shakespeare's art), the emotion works itself up until in less than half a dozen lines the stoic of few words is eloquently weeping.[34]

There is a great difference between Othello's dismissing his own past deeds in a few words, and giving eloquent utterance to the acknowledgement that his own mistaken actions have cost him all that he values in the world: the 'half-a-dozen lines' proves nothing. Close reading is much more than a matter of line counting, as Dr Leavis's best work eloquently demonstrates. Othello weeps for what he has done, and if we cannot respond to his emotion, we may well ask each other, with Dante's Count Ugolino, ' . . . and if thou weep not, at what dost thou ever weep?' (*Inferno*, Canto XXXIII). When Othello proceeds to the execution of judgement upon himself the condemnation is quite explicit. Leavis may feel that Othello is remembering his finest hour, and proving his nobility to himself by his suicide; I cannot think of anyone in Shakespeare who dies quite in the way that Eliot and Leavis suggest Othello does here, not even Brutus or Coriolanus, who might seem the most likely candidates. Shakespeare seems always to present quite seriously that action in which a man dies to prove some value:

those who see only futility and chaos in life are, like Troilus, left to live out their futility beyond the play's end, and are denied the resonance of a hero's death. There is something awesome about a man deliberately ending his life, and I very much doubt whether Shakespeare ever twists this awe to a satiric purpose. Othello, if his life as a soldier is at all real to us, must be imagined to have had many more glorious moments in battle than the killing of the traducer of the Venetian State in Aleppo. It is because he sees himself as guilty of the same sort of dishonourable offence, not against Venice alone, but against the whole world that Desdemona's love represents, that he sees himself as the traitor, the Judas, the unbeliever, the infidel, deserving only of summary justice.

But we need not share Othello's opinion of himself, for by his death he can re-establish that standard of trust, of value, that Desdemona, though dead, has proved by her fidelity to exist, the sort of value that Iago's whole life has laboured to deny. Like Posthumus, who, believing that he has brought about the death of his wife through a similar mistake, offers his own life in atonement even though he does not claim that it has the value of what has been destroyed,[35] so Othello in his last words shows that he dies for the love by which he should have lived:

> I kiss'd thee ere I kill'd thee, no way but this,
> Killing myself, to die upon a kiss.
>
> (V, ii, 359)

I hope it is clear from my account of the final scenes that this play, harrowing as it is, is not entirely pessimistic. As many critics have noticed, there is nothing at the end to suggest a return to order or good government, to provide the sort of consolation that comes at the end of *Macbeth* or *King Lear* or even *Hamlet*, which, even though it cannot in any sense make up for the heroic qualities that have been lost, at least offers a world that has returned to normal. Even in *Romeo and Juliet* there is the reconciliation of the warring families over the graves to offer some grain of comfort, inadequate though it may be. But in *Othello*, the least public of Shakespeare's tragedies, there is not this sense of a return to normal, for, apart from the interaction of the close group of figures at the centre of the play, really only Othello, Desdemona, Iago and Cassio, life has been going on normally ever since Act II, when the news came that the Turkish threat to the state had been destroyed. It is only in the private and nightmarish world which Iago first creates, and into which he then entices Othello, that normality has been destroyed. Only Othello has been made mad, and therefore only he can signal, and comment upon, his own return to sanity. As G. Hibbard points out, the ending of this play is different from the ending of all the other tragedies: the brief comment of Cassio

> This did I fear, but thought he had no weapon
> For he was great of heart . . .
>
> (V, ii, 361)

is all the epitaph Othello gets: instead of the ceremonial bearing of the dead hero from the stage, there is Ludovico's comment on the presence of the bodies of Othello and his Desdemona

> . . . the object poisons sight
> Let it be hid . . .
>
> (V, ii, 365)

All the indications are that Othello, who has always been at some remove from his society, remains so in his death: he is, as Hibbard notes, 'apart from them, . . . their reaction is that of the normal ordinary man, and as such, serves to underline for the last time the remoteness of Othello . . . he is, and always has been, a mystery and a challenge to the unheroic world in which fate and circumstance have placed him'.[36]

The audience, though, has understood, as Othello's society has not, the quality of the love that he has shared with Desdemona, has seen the torment to which he has been subjected, and can therefore respond to what has been re-established in his discovery of the truth of his love, the truth of the heart. Othello, like Troilus, has been deceived, but unlike Troilus, his whole life has not been based on a sham. This rediscovery of the integrity of his love is what he learns through his suffering, and though it is a knowledge which, when he gains it, can only lead to his death, that tragic fact does not diminish its importance. He has claimed a transcendental value for his love, lost it, and recovered and reaffirmed it in his death. For Othello it represents the difference between living in a completely chaotic world, where nothing has any value, or living in a world where in Keats' phrase 'the holiness of the heart's affections' is the great reality, mortal and vulnerable though the human heart may be.

Hibbard argues the play is so hard to bear because it is about the wanton destruction of human happiness. That seems to me to be absolutely true, and the play gains its terrible force at least in part from the way it extends our awareness of how difficult happiness of this quality is to achieve, and how easy it is to destroy. The story that Shakespeare has chosen to use, the plausibility of Iago's tactics, the very uniqueness of Desdemona, all serve to provide an undercurrent of reminder, which commands an assent in common experience, of how easily it could all have been true. The character that Iago conjures up is not Desdemona: it is Othello's great error that he comes to think it is. But as Emilia's worldly wisdom testifies, such women do exist, and had Desdemona been one of them, all Othello's ideals of love and fidelity would have been mocked and destroyed. As it is, his death, tragic though it is, is not the worst thing that could have happened, for Desdemona was true to him, and he rediscovers this at the last.

I do not mean to imply that there is any suggestion in this re-establishment of the truth of the love that any hope of reunion exists beyond death, for I feel that the play's ending will not allow any such hope. Death is final, but death cannot alter the quality of the love that has been experienced. When Othello says

> My soul hath now her content so absolute
> That not another comfort like to this
> Succeeds in unknown fate . . .
>
> (II, i, 191)

he prefaces this affirmation of complete happiness with 'If it were now to die . . . '. To establish that world as having existed, in the tragic circumstances of this play, both Desdemona and Othello have to die, as Romeo and Juliet, and Antony and Cleopatra also have to die. It is *Othello*'s great achievement that it convinces us of the possibility of that happiness, at the same time that it demonstrates its terrible vulnerability.

CHAPTER FIVE

ANTONY AND CLEOPATRA

IF WE CAN ACCEPT that *Romeo and Juliet* is a tragedy of love's intensity, and *Othello* a tragedy of love's vulnerability, then *Antony and Cleopatra* is a tragedy of love's triumph. Unlike the other pairs of lovers, both Antony and Cleopatra are aware of strong claims on their attention other than their love for each other. From one point of view, their love's progress is traced in their growing awareness of the irrelevance of all other concerns in their lives. In this sense, love triumphs, but since the two central figures cannot simply abdicate from their positions of importance in the world, their concentration on their love leaves them exposed to the worldly dangers which their political importance has attracted. It is true, though this is not the whole truth, to say that they die because they no longer care to protect themselves. It is their tragedy that their love's triumph brings about their deaths: when they die, as the play makes very clear, the act by which they acknowledge love's supreme importance ends love and life together.

It can be argued that many of the differences this play shows from the other two love tragedies stem from the difference in stature of the lovers. Romeo and Juliet are little more than children in the estimation of their society, no matter what they become to each other. Othello, though a great general, is placed in an intensely personal situation, in which his isolation from everything around him is stressed. In that play any external threat of danger, or pressure of political events, is over by the beginning of Act II. It is as an individual, shaped indeed by his past experience, but also isolated from the people around him by it, that Othello suffers and dies. For much of that play's course, only the plot-spinner, Iago, and of course the audience, know that Othello is suffering at all. But Antony and Cleopatra, by contrast, play out their roles in full view of the world's fascinated gaze. Their love affair is the topic of scandalised comment among both Antony's rivals and his own

men, for he is one of the triple pillars of the world, and his mistress is
Egypt's queen. On their fates depend the lives of many others: symbolically, their closest attendants die with them, unable and unwilling to
survive their fall. This is not the least of the suffering that Antony, in
particular, has to bear. He is forced to the realisation that though his
choices may be those that defend his integrity as a lover, the same
choices destroy his integrity as a leader of his men; he must acknowledge that he cannot act and suffer the consequences of those actions
alone. For all these reasons, the choice to die is a more difficult choice
for Antony and Cleopatra than it is for the other pairs of lovers, but
when it becomes necessary they make it quite deliberately. That they
should make such a choice at all is almost incredible to that politician
par excellence, Octavius Caesar:

> The breaking of so great a thing should make
> A greater crack. The round world
> Should have shook lions into civil streets
> And citizens to their dens. The death of Antony
> Is not a single doom; in the name lay
> A moiety of the world.
>
> (V, i, 14)

Caesar believes that he will be able to preserve Cleopatra alive to grace
his triumph in Rome, because she will want to live, but the lovers
themselves have for a long time seen their own deaths as inevitable.
More so even than do Romeo and Juliet, Antony and Cleopatra share
an underlying awareness that their love will destroy them. Antony
knows early that he must ' . . . from this enchanting queen break off '.
Cleopatra, too, though her fidelity to Antony is never seriously ques-
tioned, may at least toy with the idea of saving herself from the impending disaster by coming to some sort of arrangement with Caesar.
Antony at first tries to protect himself from the danger of too deep an
involvement, but both, in the end, acknowledge love's power, and willingly and as a direct consequence, go to meet the death that we and
they have long recognised as the inevitable consequence of caring too
much.

Because the choices they make are so important for others as well as
themselves, and because the play allows no serious possibility that they
will be able to win any kind of continuing happiness through the reconciliation of their private and public fates, it is, I think, essential if we
are to admire some heroic quality in them that we recognise that their
awareness of what they are doing, of what they feel for each other, is
qualitatively very different from the awareness of the other pairs of

lovers we have considered. We cannot say that Antony and Cleopatra are swept away by the irresistible force of a new passion, such as that which carries Romeo and Juliet so swiftly to their deaths. They are not inexperienced in love, like Othello and Desdemona; quite the contrary, they know all the tricks of what, in Cleopatra at least, has in the past come perilously close to being a trade. They feel themselves to be in command of their emotions, and we consequently feel that they know what they are doing. Antony believes that he will be able to break free from the 'strong Egyptian fetters', and Cleopatra, very clearly, fears that he may, since she devotes all her powers of attraction to holding him at her side. Because they are experienced lovers, and not at the beginning of their love affair, the quality of their love seems different, they are more conscious of love's pleasures, well accustomed to each other's company. They joke and drink and quarrel; the whole relationship seems much less obviously romantic. Apart from their opening exchange (but one ought not to forget that as an opening exchange, it does sound a most important note), there is little that could be called idealistic observable in their view of each other, at least for a long time. Cleopatra's court is openly sensual and bawdy, apparently bearing out the Roman view that the affair is no more than that, a subject for bawdy jokes or censorious comment, depending on the predilection of the speaker.

At this point in the play we are apparently being asked to see in the relationship only what outsiders see: the temptation is to dismiss it as something inferior, even slightly squalid perhaps, the not very edifying spectacle of an ageing roué and his equally ageing mistress caught in the toils of lust. But to do so would be quite wrong, for what the play shows is something much more moving and important than that, as it becomes apparent that the outsiders' view is wrong. What is gradually revealed is the absolute importance that each has for the other, an importance which systematically strips all else away from their lives, and leaves them, at the end, glad to die, in the deepest sense for each other, rather than live on alone.

This greater experience and their political importance mean that the lovers occupy the centre of a public stage, and this, in turn, means that the quality of the suffering they undergo is different from that experienced by the lovers in the other plays. Romeo and Juliet suffer the pain of physical separation, are very conscious of the brevity of their time together. Othello, as we have seen, is first made to doubt the reality of Desdemona's love, then forced to recognise that his gullibility has destroyed all that has given his life value. But Antony and Cleopatra have to endure a public humiliation as their love asserts its importance by robbing them of everything else. They are exposed to doubts and betrayals which Romeo and Juliet never know, and which in *Othello*, for all their dreadful consequence, have validity only in Othello's Iago-dominated mind. But Antony does leave Cleopatra, and marry Octavia, and Cleopatra, even if her actions are more equivocal, does flirt with Caesar's messenger, and her fleet's defection to Caesar does bring the final ruin of Antony's worldly fortunes. He comes near to complete despair after the fleet has betrayed him, for he then believes that he has given up his whole life for a love that is worthless. So it seems to Cleopatra, too, when the news of his marriage to Octavia comes to her, for she can only believe that her love for him, the central value in her life, is not returned. Antony, the greatest soldier in the world, is brought by his love to flee from battle, desert his men, ask terms from the young upstart he despises. Cleopatra's timidity, her vanity, her role-playing, which are the immediate causes of Antony's death, are all exposed, yet in spite of this the lovers achieve a nobility in their love which compels our acknowledgement that in one sense it is they who are the victors, and the rest of the world the vanquished.

Love's triumph is more stressed in this play than it is in the other two love tragedies, and it is perhaps because of this, as well as because of its place in the canon, that some critics feel that in mood and quality, this play has strong affinities with the Romances. Nevertheless, it is also true that in Antony's and Cleopatra's claim for an overriding value in the passion they feel for each other, there are obvious parallels and contrasts with what Troilus feels for Cressida. This play is clearly concerned, as so many of Shakespeare's plays are, with the whole question of value in love and how it can be estimated. It will later be an important part of my argument, when I look in some detail at the death scenes, to try to establish that in this play too, the self-defeating nature of the sacrifice the lovers make in dying for each other is not minimised, and that we are allowed no evasion of its tragic impact through refuge in belief in some undefined reunion beyond the grave. The love of Antony and Cleopatra has been so firmly founded in the physical, the sensual, that we are made fully aware that this love, no matter how strong, dies with the lovers; the final irony of Cleopatra with death, not new life, at her breast makes that conclusion inescapable.

But despite the play's being undeniably a tragedy, there is also that other note, perhaps more characteristic of the Romances, in which a quality of life and happiness is shown as having been achieved and established in spite of the mortality of the lovers, who can only lose what they have won. This aspect of the play, the feeling it communicates that the death of the lovers cannot wholly invalidate the happiness they have experienced, is of course present, but to a lesser degree, in *Romeo and Juliet* and *Othello* as well, even though the time of happiness there is so pitifully short. These plays, if I can make such a distinction, seem much more harrowing than *Antony and Cleopatra*, which though not less powerful, proceeds at a more deliberate pace, is less hemmed-in in its movement, and which, by furnishing the lovers with a representative adversary in the person of Octavius Caesar, at once allows him to be defeated by Cleopatra's suicide, and shows his material victory to be devalued by the lovers' scorning of it. At the end, the emphasis falls more on what the lovers have meant to each other than on the world that they have lost.

I realise that I have still to substantiate my reasons for reading the play in this way, and I realise too, that to do so is to ignore some weighty critical opinion. It cannot be denied that the story of the play, like that of *Othello*, sets up a situation that appears to invite moral censure. This attitude is repeatedly given voice in the play itself, and if we are to accept a reading on the lines that I have suggested, it must be by recognising a worth in Antony's and Cleopatra's love for each other that is apparent to no other characters in the play besides themselves. The situation of the play, after all, is that of a doubly adulterous affair: Antony is at first married to Fulvia, later to Octavia. He neglects his duties as one of the Triumvirs, abandons his second wife almost as soon as he has wed her, betrays the trust of those followers who remain faithful to him, loses the empire the rule of which he has shared, sets Roman fighting against Roman and, finally defeated, takes his own life, all for the sake of an ageing woman who, from the world's point of view, is vain, selfish, luxurious, cruel, deceitful, theatrical and in no way worth what he gives up for her. Neither Antony nor Cleopatra has the excuse of inexperience: they do what they do knowingly, and, if this summary of the action were to represent the true direction of the play, they would clearly deserve an end that at worst could be seen as ignominiously self-deluding, at best pitiful. But, as with *Othello*, the manner of presentation of the material radically alters its meaning. *Antony and Cleopatra* is, it is generally acknowledged, distinguished by the magnificence of its poetry, and though I know the matter can be argued in a different way, it seems to me that the direction of the play's poetic endeavour lies in a radical reversal of values within a situation that may appear at first to invite a simple moral judgement.

I am convinced that the moral problem that the play poses lies at the heart of all the differing estimates and interpretations it has attracted, for they fall into three main groups. There are those who see the play as in fact developing the line of censure that its material invites, those who, taking a completely opposite point of view, deny that moral judgements are involved, and see the play as establishing a transcendental value for the love of Antony and Cleopatra which is triumphant over Caesar's world of policy, and over death as well, and finally, those who attempt, in some measure, to reconcile these two readings.

A fairly recent study of the play, by Andrew Reimer,[1] has provided a convenient summary of the chief critical responses the play has elicited. I do not propose here to try to emulate it, but have merely selected as representative some contemporary or near contemporary writing on the play to try to focus attention on what our own century has seen as the central critical problems. Of these readings, that which sees the play as an extended demonstration of the folly of giving too much importance to love of kind is the simplest. Here again, Professor Dickey's argument,[2] firmly based on his scholarship, makes the strongest claim for our attention. He has assembled in his chapter on the play a multiplicity of examples from classical, medieval and renaissance literature, all tending to show that the story of these lovers' life and death is one of the great examples, to quote Dryden, of 'famous patterns of unlawful love' who deserve their unfortunate end. Professor Dickey is of course well aware of the fact that even if an Elizabethan audience might be expected to approach the story with certain moral preconceptions, this need not have governed the direction of Shakespeare's play, but he feels that in the light of so general an attitude, we need to find strong evidence in the play itself if we are to believe that 'the play hymns a love so great as to transcend ordinary morality'.[3] By no means unsympathetic to the lovers, he can respond to the magnificence of their passion and to the pathos of their end, but, pointing to this background, and to the adverse judgements of the lovers and their actions that are articulated within the play itself, he remains convinced that 'traditionally Antony and Cleopatra are examples of rulers who threw away a kingdom for lust, and this is how, despite the pity and terror which Shakespeare makes us feel, they appear in his play'.[4] This is a view that has found some critical support: Ribner, in his *Patterns in Shakespearean Tragedy*,[5] concurs in the view that it is the irresponsible love of Antony and Cleopatra that must be recognised as leading to their sinful destruction, while at the same time accepting that our moral condemnation is not so strong that we cannot respond to the greatness of heart of the tragic pair. Mason too, in a recent book,[6] has put the same sort of case, with rather more emphasis on the criticism he feels the play invites for the lovers.

It is the greatness of heart, though, that has tended to attract more support than the moral flaws of the lovers, and many critics have claimed a transcendental value for their love which makes moral considerations all but irrelevant. H. S. Wilson formulates this view as follows:

> *Antony and Cleopatra* is the story of empire crossed with the story of love; and the empire of the love of Antony and Cleopatra, as Wilson Knight has emphasised, extends beyond the reaches of this world, it expands to fill the universe itself, transcends the limitations of the flesh to inhabit the universe of the spirit. This is the prevailing symbolic effect of the play. It is a vision of love which glorifies man and woman, so that with all their faults of ambition and deceit, sensuality, and careless pride, they yet rise to a tragic dignity, a tragic reconciliation and severity, compared with which the dreams of eathly empire shrink almost into insignificance; ultimately, their love is everything, or all that matters, to them and to us.[7]

The acknowledgement to the work of Wilson Knight[8] fairly indicates, I think, the source of many of the readings that see in the play a transcendental triumph of love. William Wimsatt, in an essay which is more concerned with a theory of literary criticism than with giving an account of the play, uses it as an example of his argument that great art may be immoral:

> There is no escaping the fact that the poetic splendour of this play, and in particular, of its closing scenes, is something which exists in closest juncture with the acts of suicide and with the whole glorified story of passion . . .[9]

Dover Wilson, too, in the introduction to his New Cambridge edition of the play, sees it as unequivocally optimistic in its tone, Shakespeare's Hymn to Man, with 'no hint anywhere of the quintessence of dust. Man is now all fire and air'.[10] Stauffer, in *Shakespeare's World of Images*,[11] also thinks that Shakespeare has reversed the classic tragic pattern, by showing a victory for love over duty. Perhaps more conscious than some others who have shared this general view of the play of the sort of moral censure the story appears to invite, Stauffer lists what he feels Shakespeare has done in order to defeat normal moral expectations: 'reason' is shown to be mistaken, the cause of empire belittled, the passion of the lovers is made larger than the world, and the historic liaison has been 'spiritualised'. So completely does he believe that this has been done that he holds that *'Antony and Cleopatra* is less a tragedy than a victorious vision, a fulfilment of immortal longings. . . . In the sense that its protagonists finally create their own glowing worlds, the play is not the next-to-last of the tragedies, but the first and greatest of the dramatic romances'.

A variant of either view, discussed by Reimer,[12] sees not a transcendence in the final scenes, but an effective distancing of our emotions, produced by the ironic effect of Antony's bungled suicide, and by our awareness of the extravagance of Cleopatra's vision of her lost lover, which makes the play, with *Coriolanus*, of a different kind from either tragedy or romance: 'For Shakespeare . . . universal significances and metaphoric meanings lost most of their allure: it was the discovery of things as they are, in the society of men, in the world of actual and tangible reality . . . that brought his greatest powers into effect'.

Other critics, myself included, find it less easy to avoid the play's tragic implications, the universal significances of its conflict and suffering, and the finality of its ending, and look therefore for a reading that will comprehend both the tragedy and the triumph. Various ways of coming to terms with the critical dichotomy have been proposed. It may be of some value to summarise briefly some of the most interesting, before proceeding to my own attempt at a synthesis.

Eugene Waith, in *The Herculean Hero*,[13] his study of a particular aspect of sixteenth- and seventeenth-century drama, argues convincingly that Antony can be recognised as an example of the heroic character in the model of Hercules, who is ' . . . a warrior of great stature who is guilty of striking departures from the morality of the society in which he lives'. In a carefully documented study, he argues that the traditional way of regarding such a man would be based on an awareness of the paradox of his heroic potential and his human limitation—the essential ingredients of the tragic experience, albeit of a special kind, since this kind of hero's greatness has less to do with goodness than with what is called *areté* or *virtus*, which Waith interprets as 'the energy of the divine spark'. Pointing out that in the classic tragedies based on the life and death of Hercules there is never any suggestion that his suffering is a punishment for misdeeds, but rather an illustration of the hostility of the universe to the greatest of men, Waith makes out a convincing case for seeing Antony as a hero cast in this mould, a man for whom, as for his great ancestor, the greatest temptation lies in giving way to despair. Though this account of Antony, in my opinion, allows less importance than is proper to the love story, it seems to me to fulfil a most useful function in refuting those accounts of the play that see Antony as a merely corrupted man, progressively losing authority and integrity, and finding at the end a death which is miserable, and not as he deludedly believes, noble.

Norman Rabkin,[14] whose views on 'complementarity' we have already had occasion to notice, finds, not surprisingly, that *Antony and Cleopatra* affords an excellent illustration of his principle, since this play, in his opinion, reconciles the opposing views of the 'absolute transcendence' and 'utter worthlessness' of the love. The play suggests on the one hand that 'the world, as seen from the point of view of its own maximum achievement may not be worth the keeping' while on the other it offers an observation of the folly of a love 'preposterously bound to ageing flesh' that leads only to death. Two views of Rome, two views of love, are presented, but while Rabkin seems to suggest that the scales are held in exact balance, most of the other attempts to reconcile the opposing views seem to come down more heavily on one side than the other.

As Traversi notices,[15] Philo's opening statement cannot be ignored, nor can 'the sense of superhuman value apprehended through love' or what L. C. Knights calls ' . . . an immense energy, a sense of life so heightened that it can claim to represent an absolute value'[16] which Shakespeare has infused into the love story. It is true that in the end, Knights, making the point that in Cleopatra's final scene the image of the baby at the breast points ironically to death, not renewed life, believes that while Shakespeare has evoked maximum sympathy for the magnificence of the love, it is finally 'placed' and dismissed. In the same kind of way, Traversi, though seeing that the world of politics in the play is 'thoughly mean and decayed', believes that the world of the lovers is equally corrupt, and that 'rottenness becomes the ground for fertility' even though this fertility is itself 'an experience which, although dependent upon time and circumstance, is by virtue of its value and intensity commensurate with them—that is "immortal" '.[17] His account, although it strives for balance, sometimes seems written from a point of view which sees power and politics as serious, pleasure not so, and which, in the end seems to endorse a 'realistic' judgement of all the characters which makes the play read like a rather more sympathetic version of *Troilus and Cressida*.

I prefer to put my thumb in the other scale, and recognise in the play a direction which while undeniably tragic, establishes a fuller value for love than either of these two critics would allow, but before I begin my own account, I should draw attention to an essay by Robert Ornstein, 'The ethic of the imagination: love and art in *Antony and Cleopatra*',[18] which gives a most interesting account of the play's true centre of gravity, and which sees Antony and Cleopatra as possessed of an imaginative faculty in their love which rises superior to the reasonable practicalities of Octavius and Rome. In a reading of the play which allows him to give full weight to the faults and deceptions of both the lovers, Ornstein nevertheless perceives that Antony becomes a fuller man in what is, from a material point of view, his decline, and sees too

that all of Cleopatra's artifice and theatricality works to make her life
what in the end she most truly wants it to be—a dedication to her love
for Antony.

It is clear from the most cursory of investigations that the play sets up a
dynamic opposition between Rome and Egypt: the action moves between these two halves of the world, the conflict takes place between
them, the two final adversaries are Octavius Caesar, now 'sole sir' of
the world, and Cleopatra, Egypt's conquered queen. Antony, Roman
by birth but Egyptian by inclination, moves between these two worlds,
finally chooses Egypt, and is destroyed by his choice. Much depends,
therefore on how this Rome–Egypt opposition is viewed, whether it is
presented as a simple moral opposition between duty and love, or even
more extremely, between morality and corruption.

If we were to attend only to the Roman voices in the play, there
would be no problem, for those who have not been changed by following Antony to Egypt, and even some who have, have no doubt of their
virtue and of his vice. The first opinion we hear of Antony, the play's
opening words, have a decidedly Roman tone. Nothing could be more
direct than Philo's condemnation:

> Nay, but this dotage of our general's
> O'erflows the measure: those his godly eyes,
> That o'er the files and musters of the war
> Have glow'd like plated Mars, now bend, now turn,
> The office and devotion of their view
> Upon a tawny front: his captain's heart,
> Which in the scuffles of great fights hath burst
> The buckles on his breast, reneges all temper.
> And is become the bellows and the fan
> To cool a gipsy's lust. Look, where they come:
>
> Take but good note, and you shall see in him
> The triple pillar of the world transform'd
> Into a strumpet's fool: behold and see . . .
>
> (I, i, 1)

but his criticism, forceful as it is, is immediately answered by the
appearance of the lovers and the formal but tender exchange between
them

> CLEOPATRA If it be love indeed, tell me how much?
> ANTONY There's beggary in the love that can be reckon'd.
> CLEOPATRA I'll set a bourn how far to be belov'd.
> ANTONY Then must thou needs find out new heaven, new earth.
>
> (I, i, 14)

Cleopatra's first words are of her need to be loved, of her fear, half-teasingly expressed here, that it is not 'love indeed' that Antony feels for her. Antony's reply is to deny or ignore the world of responsibilities implied in Philo's speech, and to claim the transcendental value of their love—'new heaven, new earth'—as the ultimate reality, the only value by which they can live. But the confidence his answer claims needs a surer basis than Antony's awareness of his feelings can yet provide. It needs the whole of the play to establish his title to that confidence, but it is interesting to notice that even in the opening condemnatory speech of Philo's the subtlety and complexity of the poetry prepares us for that conclusion.

Antony has been a great soldier and a great general: this is what Philo, and, we later learn, Octavius too, believe he ought still to be. Philo's comparison is with the god of war himself, but even as we remember that Mars fell in love with Venus, we notice the poetry's suggestion that if a soldier is all that Antony is, then he is something less than human. 'Plated Mars' somehow suggests not only the armoured god, but because of its mechanical sound, the statue of the armoured god, with something ruthless and inhuman about it, the sort of quality with which Volumnia's praise invests her son when he returns victorious from Corioles. But Antony is no automaton, and there is an underlying awareness in the speech that it is his human qualities that have made him the great general he is. It is his 'Captain's heart' impatient of all restraint, that has given him his courage; the same heart is the source of his love. In the same way, the words used to describe his ordering of the battle suggest a very different sort of ordering activity, so that the phrase, 'the office and devotion of their view', applied to his eyes, can look forward to the other object of his life, his love, and so imply an almost religious devotion. It is in the bitterness of phrases like 'tawny front', 'a gipsy's lust', and 'a strumpet's fool' that Philo, or any outsider, shows he is least competent to judge. Love, provided it is not based on absolute delusion, creates its own value in the object of that love, and that value in turn, creates more love. Only time can show whether or not the love *is* a delusion. The contradiction inherent in the irony of

> . . . the bellows and the fan
> To *cool* a gipsy's lust . . .

is a revealing one, for as it suggests the blowing up and heating of a furnace at least as strongly as it does the cooling process, it is, unwittingly perhaps, an admission of the strength of Antony's passion.

The audience may recognise, even if Philo cannot, that Antony loves greatly because of the greatness of his heart, as his instinctive and generous answer to Cleopatra's question reminds us: 'there's beggary in the love that can be reckoned'. Nevertheless, Philo's view of what he sees before him is the first statement of that judgement of Antony, articulated most forcefully by Octavius, against which any claim for his nobility must be established.

All would be very much clearer if we could feel that the Roman view, and the thoughts and actions of the Romans in this play, could be equated with the traditional Roman virtues, if we could feel that the life of Rome was undoubtedly morally superior to the life of Egypt. Shakespeare seems to take pains, however, to make it clear that Octavius' assumption of moral superiority rests on nothing more solid than his conviction that the things he wants, political power, the sole control of the Roman empire, the desire to be recognised as 'the universal landlord', are more admirable than the things that Antony wants. Romans in the play make frequent reference back to their noble heritage, to the virtues of fidelity, courage, endurance, honourable conduct, but the Rome we are shown is a very different place. Octavius can show contempt for Antony's 'lascivious wassails', feel that Antony has wounded his own honour, broken faith, and renounced his Roman nobility, but his own conduct, though its purpose is different, is as unscrupulous as Antony's could ever be accused of being. That he breaks faith with Pompey, defeating him, and then turns on his ally Lepidus, deposing and imprisoning him, is perhaps only to be expected of a man so accomplished in the techniques of the savage world of power politics. Much more chilling is his use of his own sister, Octavia, in what I think we must see as an ensnaring of Antony, a successful plan to provide a cause for war against him. It is true that the actual marriage is proposed by Agrippa, one of Caesar's lieutenants, but even if we can imagine that such a man would make such a suggestion without first discussing it with his master—Octavius shows no surprise—it is a suggestion that is at once accepted. And the man who accepts it is the same Caesar who is so skilled in calculating the weaknesses of others, who has so roundly condemned Antony's revels in Egypt and thinks him

> A man who is the abstract of all faults
> That all men follow.
>
> (I, iv, 8)

To marry his sister to a man for whom he feels such distaste in order to secure him as an ally is itself bad enough, but if we realise what I

believe the play suggests, that Octavius does it expecting that Antony
will go back to Egypt and so give Caesar cause for the war that will
settle the mastership of the world, then it becomes much worse. After
all, Enobarbus and his professional acquaintances, the followers of
Lepidus and Octavius, see well enough what the likely outcome will be,
and Caesar, in an affair of state of this kind, is not likely to be less
perceptive than they. His first mention of Antony in the play is of 'Our
great competitor'; his quarrel with Antony is on the grounds that Fulvia has opposed him on Antony's behalf. Immediately before Agrippa's
suggestion of the marriage, so immediately indeed that the effect is one
of contrivance, he is saying

> . . . for't cannot be
> We shall remain in friendship, our conditions
> So differing in their acts. Yet, if I knew
> What hoop should hold us staunch, from edge to edge
> O' the world I would pursue it.
>
>   (II, ii, 112)

Then comes the arrangement of the marriage. When they part it is with
the public caution from Octavius that any slighting of his sister will be
regarded as what is now called an hostile act (III, ii, 25). For all his
professions of caring for her, Caesar sees Octavia only as a means to an
end, a pawn in his political game: his true appraisal of his relationship
to Antony emerges when he has won, when Antony is dead, when he
can say

> . . . I must perforce
> Have shown to thee such a declining day,
> Or look'd on thine; we could not stall together
> In the whole world: . . .
>
>   (V, i, 37)

Caesar gets what he wants, and we have to admit that he is most
efficient at getting it. Before battle, deserters from Antony's army are
set in the van of his own, so that his own forces may be preserved, and
the enemy disheartened; he fights his battles, as Antony scornfully
remarks, by calculation, keeping himself withdrawn, contemptuously
dismissing Antony's challenge to individual combat with

> Let the old ruffian know
> I have many other ways to die:
>
>   (IV, i, 5)

He prefers to reply with promises of reward, which he has no intention of honouring, if Cleopatra will kill Antony for him. But though he wins the decisive battles, he is outwitted and defeated by Cleopatra in the end. She, who needs to be preserved alive to grace his triumph in Rome, sees through his deception and lies, and wins her way through to being able to call Great Caesar 'ass unpolicied'.

Octavius cannot be thought of simply as a villain; he is a reasonable man, perfectly in command of himself—he hates the drinking bout on the barge because it lessens that command—cold, not to the point of absolute inhumanity, certainly, but calculating, using everyone for his own ends, and not counting the cost of any action in human feelings. If indeed he does sometimes seem to verge on the inhuman, it is in contrast to the warmth, the flamboyance, of Antony, whose style of life is the very opposite of Caesar's. Caesar's followers share with him what the play discloses is only a surface conformity to the Roman virtues: Proculeius, whom Antony with his dying breath advises Cleopatra to trust, betrays her and brings about her capture. Menas the Roman advises Pompey the Roman to put to sea, cut his guests' throats, and become the world's master, and Pompey can only reluctantly resist this temptation:

> Ah, this thou shouldst have done,
> And not have spoke on't! In me 'tis villainy;
> In thee't had been good service. Thou must know,
> 'Tis not my profit that does lead mine honour;
> Mine honour, it. Repent that e'er thy tongue
> Hath so betray'd thine act: being done unknown,
> I should have found it afterwards well done;
> But must condemn it now. Desist, and drink.
>
> (II, vii, 74)

This is not honour that speaks, though Pompey may think it is; Menas' response is to look for some more sensible master; Caesar perhaps? Rome, in this play, is a world about which neither Caesar nor Antony has any illusions. When Antony hears of Pompey's threat, he can comment

> . . . Sextus Pompeius
> Hath given the dare to Caesar, and commands
> The empire of the sea: our slippery people,
> Whose love is never link'd to the deserver
> Till his deserts are past, begin to throw
> Pompey the Great and all his dignities
> Upon his son; who, high in name and power,
> Higher than both in blood and life, stands up
> For the main soldier . . .   (I, ii, 184)

'Our slippery people' is a description of the members of the Roman
state that is echoed by Octavius

> . . . This common body,
> Like to a vagabond flag upon the stream,
> Goes to and back, lackeying the varying tide,
> To rot itself with motion.
>
> (I, iv, 44)

Whatever it is that calls Antony back to Rome, or leads Caesar to make
war on him, it is not a concept of high duty, and though at the play's
end Caesar may look for a little easy admiration from his followers,
which they dutifully provide, by claiming that it was his destiny,
fulfilled in sorrow rather than anger, to have been Antony's conqueror,
for the most part they all admit quite frankly that it is political power
they seek. Scarus, Antony's lieutenant, can see the outcome of the
battle as the loss of 'the greater cantle of the world' and the Romans on
Antony's side are as apt as any Egyptians to 'follow their reason' and
desert to Caesar.

It is thus difficult to see the Roman side of Antony's life as the clear
depiction of a duty that his love for Cleopatra makes him neglect,
though a superficial impression of Cleopatra's Egypt, lascivious, luxurious, easy-going, corrupt, makes that seem to fit much more exactly
into the other half of the moralist's paradigm.

Just as Caesar is the chief representative of Rome, so Cleopatra is of
Egypt, but as with Caesar, as the play unfolds, it is clear that
Cleopatra's role cannot be understood as simply symbolic, in her case,
of an easy and luxurious life. Early impressions of her, and of Egypt,
seem to bear out Caesar's description of it as a place of 'luxurious
wassails' but that, if true, is only part of the picture. The setting for the
love story, the background for the 'new heaven, new earth' that Antony
has claimed for them, is quite mundane: Antony, encouraged by
Cleopatra, refuses to hear the messages from Rome:

> There's not a minute of our lives should stretch
> Without some pleasure now. What sport tonight?
>
> (I, i, 46)

and Enobarbus, in his role of detached observer can comment that

> Mine, and most of our fortunes tonight, shall be— drunk to bed.
>
> (I, ii, 45)

The tone for the Egyptian background seems set by Act I, scene ii, where Cleopatra's women jest with the soothsayer; they are gay, bawdy, irreverent, but we should not fail to notice how closely their liveliness is linked with a sense of foreboding and death, how the solemnity of the soothsayer's reply to Charmian's mocking

>   Is this the man? Is't you, sir, that know things?
> SOOTHSAYER   In nature's infinite book of secrecy
>   A little I can read . . .
>
>   (I, ii, 8)

makes the point of the uncertainty of all life, and thus gives an underlying seriousness to all their gaiety. 'O excellent, I love long life better than figs . . .'(I, ii, 31) replies Charmian to the soothsayer, who has prophesied the literal truth that she will outlive her mistress. At the play's end she will forgo her chance of long life to die with Cleopatra, and like Enobarbus and Iras, like Antony and Cleopatra themselves, prove the truth of the attitude, characteristic of Egypt in this play, that the quality of life is more important than its duration. It may seem that I am straining to hang too heavy a significance on what is after all a light-hearted scene, one that is cheerfully amoral, but it does seem true of the play as a whole that the Egyptian court for all its bawdiness, flippancy, occasional cruelty, and some critics might add, corruption, is closer to the realities of individual life and death than is Octavius Caesar's camp, for all *its* firm grasp on the realities of political power.

As we have already noticed, many critics have seen a fertility principle underlying the Egyptian scenes, which is closely linked by the play's imagery with notions of both life and death: life springs from Nilus' slime, and returns to it with the dissolution of the physical. It is perhaps not too much to see Cleopatra, with her 'infinite variety', and Antony too, with all his vacillation and changing moods, as being more in tune with the inevitable changes that comprise life than the marble-like Caesar, his will unalterably fixed, his emotions perfectly controlled. Cleopatra's court is devoted to the pursuit of pleasure; life there, to say the least, is eventful; and Cleopatra in reliving its glories can remember the visits of Julius Caesar and Cneius Pompey, as well as the fishing expedition when her diver hung a salted fish on Antony's hook. Antony too, by his own admission, seems to have given himself wholly over to sensual gratification, a point neatly underlined early in the play by the Roman soldier Enobarbus, who responds to Antony's call with 'What's your pleasure, sir?' (I, ii, 128).

Antony is like Mars, Cleopatra is like Venus (the identifications are explicitly made in the play); together or apart, they dominate their world in a way that Caesar does not, although he may hold the political power, and what is more, they can both inspire an affection and a loyalty which is strangely lacking from the Roman world, with its multiple intrigues and betrayals. Antony and Cleopatra can be betrayed, too, but significantly, those Romans or Egyptians who do so identify themselves with the Roman cause by going over to Caesar. The examples of courage and nobility are all on the side of Antony and Cleopatra, and they alone can inspire the truly Roman devotion to a master, or an ideal, that makes Enobarbus die of a broken heart after he realises what his betrayal of Antony means, makes Eros kill himself rather than kill his master, makes it unthinkable for Iras and Charmian to live longer than their queen. And, finally, this devotion makes Antony and Cleopatra die for each other 'after the high Roman fashion' in a way that finally establishes their integrity as individuals and the integrity of their love.

Since all the devotion of the Egyptian court and all its attention focus on Cleopatra, the best way to define this Egyptian quality is to attempt the definition of hers. The obvious place to start is with her variety: she is mocking, shrewish, bawdy, cruel, affected, argumentative, fierce, cowardly, familiar, dignified, tender, despairing, triumphant, in the most bewildering succession. As Bradley has it,

> Many unpleasant things can be said of Cleopatra; and the more that are said the more wonderful she appears.[19]

In the play, once Philo has voiced his initial condemnation of her, almost everyone else who meets her seems to fall under her spell. She can, even in her grief and near despair after Antony's death, charm Dolabella into revealing the truth of Caesar's plans for her. We know most about her through her relationship with Antony, of course, and this must be considered in detail, but Enobarbus' view of her is hardly less interesting. Of all the outside comments on the love affair, I find that offered by his role in the play the most interesting. Like Mercutio in *Romeo and Juliet*, and somewhat like an unmalicious Iago, if such a thing is imaginable, Enobarbus represents what he himself would call an intelligent, realistic reasonable point of view, and like them, he reveals the limitations of such an attitude. He prides himself on his bluntness, on his ability not to be taken in by appearance. He is cynical about most things, and not in the least inclined to romanticise, though he can tell a good story for the benefit of his soldier friends back in Rome. But what makes him most interesting is that he loves and admires Antony, and he sees and reports what the play makes clear for us, that it is Antony's love for Cleopatra that is destroying him as a general, as a ruler, as a man of power. So to a certain extent, he shares the attitude to the love affair of the severest of Antony's critics, just as he thinks he would like to share their common-sense view of the world. Two aspects of his role are particularly worthy of close attention: his attitude to Cleopatra, and his struggle with himself as he watches the growing certainty of Antony's fall.

Enobarbus, like his master, enjoys life in Alexandria, but he is not in love with Cleopatra. It is because of this, because of the disinterested nature of his testimony, that his account of Cleopatra's almost irresistible attraction carries so much weight. I am thinking at present not primarily of his great set piece, the description of the barge on the river Cydnus, but rather of his response early in the play when Antony, having had news of Fulvia's death, determines to return to Rome. Feeling now the threat of his relationship with Cleopatra to his position of power, Antony fears himself trapped

> These strong Egyptian fetters I must break
> Or lose myself in dotage.
>
> (I, ii, 116)

Enobarbus reminds him of the fury of the response that this decision will evoke from Cleopatra, but when Antony complains 'She's cunning past man's thought', Enobarbus' reply makes it clear that he understands Cleopatra a good deal better than do many of the play's critics, for he sees that all her acting of parts and changes of mood are natural to her:

> Alack, sir, no, her passions are made of nothing but the finest part of pure love. We cannot call her winds and waters sighs and tears; they are greater storms and tempests than almanacs can report. This cannot be cunning in her; if it be, she makes a shower of rain as well as Jove.
>
> (I, ii, 150)

Even allowing for the ironic tone of Enobarbus' tribute, there is considerable truth in his perception that she does not feign her emotions, but becomes what her emotions make her. And yet, as the ironic tone makes us realise, she is 'cunning' too, for almost everything she does is directed to the single end of making sure of Antony's love for her. To take up her own phrasing, she lives in a world of becoming rather than of being: what she aspires to is the security and perfection of Antony's love for her, and hers for him. Her life is change and movement, and it is her tragedy and his that the final testimony of his love can only come by his death, just as she can only make good her claim to be his wife

and not merely his mistress by stilling all the change and movement by
her own death.

What might be called the naturalness of Cleopatra's role-playing,
her openness in it, is, I think, something that has not had enough
critical attention. It has been suggested, for instance, that Enobarbus'
description of her entrance into Antony's life, on the river Cydnus,
contains so striking an element of artificiality that we (unlike Antony)
are insulated from too easy a surrender to her charm. We can easily
agree that the whole elaborate tableau is devised by Cleopatra to show
herself off in the most attractive way, but not, I think, that her care
defeats its own object. Shakespeare's Cleopatra, unlike Plutarch's, who
is described as being 'at the age when a woman's beautie is at the
prime', is very conscious throughout the play that she is ageing, not as
beautiful as she was.

> . . .Think on me,
> That am with Phoebus' amorous pinches black
> And wrinkled deep in time . . .
>
> (I, v, 28)

she says of herself, and knows that she must use art to show herself off
to best advantage. Even when she dies, she is concerned with what she
should look like; it is part of her nature that she should be so, but we
should notice that when she stages her last scene it is to that supreme
moment of her life that her thoughts return—'I am again for Cydnus'.
Enobarbus, when he tells the story, sets out, of course, to make an
impression on his rivals, who, gossipy as professional soldiers often are,
are only too eager to hear of the goings-on in Egypt:

> Eight wild-boars roasted whole at a breakfast, and but twelve persons
> there; is this true . . .
>
> (II, ii, 180)

asks Maecenas, but I find nothing either in the speech or in the hearers'
reception of it to suggest that it is not what it seems to be, an admiring
tribute to the marvellous mistress his captain has found. The magnifi-
cent poetry of the speech itself, all the more remarkable for staying so
close to its source in North's translation of Plutarch, and yet investing it
with a raptness of tone and sense of great excitement, is sufficiently
well-known to make lengthy quotation unnecessary. We must beware
though, of attaching to it the kind of association of artificiality and
sterility that T. S. Eliot imposes on his own echoing of it in *The Waste
Land*. In the play, the qualities of richness, harmony, beauty, royalty,

passion, gentleness are what the speech conveys, so woven together
that when the explicit comparison is made, 'out-picturing that Venus',
it can be willingly accepted, as can the later comparisons of Antony
with Mars, or Hercules. He and Cleopatra seem at times almost
superhuman, but their tragedy is that they are very human indeed, and
therefore vulnerable. Here the chief impression made by Enobarbus'
description is of a beauty and a power of attraction too great to be
resisted. Even the air

> . . . but for vacancy
> Had gone to gaze on Cleopatra too
> And made a gap in nature . . .
>
> (II, ii, 225)

The exclamations of his hearers make it clear that he has conjured up
for them the picture of a splendid mistress: 'O rare for Antony', 'Rare
Egyptian' and 'Royal wench' all indicate admiration, mixed with envy
for Antony's good luck, rather than a sympathy for one who has been
patently deceived. Nor should it be forgotten that this is not the end of
Enobarbus' description, though it is the point at which quotation
usually stops. It is her unpredictability just as much as her contrivance
that gives Cleopatra her charm: whatever she does becomes her. The
play never shows us anything to make us seriously doubt the truth of
Enobarbus' commendation

> . . . I saw her once
> Hop forty paces through the public street
> And having lost her breath, she spoke, and panted,
> That she did make defect, perfection,
> And breathless, power breathe forth . . .
>
> (II, ii, 228)

Then comes the summing-up of why Antony cannot resist her: she has
the freshness and variety, the self-renewing quality of life itself.

> Age cannot wither her, nor custom stale
> Her infinite variety; other woman cloy
> The appetites they feed, but she makes hungry
> Where most she satisfies . . .
>
> (II, ii, 235)

Enobarbus sees that it is to Cleopatra that Antony will be drawn,
regardless of the marriage that policy makes him contract in Rome, and
though Antony, at this stage of the play, may still think of his return as

merely indulgence—'I' the East my pleasure lies'—he is steadily made aware that what holds him to Cleopatra is something much more enduring than that.

As we shall see more fully later, when we explore the value that each of the lovers discovers in the other, it is Cleopatra's ability to become what she feels that lies at the heart of her character. For all her pretences and play acting, she wears her heart on her sleeve, for in the truest sense, she is what she seems to be. It is Octavius, the honest Roman, who is the master of concealment, who always erects a shield between his emotions and the world. In the opposition between the worlds they represent, worlds which in the first half of the play contend for Antony's attention, it is therefore very misleading to see the conflict as one between duty and pleasure, fidelity and lust, morality and moral anarchy. In this play, it is perhaps misleading to refer at all to the world of the ancient Roman virtues, so lacking are they from the behaviour of the Romans we see, but if courage and loyalty remain, it is at the court of Antony and Cleopatra, rather than in Octavius Caesar's councils that they are to be found.

Antony tries first to live in both worlds, vacillates between them, then finally realises that he must choose. On the implications of his choice rest the issue of his degeneration, or his integrity as a man. As we consider this, we ought perhaps to remember that an audience more familiar with Roman history would certainly not assume, as a modern audience or undergraduate class is perhaps too apt to do, that his surrender to the softer pleasures is something that dates from his meeting with Cleopatra. Shakespeare's most direct source, North's translation of Plutarch's *Parallel Lives of the Greeks and Romans* makes it clear that Antony had the name of a libertine before he ever saw his Egyptian queen, that he had the reputation of 'enticing men's wives', that he could be cruel and arrogant on occasions, but that his courage, his soldiership, and above all his magnaminity made men ready to forgive him for his faults. It is true that Plutarch also holds that Cleopatra (in North's translation) ' . . . did waken and stir up many vices yet hidden in him, and were never seen to any; and, if any spark of goodness or hope of rising were left in him Cleopatra quenched it straight and made it worse than before'[20] but that is a somewhat different thing from the impression that Octavius seeks to convey, of a noble soldier unmanned by lust. We are shown Antony making a choice that sets him at odds with the rest of his world, but the very fact that it does so should make us careful about accepting the rest of that world's judgements of his actions.

That Antony, at the play's opening, is still poised between Egypt and

Rome is made apparent by Cleopatra's anxiety to keep him at her side.
She teases, cajoles, mocks, plays on his vanity to get him to dismiss the
messengers from Rome, for she sees the whole of his life there, rather
than just for the claims of his wife Fulvia, as her rival. There is an
uneasiness in their relationship, an uncertainty in their evaluation of its
importance that appears both in the rhetorical flourish of the ending to
Antony's speech:

> Let Rome in Tiber melt, and the wide arch
> Of the rang'd empire fall! Here is my space,
> Kingdoms are clay: our dungy earth alike
> Feeds beast as man: the nobleness of life
> Is to do thus; when such a mutual pair
> And such a twain can do't, in which I bind,
> On pain of punishment, the world to weet
> We stand up peerless . . .
>
> (I, i, 33)

and in Cleopatra's immediate comment on it—'Excellent falsehood'—for while it is the sort of declaration she wants to hear, as any
lover would, the spaciousness of the arch image, the very reference to
kingdoms, suggests that political power can still attract Antony, though
he seeks to drown out its call in the self-advertising gesture of his
concluding lines. Cleopatra, at all events, is not wholly convinced, and
returns to the attack, to make sure that the messengers from Rome are,
for the present, dismissed; even she cannot postpone their reception
indefinitely. Later, Antony's attention does return to Rome, as she
ruefully acknowledges:

> He was disposed to mirth, but on the sudden
> A Roman thought hath struck him.
>
> (I, ii, 79)

This air of an apparently greater seriousness is sustained by the mood
in which Antony receives the bad news from Rome, but even if we
admire the coolness with which he (unlike Cleopatra!) can control his
emotions

> Things that are past are done, with me. 'Tis thus:
> Who tells me true, though in his tale lie death,
> I hear him as he flattered . . .
>
> (I, ii, 94)

we are soon brought to realise that the 'Roman thought' that has struck
Antony has regard to his prestige and power in the world, rather than

to any high sense of duty. It is not his neglected promise to the other Tribunes that pricks his sense of honour, but the news that his possessions are being attacked, and it is to defend them that he feels he must break the 'strong Egyptian fetters'. There is something very engaging about Antony's honesty with himself when he gets the news of Fulvia's death; he can be self-critical, examine his own response to the news, and wryly pay the dead woman her exact due. 'There's a great spirit gone . . . ', without attempting to feign what Enobarbus would call an onion-eyed sorrow.

Much less admirable is his attempt to placate the now furious Cleopatra with the news of Fulvia's death, so that he may win her consent to his leaving. The contrast between them is very marked at this point; he may be able to persuade Cleopatra and perhaps even himself, that he goes to Rome to fight on her behalf:

> I go from hence
> Thy soldier, servant, making peace or war
> As thee affects . . .
>
> (I, iii, 69)

but his thoughts before this declaration and his actions when he gets to Rome make it clear that this is a deceit. Cleopatra, by contrast, has no doubt where the centre of her life lies. From her first appearance in the play her whole endeavour has been to keep Antony with her. Here she sees how strongly he is pulled away from her, and her rebuke of him, scornful as it is, is nevertheless a moving statement of the value their love holds for her:

> Nay, pray you, seek no colour for your going,
> But bid farewell, and go: when you sued staying,
> Then was the time for words: no going then;
> Eternity was in our lips, and eyes,
> Bliss in our brows' bent; none of our parts so poor,
> But was a race of heaven. They are so still,
> Or thou, the greatest soldier of the world,
> Art turn'd the greatest liar.
>
> (I, iii, 32)

It may be that Cleopatra is using the regal plural to refer to herself, but even if this is so, the effect is at least as much of a tribute to their mutual love, whose rarity and self-sufficiency is beautifully suggested in the image of time suspended for the kissing lovers. She knows that he has determined to go, and she is too wise to push her demands for him to stay to the point where he must defy her, but she has a great need to prove that her importance to him has not been diminished. So with her own personal and appealing mixture of affectation and quick emotion, she collapses even before he can break the news of his intended departure, taunts him with his lack of fidelity to her, and to Fulvia, for the pleasure of hearing him protest that he loves her, and seeing him grow angry:

> Look, prithee Charmian,
> How this Herculean Roman does become
> The carriage of his chafe.
>
> (I, iii, 82)

But when she has teased him enough, she shows, in poetry whose conviction the later action of the play bears out, that though she knows very well what his absence will mean to her, she recognises that she must let him go. The exchange beginning

> Courteous lord, one word: .
> Sir, you and I must part . . .
>
> (I, iii, 86)

is taken by Antony as yet another delaying tactic, but he is rebuked by her:

> 'Tis sweating labour
> To bear such idleness so near the heart
> As Cleopatra this. But sir, forgive me;
> Since my becomings kill me when they do not
> Eye well to you: your honour calls you hence;
> Therefore be deaf to my unpitied folly,
> And all the gods go with you! Upon your sword
> Sit laurel victory, and smooth success
> Be strew'd before your feet.
>
> (I, iii, 93)

When he is gone, her centre of being is gone too, and what is left is 'a great gap of time' that must be filled up somehow until he comes back. Bearing that idleness, as she knows, will be bad enough, but worse than that is the present pain of his departure. But the way she masters her confusion and adopts the role of the noble Roman matron, sending him away from her with a valediction suitable for the part *he* is playing, show how she strives to keep control of herself, to make his unavoidable departure easy, so that, as she hopes, his return will be speeded.

When Antony gets back to Rome, he begins to learn that the whole business of the exercise of power is no longer as attractive as he had remembered it to be. It is important, I think, to notice that he is still good at it; that, in a sense, his return to Cleopatra is his relinquishing of power, rather than the retreat of a man whom power is already beginning to leave. Away from Cleopatra, his actions are, as defined in the context of this play, certainly Roman, but by no means admirable. Yet even here, I think, it is necessary to make a distinction between his personal and his public actions.

Much of Act II is in this sense very largely Roman in mood: after Pompey, Menecrates and Menas have, with some trepidation, for 'his soldier-ship / Is twice the other . . .' (II, i, 34), discussed Mark Antony's return, there is the meeting between Antony and Caesar, with Lepidus weakly trying to smooth over the quarrel between them. This scene has been read in very different ways, with some critics holding that Antony shifts and prevaricates in his excuses, and shows up very badly. In my opinion, though, Caesar is reminded, just as Lepidus is reminded by Enobarbus, that Antony in this sort of situation is still very much the man he was. Antony is prepared to go as far as his pride will let him in an apology that will heal the breach between them: it is true, as the audience knows, that he has not been using Fulvia to ferment a quarrel with Ceasar;

> . . . As for my wife
> I would you had her spirit in such another:
> The third o' the world is yours, which with a snaffle
> You may pace easy, but not such a wife.
>
> (II, ii, 61)

This rueful admission of his inability to control Fulvia seems to me also to contain a hint of warning to Caesar to be content with what he has, which, when Caesar questions his honour directly, is reinforced by a menace that is umistakable.

> CAESAR   You have broken
> The article of your oath, which you shall never
> Have tongue to charge me with.
> LEPIDUS   Soft, Caesar!
> ANTONY   No Lepidus, let him speak;
> The honour is sacred which he talks on now
> Supposing that I lack'd it. But on, Caesar
> The article of my oath.
>
> (II, ii, 81)

This touch of steel seems all that is needed: Caesar accepts the explanation, which really can hardly be called an apology, and a sort of amity is restored, for at least as long, as Enobarbus points out, as

Pompey remains a threat to their joint interest. When Caesar tries to reassert himself by mocking Antony's relationship with Cleopatra he is warned off with one curt phrase 'I am not married, Caesar' as Antony slips back naturally into the habit of command. Now for a while he is resettling himself into the masculine world of Rome, and it is in this Roman mood that the marriage with Octavia is arranged. Of all Antony's actions, this one, a marriage between Romans, arranged and approved by Romans, is the least defensible. We have already speculated on Caesar's motives for suggesting the match: Antony's, whatever they are, are hardly more admirable, for even if we accept at its face value his awkward attempt at sincerity with his new wife:

> My Octavia
> Read not my blemishes in the world's report;
> I have not kept my square, but that to come
> Shall all be done by the rule . . .

(II, iii, 4)

we cannot forget so easily his protestations to Cleopatra, or her concern for him so all-engrossing that even in his absence her first words to a messenger from him are 'How much unlike art thou Mark Antony!' (I, v, 35).

One or other woman must be betrayed by the marriage, cold-bloodedly undertaken as a marriage of policy, perhaps with Antony himself hoping that it will prove an antidote to the charm of Egypt, perhaps only as a passing expedient, to win time for himself in the impending quarrel with Caesar. Either way it is an action that can only reflect unfavourably on him, and one furthermore that is most unlikely to succeed, if it is a real attempt to abandon the life of pleasure. Enobarbus understands quite clearly what his master's reaction is likely to be, and why the marriage must surely fail.

ENOBARBUS Octavia is of a holy, cold and still conversation.
MENAS Who would not have his wife so?
ENOBARBUS Not he that himself is not so; which is Mark Antony. He will to his Egyptian dish again: then shall the sighs of Octavia blow the fire up in Caesar; and (as I said before) that which is the strength of their amity shall prove the immediate author of their variance. Antony will use his affection where it is. He married but his occasion here.

(II, vi, 119)

Enobarbus' prediction is soon proved correct. I find it difficult to know what to make of the scene with the soothsayer that is the immediate cause of Antony's return to Egypt, whether Antony snatches at any excuse to make the return that the gusto with which he has enjoyed the feasting on Pompey's barge has already prepared us for, or whether he believes the prediction and naïvely seeks to avoid the clash with Caesar. If the latter, then the irony of the words whereby he announces his decision is strong indeed

> I will to Egypt:
> And though I make this marriage for my peace,
> I' the east my pleasure lies . . .

(II, iii, 37)

for the combination of this marriage, made for his peace, and his return to Egypt is what gives Caesar the excuse to war with him. At this point in the play Antony may think his return is merely for the sake of his pleasure, but in fact it is the decisive choice of his life. Having made it, its political consequences force him to the realisation that Cleopatra's love is not only his pleasure, but all that gives him his being.

Two interesting points emerge as consequences of Antony's journey to Rome and his return to Egypt. The first, as we have seen, is that it might be argued that what brings about his political overthrow is not his infatuation with Cleopatra, but his political marriage, his flirtation with Caesar's rather than with Cleopatra's values. The second is that hereafter Rome and what it represents seem to attract him less and less, as if he needed only to experience its ethos once more in order to be cured of its fascination. The carousing scene on the barge, with Lepidus incapably drunk, and Octavius, with some distaste, doing what is expected of him, shows Antony trying to turn Rome into Egypt:

> ENOBARBUS Ha, my brave emperor,
> Shall we dance now the Egyptian Bacchanals
> And celebrate our drink? . . .
> ANTONY Come, let's all take hands
> Till that the conquering wine hath steep'd our sense
> In soft and delicate Lethe.

(II, vii, 102)

Once he goes back, he acknowledges that his destiny is linked with Cleopatra's; if he wins his battles the prize will be life with her; life without her is no longer a possibility. We do not have the impression that Antony is fighting Caesar for the possession of Rome or the world, though this may be what many of his followers want him to do, and why they defect to Caesar when Antony is seen to be losing.

I do not want to give the impression, though, that I think Antony and Cleopatra toss the world lightly aside. The exercise of a power that

has been well nigh absolute is something that they both enjoy, something that they can hardly imagine being without. It is even arguable
that Cleopatra's indulgence in her emotions is in part the reaction of
one who has always had what she has wanted, and that it is the loss of
this absolute authority, as much as their love for each other, that makes
them ready to die rather than live with diminished fortunes. This view
of the royal pair certainly has something to commend it: the almost
ridiculous sound of Antony's request to the victorious Caesar to be
allowed to live on as a private citizen shows very clearly that while he
and Cleopatra may dress up as common people, for sport, they can
never become commoners. When Antony has returned to Egypt, his
attempt is clearly at first to hold his authority, and be with Cleopatra.
It is only when he is forced to see that he cannot have both that the
agonising nature of the choice he has so lightly made—'I' the East my
pleasure lies'—becomes plain to him.

I have already suggested that it is in the nature of the suffering that love
exacts that this play chiefly differs from the other love tragedies: more
complex than either of them, it unites the world without with the world
within. Both Antony and Cleopatra have to face a material
impoverishment of their lives, which up to now have been lived and
enjoyed without moderation or restraint; both have to face defeat and
failure, experiences new to them, and both, within the bounds of the
love affair for the sake of which they endure these losses, have to
recognise the possibility of the infidelity of their partners.

Cleopatra's humiliation comes first. All her vitality and expectancy
has been directed towards Antony's return, but she receives instead the
news of his marriage to Octavia. It is a bitter blow, for throughout the
play, she shows an interesting preoccupation with the question of marriage, from her early 'What, says the married woman you may go?' (I,
iii, 20) through her fury when she hears of Antony's remarriage, to her
final claim that by her suicide she earns the title of Antony's wife. Her
affairs with Caesar and Pompey can be dismissed airily as the indis-
cretions of her 'salad days' when she was but 'green in judgement';
from Antony she wants something more; she wants to be his partner in
all things, in battle as well as bed, and will not be satisfied with the role
of his 'pleasure' to which he at first seeks to assign her. She feels that
the news the messenger from Rome brings is shattering to her, and it is,
of course, a public humiliation, a rejection by the man she has so
extravagantly praised, in front of those courtiers to whom she has
praised him. Her passion vents itself, quite unfairly, on the bearer of
the news. She is wild and cruel and rueful all at once, but though the

figure she cuts comes close to being ridiculous, she is redeemed and given an underlying dignity (and I use the word advisedly) by the way in which, even under this crushing blow, her love for Antony is not seriously shaken. Nor, in spite of her quite extraordinary performance, does she seem unlike herself, though she drags the unfortunate messenger about by the hair, and even offers to kill him herself if he persists in his report. Her reply to Charmian's

> Good madam, keep yourself within yourself
> The man is innocent . . .
>
> (II, v, 75)

characterises her emotions very well. As she truly remarks, and as life, and Shakespeare's plays, repeatedly show, fairness is not something that can be confidently expected by everyone. Muttering 'some innocents 'scape not the thunderbolt . . .' she goes on, in a curious echo of Antony's 'Let Rome in Tiber melt . . .',

> Melt Egypt into Nile! and kindly creatures
> Turn all to serpents! Call the slave again
> Though I am mad, I will not bite him, call!
> CHARMIAN He is afraid to come.
> CLEOPATRA I will not hurt him.
> These hands do lack nobility, that they strike
> A meaner than myself; since I myself
> Have given myself the cause . . .
>
> (II, v, 82)

Like Troilus, she wants things to be other than what they are; like him too 'Though I am mad . . . ' she feels that Antony's betrayal of her has made chaos around her, but she can regain the grip upon herself, and she can bend her energies to what she has to do to win Antony back again. What gives her her dignity is, I think, the sincerity of her reactions. She is not acting out a part for the benefit of anyone: what she feels she says and does, and she is too honest to pretend that anything, grief, hurt pride, any feeling of rage or self-pity (and as the scene so clearly demonstrates, she experiences all these emotions) can take precedence over her love for Antony and her need to get him back again. If she has chosen wrongly, she has nobody to blame but herself, a much more healthy reaction, surely, than Troilus' rantings at a universal betrayal and a universal corruption. It all merges together beautifully in the last speeches of the scene:

CLEOPATRA	In praising Antony, I have disprais'd Caesar?
CHARMIAN	Many times, madam.
CLEOPATRA	I am paid for't now. Lead me from hence. I faint,

O Iras, Charmian! 'tis no matter
Go to the fellow good Alexas, bid him
Report the feature of Octavia; her years,
Her inclination, let him not leave out
The colour of her hair: bring me word quickly.
Let him for ever go, let him not—Charmian,
Though he be painted one way like a Gorgon,
The other way's a Mars. Bid you Alexas
Bring me word how tall she is. Pity me, Charmian,
But do not speak to me. Lead me to my chamber.

(II, v, 108)

Everything is completely in character, including the final imperious demand for silent sympathy. Running through it all is her admission that whatever Antony does, she cannot stop loving him. There can be no doubting that both the intensity of her passion and the impulsiveness of her responses are wholly directed towards Antony, as are the resilience and resource she shows in needing to know exactly what her rival is like, for the better planning of the next stage of her campaign to get him back. Her love is based not on illusion, rather on the recognition that life without Antony is not worth contemplating. When he does return, it is significant that she wants to be everything to him, fellow soldier, armourer, wife, as well as mistress; once he has returned and the initial battle has been lost she can see very clearly where events are taking him, but it does not seem to me that what are sometimes called her intrigues with Caesar and his messengers are intended to do any more than win a little time for them both.

Ironically, the increasing closeness of their relationship helps directly to bring about their material destruction, for when Antony returns to Cleopatra, he admits her to his councils of war as his equal. It is Enobarbus again, who can point to the folly of this, in his usual blunt way:

If we should serve with horses and mares together the horses were merely lost; the mares would bear a soldier and his horse.

(III, vii, 7)

Enobarbus sees love and war as mutually opposed values, as they traditionally are, and sees too, that Antony's attempt to include Cleopatra, in his rather endearing mixture of tenderness and professional soldiership

> Is it not strange, Canidius
> That from Tarentum and Brundisium
> He could so quickly cut the Ionian sea
> And take in Toryne? You have heard on't, sweet? . . .
>
> (III, vii, 20)

must affect his judgement as a general. He is quite right, as the flight from the sea battle proves. Antony accepts Caesar's dare to fight by sea, because of his desire to appear well in Cleopatra's eyes, and in spite of all reason, even in the face of an appeal from one of his own veteran soldiers, he will neither change his decision nor consider its possible consequence. Cleopatra wants to fight by sea, and bear her share, and when, predictably, 'that great face of war' as Enobarbus calls it, frightens her, and she takes flight, Antony's love carries him after her. His followers, disheartened by his example, give up. The decisive battle is lost, and hereafter there is no chance whatsoever that Antony and Cleopatra will be finally victorious, and allowed to live out their love.

This instinctive following of Cleopatra from the battle is Antony's second decisive action, again made apparently without heed of its consequences. Poised as he still is in his consciousness between love and power, he can interpret this action in two ways, but to his followers, it means only one thing, defeat. His reputation for invincibility is lost, his lieutenants no longer trust his generalship, and, anxious to be on the winning side, desert to Caesar. Canidius goes, and so do many of the kings in his train, the roll-call of whom had earlier made such a brave impression of power. To his men, it seems an action of almost unbelievable cowardice:

> . . . Yon ribaudred nag of Egypt,—
> Whom leprosy o'ertake!—i' the midst o' the fight,
> When vantage like a pair of twins appear'd
> Both as the same, or rather ours the elder,—
> The breeze upon her like a cow in June,
> Hoist sails and flies . . .
> She once being loof'd,
> The noble ruin of her magic, Antony
> Claps on his sea-wing and (like a doting mallard)
> Leaving the fight in height, flies after her:
> I never saw an action of such shame;
> Experience, manhood, honour, ne'er before
> Did violate so itself.
>
> (III, x, 10)

The contempt that Scarus feels for Cleopatra is clearly expressed in the degrading image of the cow on the gad, yet oddly, the lines that

describe Antony's following of her have their own beauty, even though
Scarus so roundly condemns the action. It is interesting too, to notice
with what care Shakespeare makes the points that Antony is not
defeated, nor has he yielded to fear. Judged from his soldiers' point of
view he is doubly condemned, his manhood and his honour are viol-
ated, but this is not the way the consequences necessarily appear to us.

It is because Antony has been a great soldier and leader that his
choice exacts so great a price from him. Were he merely an individual,
his decision would be an individual matter, but he has to learn that his
love is all-demanding. His reputation, and his pride in himself as a
soldier are the first things to go, along with almost all his power. The
shame he feels at his betrayal of his men, and at himself, is so great that
at first he does not even notice Cleopatra's presence, for whose love he
must bear it all.

> ANTONY   Hark, the land bids me tread no more upon't
> It is ashamed to bear me. Friends, come hither,
> I am so lated in the world that I
> Have lost my way for ever . . .
>
> (III, xi, 1)

To have to yield to Caesar without himself having been beaten by him
seems almost unendurable, and all the fighting soldier's scorn for a
man who has not fought comes out in

> . . . he, at Phillipi kept
> His sword e'en like a dancer, while I struck
> The lean and wrinkled Cassius; and 'twas I
> That the mad Brutus ended: he alone
> Dealt on lieutenantry, and no practice had
> In the brave squares of war: yet now—No matter.
>
> (III, xi, 35)

His anger and disgust with himself are intense, but he is coming to
realise through his humiliation where the true purpose and centre of his
life lies: his bitterness at himself is not here turned against Cleopatra.
Addressing her formally by her title, as he is to do again, most movingly, when he is dying, he shows how far his view of what has occurred
differs from that of his followers. He tells her only that he loves her, that
she might have foreseen the consequences of her flight. Now, at a
moment when he is most keenly aware of what his love for her is costing
him, he reaffirms the value of that love.

> Fall not a tear, I say; one of them rates
> All that is won and lost. Give me a kiss,
> Even this repays me.
>
> (III, xi, 69)

This is very different in tone from the bravado of some of his earlier
declarations, for there is a sort of weariness here that is most revealing.
He has begun to recognise the progressive shedding of his political
ambitions that his return to Egypt has implied, but he cannot yet
reconcile himself to the loss of what he thinks of as his honour. There is
a note of self-pity in much of what he does, until he can feel that he has
repaired that honour by fighting again, and winning. For the present,
he is reduced to sending his schoolmaster to Caesar, to sue for peace
and to ask to be allowed to live as a private citizen, but Caesar,
confident of his power, ignores the request, thus stinging Antony into
his offer of single combat. It is wrong, I think, to treat this challenge
solely as a piece of desperate bravado, and to dismiss it with Enobarbus' comment

> Yes, like enough high-battled Caesar will
> Unstate his happiness and be staged to the show
> Against a sworder! I see men's judgements are
> A parcel of their fortunes, and things outward
> Do draw the inward quality after them,
> To suffer all alike. That he should dream,
> Knowing all measures, the full Caesar will
> Answer his emptiness! . . .
>
> (III, xiii, 29)

or with Caesar's contemptuous

> . . . let the old ruffian know,
> I have many other ways to die, meantime
> Laugh at his challenge.
>
> (IV, i, 4)

Individual integrity is now of far more concern to Antony than political
or military success. Because he feels that he has lost his own integrity,
and feels keenly the need to re-establish it, he credits Caesar with
something of the same sense of honour. The terms of his challenge
strike us as absolutely true of Caesar's position:

> . . . tell him he wears the rose
> Of youth upon him; from which, the world should note
> Something particular: his coin, ships, legions,

> May be a coward's, whose ministers would prevail
> Under the service of a child, as soon
> As i' the command of Caesar:
>
> (II, xiii, 20)

but so far has Antony's interest removed from the power game that he has forgotten that Caesar cares far more about his position, and possessions, than about what he himself is. Enobarbus is right when he calls the challenge foolish, but Antony, who is beginning to inhabit a different world, is right too.

It is, as I have already suggested, an important part of Antony's tragedy that he is not allowed to be the sole sufferer of the consequences 'of his choices. He holds the allegiance of many men, who fall as a result of the change of direction in his life, and keenly feels what he sees as his betrayal of their loyalty, as his own fall puts them in the position of having to fall with him, or desert to Caesar. His reception of the news of Enobarbus' defection makes clear the generosity of spirit that takes the blame upon itself

> ANTONY   Is he gone?
> SOLDIER   Most certain.
> ANTONY   Go Eros, send his treasure after, do it,
>   Detain no jot, I charge thee: write to him—
>   I will subscribe—gentle adieus, and greetings;
>   Say, that I wish he never more find cause
>   To change a master. O, my fortunes have
>   Corrupted honest men. Despatch—Enobarbus!
>
> (IV, v, 12)

In the end, he cannot even choose to die alone, for his last follower, Eros, kills himself rather than have to kill his master. As he moves toward his death, he has to recognise that love strips him of everything that he has previously valued; he loses power, even the desire for power, his reputation, his honour, his own integrity as a soldier and as a leader, yet even as he undergoes this ordeal for love, he moves closer to his new-found integrity in his love for Cleopatra, discovering that he cares more about her than he does about himself. It is this rivalry for first place in Antony's heart, I think, that most distinguishes him from Romeo or even Othello. Cleopatra wins her primacy against other powerful concerns, some of which, like his pride in his soldiership and his loyalty to his followers, are both enduring and admirable.

It is most noticeable that in the scenes in which Antony is shown coming to realise that his power in the world is slipping away from him, he expresses no bitterness toward Cleopatra, or even towards love itself, at the heaviness of the price. There is an elegiac note to the poetry that we shall have occasion to look at later in more detail, merely noting here that the curious scene in which his soldiers hear music under the earth, which they believe signifies that 'the god Hercules, whom Antony loved / Now leaves him . . . ' (IV, iii, 15) is very much in this mood. But if Antony had only to suffer this loss of a place in a world about which he no longer greatly cares, the play as a whole would be much gentler and less searching than it actually is. Much more painfully, he is also made to doubt the reality of the love which exacts so great a sacrifice from him. He must face the possibility, which his greater experience, his knowledge of Cleopatra's past, and the immediate circumstances of his defeat all suggest to him may even be a probability, that she does not love him in defeat, and is betraying him to his enemy.

The greatest threat to Antony's integrity comes from the circumstances which make him unconfident of Cleopatra's love. We have already seen that her leading of him from the battle has made him more reproachful of himself than of her; he can be sure of himself when he is sure of her, even to the extent of at once communicating to her Caesar's suggestion that she save herself at the expense of his life.

> ANTONY   The queen then shall have courtesy, so she
> Will yield us up?
>
> EUPHRONIUS   He says so.
>
> ANTONY   Let her know't.
> To the boy Caesar send this grizzled head,
> And he will fill thy wishes to the brim
> With principalities.
>
> CLEOPATRA   That head, my lord?
>
>   (III, xiii, 14)

Her reply, which implies a wealth of shared affection and tenderness in its simplicity, is all that is necessary here to reassure him, but it is a very different matter when he finds Caesar's messenger kissing her hand.

> Favours? By Jove that thunders!
> What art thou fellow? . . .
> Take hence this Jack and whip him.
>
>   (III, xiii, 85)

Now he does feel that Cleopatra is demeaning, perhaps even betraying, their love; his anguish expresses itself in his cruelty to the messenger,

just as Cleopatra's did, when she had the news of his marriage to
Octavia. In the insecurity he feels he senses the possibility of having
given up all that he had, for a love that may have been occasioned by
his position and not been for himself as a man.

> . . . Now, gods and devils
> Authority melts from me: of late, when I cried 'Ho!'
> Like boys unto a muss, Kings would start forth,
> And cry 'Your will?' Have you no ears?
> I am Antony yet.
>
> (III, xiii, 89)

The cruelty of his attempt to reassert the old authority, to reverse the
transformation that his love is demanding, shows Antony at his least
sympathetic, even if we can understand the cause of the fury with
which he turns on Cleopatra

> You were half blasted ere I knew you: ha?
> Have I left my pillow unpress'd in Rome,
> Forborne the getting of a lawful race
> And by a gem of women, to be abus'd
> By one that looks on feeders? . . .
>
> (III, xiii, 105)

His sexual bitterness, his revulsion from what he also most desires, is
reminiscent of Othello, or Hamlet; his pride is hurt, he is sorry for
himself, and we must recognise that he is venting some of his humiliation and anger at the disgrace he has exposed himself to by following
Cleopatra from the battle, on her now, under cover of another pretext.
If the energy of his anger and anguish were not so great, his attempt to
strike a moral attitude '. . . I am sure / You can guess what temperance
should be / You know not what it is' would be laughable. But running
through it as well as ample evidence of his own hurt, there is a concern
for Cleopatra herself, who degrades herself from what she really is by
this baseness:

> ANTONY   Alack, our terrene moon
>   Is now eclipsed, and it portends alone
>   The fall of Antony.
> CLEOPATRA   I must stay his time.
> ANTONY   To flatter Caesar, would you mingle eyes
>   With one that tied his points?
>
> (III, xiii, 153)

I should, in passing, make it clear that I think Antony quite misun-
derstands the situation that is here the occasion for his rage. He has not

heard what I take to be Cleopatra's elaborately acted surprise at the
news from Caesar that she

> . . . embrac'd not Antony
> As you did love, but as you fear'd him . . .
>
> (III, xiii, 56)

or her gross flattery of Caesar as she appears to accept his suggestion
that her '. . . honour was not yielded / But conquered merely'. She is
surely playing for time, as she does in her later dealings with Caesar,
time which Antony badly needs to recover himself after the shattering
experience of his defeat. Conclusive, to my mind, is the fact that she
takes care to receive Caesar's embassy in the presence of Enobarbus.
Nobody could call Cleopatra stupid, and she would have to be that if
she openly made plans to betray Antony in the hearing of his closest
follower.

But be that as it may, Antony, who is after all close to despair at this
point, feels that she too has turned against him, and in his despair, is
something less than himself. It takes Cleopatra's solemn oath, in
response to his demand 'Cold hearted towards me?' to convince him
that their love is as it was.

> CLEOPATRA   Ah, dear, if I be so,
> From my cold heart let heaven engender hail,
> And poison it in the source, and the first stone
> Drop in my neck: as it determines, so
> Dissolve my life; the next Caesarion smite
> Till by degrees the memory of my womb,
> Together with my brave Egyptians all,
> By the discandying of this pelleted storm,
> Lie graveless, till the flies and gnats of Nile
> Have buried them for prey!
>
> (III, xiii, 159)

The sincerity this avowal carries comes from its complete awareness of
what a betrayal of their love would mean to her. Not only are there the
cold and destructive associations of the hail, there is also her conviction
that if the love which is her life were poisoned at the source (again an
echo of *Othello* imagery) life itself would be impossible, for the heart,
instead of supporting life, would dispense poison. Everything about her
would lose form, dissolve, 'discandy', in the very image that Antony is
to use of himself later in the play, for without her love for him, and his
for her, there is no fixed point of reference in her world by which she
may know herself. Antony can accept this reassurance because it states

so explicitly the chaos that threatens him when he loses faith in the mutuality of their passion. Believing in Cleopatra's love, he can become a full man again, and even win the victory in battle that restores his faith in himself, though it cannot change the eventual outcome of the war. In his ability to quell his doubts, to regain his faith in Cleopatra's fidelity to him, Antony seems closer to the heroes of the Romances than he does to Othello. It is true that like Troilus, he believes that what he most needs to believe is true, but he makes great sacrifices for that belief, the final one being his own life, and the play does not give him the lie.

The final, severest test of his faith is his suspicion that Cleopatra is to blame for the treachery of his fleet, when it goes over to Caesar, and that this betrayal reveals that Cleopatra has all along been deceiving him. I would like to postpone detailed consideration of this scene until later in the chapter, but it is clear enough that once again the consequence of this loss of faith in what has become the supreme value in his life, is, after his immediate fury against Cleopatra has expended itself, a feeling of being lost, of having lost his own identity, so that he drifts, purposeless, unable to live or to die. The news of Cleopatra's pretended death, itself a falsehood, is a paradox that brings him to the the truth. If she has killed herself, as he at first believes, then she must have loved him; but even if her death is only a pretence, then the deception itself is proof of her caring still for him, and no word of reproach is uttered at the trick that costs him his life, because the value of his love is recreated by it.

After his death, as Cleopatra moves towards hers, her grief at his loss is passionate and moving, but at least it is a grief that comes from a physical loss, not the agony of perhaps having to recognise that she has lived a lie. Cleopatra can and does take comfort in her vision of Antony. She is going to die because she cannot live without him, it is true, but she has also been splendidly happy with him, and it is the quality of that past happiness that modulates the tragic tone of the fifth act into something different and makes this play in its final effect quite unlike the other two tragedies.

The whole question of the value that Antony and Cleopatra find in each other is for me the principal interest in the last two acts, which see the re-establishment of Antony as a man and as a lover after his near-despair following the battle of Actium, his suicide, and Cleopatra's evasion of Caesar's deceptions as she struggles to find a way to join Antony in death.

I have already suggested that one of the reasons why we can accept the valuation that each of the lovers puts on the other, in spite of its obvious subjectivity, is that it is recognisably true to what the play has shown of them. That they should find each other worth dying for is not surprising when those who serve them can die for them too, Eros and Charmian by their own hands, Enobarbus and Iras because their hearts will not sustain the breach of loyalty that living on would imply. The quality that attracts Cleopatra to Antony, his greatness of heart, his magnanimity, has been amply demonstrated by his actions, and it is a quality, moreover, that is testified to by his enemies as well as his friends. Acknowledgement of it, after he has deserted Antony, breaks Enobarbus' heart, and kills him. It is a quality that shows through almost everything Antony does, and though Cleopatra has ample reason to know that he has other qualities as well, that he has wavered in his love for her, and deceived her, she still loves him for this one great essential quality: even his rage, even when it is directed against her, she finds almost irresistible.

As for Cleopatra, we must remember that Antony loves her for what she is shown to be in the first four acts. Even if it were thought that she is unjustifiably ennobled and made more sympathetic by her response to his death—which I do not accept—this would be an aspect of her that Antony could never know. He loves her for what she is, when she is the 'wrangling queen / Whom every thing becomes . . .' and he cannot stop loving her even when he believes she has been false to him. Her charm is understandable enough: Enobarbus supplies his splendid testimony; Charmian in a final memorable phrase, calls her 'a lass unparallell'd'; even Caesar, though he characteristically sees it as a snare, can play tribute to her beauty in death:

> As she would catch another Antony
> In her strong toil of grace . . .
>
> (V, ii, 345)

Cleopatra's openness, like Antony's, makes her faults unhidable: he loves her because of what she is, aware of what his loving her is costing him. It is in this that both he and she differ from the world around them, which cannot comprehend why the lovers should give up so much for each other, and is unable to see that Antony and Cleopatra are not deceived about each other, but are judging and directing their lives to a different purpose from the world's aims. I believe that if the play is read with care, it is easy enough to accept that Antony finds Cleopatra's love worth dying for, not as an escape from a world that has already rejected him, but as a final positive heroic action by which he can demonstrate the central value of his life, his feeling for Cleopatra. This centrality is a position Cleopatra is well fitted to occupy.

Everything about her, all her actions, all her words in the play, are, I believe, directed to making clear four basic attributes. The first, and that which governs all the rest, is that everything she does can be explained by her love for Antony and, after his death, by her sense of the disaster of his loss. Her reply to Charmian's well-meaning advice

CHARMIAN	Madam, methinks if you did love him dearly You do not hold the method, to enforce The like from him.
CLEOPATRA	What should I do, I do not?
CHARMIAN	In each thing give him way, cross him in nothing.
CLEOPATRA	Thou teachest like a fool: the way to lose him . . .

(I, iii, 6)

makes the point early on that all her changes of mood, her taunting, teasing, railling, feigned anger, sickness, are not a wanton demonstration of her power over Antony, but her attempt to keep him for her own. The second quality about her presentation is that, paradoxically, she is an honest person: I have already commented that even Enobarbus seems to agree that far from being hypocritical, she *becomes* all things in turn, that her emotions direct her whole life. She reacts in word and deed in the way many of us would like to do, if notions of propriety and decorum did not hold us back. This is not to say that all her reactions are admirable, by any means, but at least, unlike others in the play, she is what she seems. Moreover, she is honest with herself, she demands love, admiration, sympathy, but she does not attempt to deceive herself into thinking that all will be well simply because she wants it so. Thirdly, there is a tremendous sense of enjoyment in everything she does, she can relive in memory the moments of her greatest triumphs, she can jest with her women about her old conquests, appraise her own charms without illusion; she can even stage-manage her own death, and relish the thought of Caesar's consternation when he discovers that far from tricking her, she has tricked him. And finally, like Antony, she has the power to inspire absolute devotion. She can be cruel (she is particularly so to poor Mardian, the eunuch, and we can see why), conceited, self-pitying, cowardly, overbearing and undoubtedly of loose sexual morals, but she can inspire absolute devotion. Those who love her will die for her, as men will for Antony. Those with only an eye for the main chance will desert to Caesar, and find incidentally, that they miscalculate even here, because he is far too politic to trust them. It is impossible to imagine anyone staying with Octavius in defeat, and the contrast is obvious.

Acts IV and V are particularly interesting because they establish the quality of feeling the lovers share, and it is this quality that decides whether or not we feel that their suicides establish any sort of victory for them and set a seal upon their love, or whether, as some critics believe, Shakespeare intends us to see them taking refuge from the collapse of their material fortunes in a golden haze of romantic self-delusion. Because they are very different temperamentally, Shakespeare makes a very definite separation in the mode of their tragedies. Antony has to recover his command of himself before any action, even self-ending, can be meaningful, while Cleopatra, once he is dead, has to triumph over her own timidity, over her zest for life, in order to be able to join him in the oblivion of death.

It is from the point of view of Antony's re-establishment of himself that Shakespeare's handling of the second battle is so important. Antony's victory here, though there is never any suggestion that it can change the outcome of the war—indeed the contrary is implied in 'Had we done so first, we had droven them home / with clouts about their heads' (IV, vii, 5)—is given vastly more emphasis than the relating of this successful but minor sally enjoys in North's *Plutarch*. It is after Cleopatra's terrible vow of fidelity that Antony determines to redeem what he feels is the loss of his honour by fighting again, to show himself worthy of her. That he is far from confident of victory is shown by the images of death, the undertone of finality that runs through all his resolve:

> Come,
> Let's have one other gaudy night; call to me
> All my sad captains; fill our bowls once more
> Let's mock the midnight bell . . .
>
> (III, xiii, 183)

> . . . tonight I'll force
> The wine peep through their scars. Come on my queen
> There's sap in't yet. The next time I do fight
> I'll make death love me; for I will contend
> Even with his pestilent scythe.
>
> (III, xiii, 190)

Enobarbus thinks this merely the bravado of despair

> . . . I see still
> A diminution in our Captain's brain
> Restores his heart; When valour preys on reason,
> It eats the sword it fights with: I will seek
> Some way to leave him . . .
>
> (III, xiii, 197)

but Antony's victory proves him wrong, because Antony is fighting for
something beyond mere military success. Through the speeches of his
resolve, images of life and death mingle and merge; words like 'force',
'sap', 'love', the blood-red wine that will peep through the scars, merge
with images of wounds, fighting, death and his 'pestilent scythe'. What
Antony is saying in effect, is that at least he will live until he dies, the
only sort of victory over death that any mortal can win. He can with
perfect honesty, and without diminishing the importance of his love,
say

> Tomorrow, soldier,
> By sea and land I'll fight: or I will live,
> Or bathe my dying honour in the blood
> Shall make it live again.
>
> (IV, ii, 4)

Honour and love, which had in the earlier battle beckoned him down
diverging paths, now come together again. To be worthy of Cleopatra,
to love as a complete man, he must regain his honour, but in the tragic
situation in which he finds himself he can only redeem his honour by
dying for it, and love cannot survive death. Nevertheless, this battle is
fought for love. After Enobarbus' desertion, Eros becomes his closest
companion, and the name takes on an increasingly symbolic value.
Eros and Cleopatra help Antony put on his armour, the god of love,
and the armourer of his heart, as Antony calls her, while, in tones very
different from the mixture of self pity and somewhat desperate resolve
of the previous night, Antony contemplates with pride but without
boastfulness his own worth as a soldier. 'Workman', the unlikely word
which marks the climax of this speech, is a word quite devoid of military glamour, but it suggests with great force his confidence, not that he
will win, but that he will acquit himself well, as a master of his craft.

> He that unbuckles this, till we do please
> To daff't for our repose, shall hear a storm.
> Thou fumblest Eros, and my queen's a squire

> More tight at this than thou: despatch. O love,
> That thou couldst see my wars today, and knews't
> The royal occupation, thou shouldst see
> A workman in't.
>
> (IV, iv, 12)

It could hardly be clearer that he goes to find himself: Cleopatra, too, knows in her heart, whatever the day's outcome, what the certain end for both of them will be.

> He goes forth gallantly: that he and Caesar might
> Determine this great war in single fight!
> Then Antony—; but now—Well, on.
>
> (IV, iv, 36)

What are nowadays called the opposed life-styles of Antony and Caesar are clearly contending here: Antony is supported by those followers who have remained faithful to him, including the old soldier whose advice he has previously disregarded; Caesar fights his battle by calculation, putting the deserters from Antony's army in the van, to dishearten his opponents; so confident of his success that he gives instructions for Antony to be taken alive, as he later wants Cleopatra taken, for his triumph. But Caesar is beaten, for his men have no stomach for the fight against the courage and generalship of the complete Antony, who is not now being pulled in different directions by love and honour. By the re-establishment of his honour, Antony feels himself again worthy to love and be loved. His victorious greeting to Cleopatra conveys fully his exhilaration in his triumph, but also the way in which love and death are drawing closer together, for all his victory.

> ANTONY   . . . O thou day o' the world,
>   Chain mine arm'd neck, leap thou, attire and all,
>   Through proof of harness to my heart, and there
>   Ride on the pants triumphing!
> CLEOPATRA   Lord of lords,
>   O infinite virtue, com'st thou smiling from
>   The world's great snare uncaught?
>
> (IV, viii, 13)

Cleopatra sees his return as an almost magical deliverance, wrought by love and courage, but even in the wonder and exhilaration there is the realisation that this is not a permanent victory. The strongly orgasmic tone of the imagery, perhaps carrying an implied pun on the sexual sense of 'dying', a repeated play on words that becomes more overt as the paths of love and death converge, provides an implicit recognition of what Cleopatra's words make explicit: the world, in which once they delighted, has become the 'great snare' that seeks to accomplish their destruction. Even the negative form, 'uncaught', strengthens the suggestion that this escape cannot be permanent, though it is embraced now as a fortunate chance. The autumnal ironies of this speech, with its moving suggestions of the fleetingness of life and time, perhaps also express something of the resentment of the old at being replaced by the young,

> . . . What girl! though grey
> Do something mingle with out younger brown, yet ha' we
> A brain that nourishes our nerves, and can
> Get goal for goal of youth . . .
>
> (IV, vii, 19)

and make it clear that in spite of the triumph which proves that Antony the man is no wreck, the sands are running out for the lovers, and they know it. The next day's battle sees not a personal defeat for Antony but the surrender of his fleet to Caesar, and thus the final ruin of any hope of escape.

It must be admitted that the play does not make clear whether or not this defection of the fleet means that Cleopatra has betrayed Antony's trust and love, though I feel that the strong supposition is that she has not. Cleopatra certainly is not stupid, and it seems most unlikely that she, of all people, would not have the wit to put a safe distance between herself and the man she has betrayed, since she has already experienced a taste of his despairing fury. After Antony's death, moreover, she is well aware that she can expect no favours from Caesar; had she such a trump card to play in her dealings with the victor, we cannot imagine that she would hesitate to play it. But for Antony, the final recognition that love has stripped him of everything that he was again brings him near to despair. For a man who habitually shows and expects loyalty, his own betrayal by others is something that he finds barely comprehensible. The parallel that Eugene Waith traces with the figure of Hercules is nowhere more convincing than here, as Antony, knowing that he has been betrayed, not vanquished, feels himself to be wearing the shirt of Nessus. Fearing again that Cleopatra has betrayed him, he gives way to despair (the great temptation for the Herculean figure, who finds his own strength powerless) and dismisses all his forces. Again, the stable centre of his life seems gone, and, tasting the bitterness of an imagined betrayal in love, he loses all judgement, looking, in a way reminiscent of Othello, only for revenge on Cleopatra:

> . . . Triple turn'd whore, 'tis thou
> Hast sold me to this novice, and my heart
> Makes only wars on thee. Bid them all fly:
> For when I am reveng'd upon my charm,
> I have done all. Bid them all fly, be gone . . .
>
> (IV, xii, 13)

and a little later

> The shirt of Nessus is upon me . . .
> . . . The witch shall die,
> To the young Roman boy she hath sold me, and I fall
> Under this plot: she dies for't.
>
> (IV, xii, 43)

It seems to me that it is because he once more doubts the reality of his love that his thoughts can turn again to what he has given up for it, his reputation, his power, yielding the victory to 'the young Roman boy' for whom he feels such contempt. If Antony were to die in this state, feeling himself betrayed, self-pitying, even self-dramatising to some extent, the effect of his death would be vastly other than what it actually is. But even in this, his nearest moment to despair, his lament for what has been lost shows (as do Othello's laments for what has been lost with Desdemona's falling off) the quality of the love that has meant so much to him.

> O sun, thy uprise shall I see no more,
> Fortune and Antony part here, even here
> Do we shake hands. All come to this? The hearts
> That spaniel'd me at heels, to whom I gave
> Their wishes, do discandy, melt their sweets
> On blossoming Caesar: and this pine is bark'd
> That overtopp'd them all. Betray'd I am.
> O this false soul of Egypt! this grave charm,
> Whose eye beck'd forth my wars, and call'd them home;
> Whose bosom was my crownet, my chief end,
> Like a right gipsy, hath at fast and loose
> Beguil'd me, to the very heart of loss.
> What, Eros, Eros!
>
> (IV, xii, 18)

This marvellously complex speech shows very clearly the folly of any simple interpretation of Antony's mood at this point, when everything seems lost, when nothing familiar around him holds its form. As he looks back at what has gone, he remains fundamentally true to the new vision his love has given him, for he cannot view the world of power with his old enthusiasm. The fawning courtiers, 'the hearts / That spaniel'd me at heels', whom he sees now as being worthy only of contempt, for the hearts which should have been the seats of loyalty and affection, the hearts to which he gave their wishes (not only in the sense of granting their suits, but more fundamentally in the sense of creating in them these wishes, giving their lives shape and form by his own) he sees as dissolving into the cloying flatteries they heap on the 'blossoming Caesar'. Caesar is the man of the time, before whose flowering even the rugged strength of the pine must give way, because it has outlived its time. Again we can feel the resentment of the older man at being pushed out by the younger, the solitary strength being pulled down by the many, but it is the sense of the betrayal of what is of far more worth to him than his lost power that floods his speech. If his love is not real, then all reality is lost, his life has been a mockery. Again, the similarity with Othello's feelings of despair is very striking. It is not so much that his 'grave charm' has led him to death; it is even more bitter for him to accept that the aim and purpose of his actions, his love for Cleopatra, has been based on a sham. His wars have been fought for her eyes, and, he might add, lost because of them; the victor's crown he has sought has been the lover's, his head between her breasts. If she is false, then he has been brought to 'the heart of loss' in the destruction of his own heart. His cry to Eros is not simply a call to his squire, but a cry of bewilderment to love itself, which has, as he thinks, brought him to the point of destruction of the world about him and of his sense of his own identity.

His exchange with Eros conveys his almost bemused sense of this meaningless drift towards his life's end:

ANTONY   . . . thou hast seen these signs
            They are black vesper's pageants.
EROS   Ay, my lord.
ANTONY   That which now is a horse, even with a thought
            The rack dislimns, and makes it indistinct
            As water is in water.
EROS   It does, my lord.
ANTONY   My good knave Eros, now thy captain is
            Even such a body: here I am Antony,
            Yet cannot hold this visible shape, my knave.
            I made these wars for Egypt, and the queen,
            Whose heart I thought I had, for she had mine:
            Which whilst it was mine, had annex'd unto't
            A million moe, now lost: she, Eros, has
            Pack'd cards with Caesar, and false-play'd my glory

> Unto an enemy's triumph.
> Nay, weep not, gentle Eros, there is left us
> Ourselves to end ourselves.
>
> (IV, xiv, 7)

There is the ominous image of the night closing in, and very interestingly, the suggestion of thought being the power that creates or destroys the world's coherence. His love has given life both pattern and meaning; with that gone, he can no longer believe in the reality of anything, not even of himself. In the image of the anonymity of water, curiously like that early image from *The Comedy of Errors*, the slipping away of his identity is acknowledged. If he were to kill himself now, that is all the act would signify, a final negation of the individuality he feels is already effectively gone with the loss of his belief in Cleopatra.

But as it is to Othello, and to the great Hercules whom Antony claims as ancestor, it is granted to Antony himself not to have to die in this state of despair. The tragic paradox is that it is the news of Cleopatra's death that allows the great value of his life to be reborn, phoenix-like, in its own destruction. If she has killed herself, then their love has been a true thing, but though its reality has been reestablished it has also been lost, for she is dead. He no longer has anything to live for, but at least he has a value to die for, even if the very fact that this is so poses the question, not for Antony, but for the audience, of the self-destructive nature of a love for which he must die. The impression of waste, which is part of the tragic impression, is strengthened by our awareness that the report of Cleopatra's death is a false one, but we are also aware that there is in any case no hope of escape for the lovers, for the world will not allow them to live. The report, which incidentally is the result of Cleopatra's taking Charmian's advice for the only time in the play, is false, but there is no sense that Antony dies needlessly. The paths of love and honour have come together again and lead straight to death, which is the price that the world exacts for having been rejected by the lovers, as it was the price it demanded of Romeo and Juliet. Just as the news of Juliet's death gave Romeo a purpose and a decision he could not find before, so Antony is saved from his despairing drift; he has no more doubt or hesitation about what he must do:

> ANTONY Dead, then?
> MARDIAN   Dead.
> ANTONY Unharm, Eros, the long day's task is done,
> And we must sleep. That thou depart'st hence safe,
> Does pay thy labour richly; go.
> Off, pluck off,

> The seven-fold shield of Ajax cannot keep
> The battery from my heart. O, cleave, my sides!
> Heart, once be stronger than thy continent,
> Crack thy frail case! Apace, Eros, apace!
> No more a soldier: bruised pieces, go;
> You have been nobly borne . . .
>
> (IV, xiv, 34)

The dignity of the man rings out in this courageous facing of the fate that has for so long been approaching. The god of love too, may now unarm, there is nothing further he can do, as, in a dramatic echoing of the play's opening speech, the heart, always too strong, must now accept its fate, and kill the body. It is the essential tragedy that the accomplishment of the perfect pattern of integrity of Antony's love is also its termination: all his life now has relevance and shape, but one side has already ended, and the other is now ending. Once again he can look back with pride on his soldiership, but he has no regret for its loss: it belongs to another world, one that contained the living Cleopatra. All the strength and courage he has used in action, implied by the 'bruised pieces' of armour, are to be put aside. Only by dying can he prove his love for Cleopatra, and make atonement for doubting her.

> I will o'er-take thee Cleopatra, and
> Weep for my pardon. So it must be, for now
> All length is torture: since the torch is out.
> Lie down and stray no further. Now all labour
> Mars what it does: yea, very force entangles
> Itself with strength: seal then, and all is done.
> Eros!— I come, my queen:—Eros!—Stay for me,
> Where souls do couch on flowers, we'll hand in hand.
> And with our sprightly port make the ghosts gaze:
> Dido and her Aeneas, shall want troops,
> And all the haunt be ours.
>
> (IV, xiv, 44)

From now until his death, all Antony's thoughts are for Cleopatra, who has been the light and warmth of his world, and after whose loss, only emptiness remains.

I find it difficult to decide whether Antony himself feels that by his death he goes to an actual reunion beyond the grave, though I rather doubt that he does. I am sure that the play intends these words as an affirmation of the absolute worth that love has held in his life, for the physical suffering of his suicide, and more particularly the dramatic ironies of Cleopatra's final scenes, hardly allow any consoling belief in love's continuance after death. Here the admiring ghosts, like the world that earlier had been commanded to acknowledge the unique supremacy of the lovers, are a measure of Antony's own feeling, and an image for the purpose of the action to which his love and his sense of honour now urge him

> Since Cleopatra died,
> I have liv'd in such dishonour that the gods
> Detest my baseness . . .
>
> (IV, xiv, 55)

and

>   . . . I will be
> A bridegroom in my death, and run into't
> As to a lover's bed.
>
> (IV, xiv 99)

As the spectacle of Eros' death has just made us aware, what he has to do is something very different from running to 'a lover's bed'.

It has been urged by some critics that the circumstances of Antony's suicide, first of his needing to be taught by Eros' example what he should do, and even then failing to carry it out satisfactorily, cast a satiric light on his protestations of love and honour; that there is an element of the grotesquely comic, and therefore of the anti-romantic, in his failure to kill himself cleanly. I disagree with this reading absolutely; it is surely only an age grown accustomed to the projection of real and imaginary horrors into its living rooms in the name of entertainment that can adopt a position of superiority while watching the agonies of a man wounded to death, but not yet dead. Not in the immediate sense of his words and certainly not in the reactions of others—his guard are so awed by what they see that they behave as if they were watching the death of a god—do I find any suggestion that we are invited to distance ourselves from his suffering, much less be amused by it. On the contrary, nothing in the play is more eloquent of the strength of his love than his refusal to waste even one word of reproach on the pretence that causes his death agony, or in railling against the chance that is destroying him. His reception of the news that Cleopatra is alive is, in its simplicity, one of the play's great moments;

> DIOMEDES   . . . for when she saw—
> Which never shall be found—you did suspect
> She had dispos'd with Caesar, and that your rage
> Would not be purg'd she sent you word she was dead;
> But fearing since how it might work, hath sent
> Me to proclaim the truth, and I am come
> I dread, too late.
> ANTONY   Too late, good Diomed: call my guard, I prithee

> . . . Bear me, good friends, where Cleopatra bides,
> 'Tis the last service that I shall command you.
>
> (IV, xiv, 121)

He asks only to be brought to where she is, and his last words are expended in care for her. This death scene, with its steady shift of attention away from the dying Antony to the mourning Cleopatra, is unlike anything else that Shakespeare had written in the tragedies up to this point, and its very difference has perhaps deceived some critics into a search for a satiric intention, which they identify in a Cleopatra so self-centred that she will not risk her safety by opening the doors of her monument, rather subjecting Antony to the pain of being hauled up, and when she gets him to her side, talking so much herself that she hardly allows him his dying words. The scene can be forced to bear this interpretation, could indeed be played this way, but only, I think, by ignoring and distorting the effect of the poetry. It is a complex scene, and we must resist any inclination to simplify it by attempting to make it simply satiric or simply triumphant, or even simply tragic. Neither Antony nor Cleopatra has seriously expected anything but death from the time the first battle was lost, so in a sense, what happens now is only expected, but Cleopatra, as did Antony when he heard the news of her supposed death, realises when she sees her dying lord just how empty and meaningless a world without him will be.

> O sun
> Burn the great sphere thou mov'st in, darkling stand
> The varying shore o' the world. O Antony
> Antony, Antony!
>
> (IV, xv, 10)

Yet at this moment of tragedy she is not magically ennobled: she remains very recognisably the woman she has always been; she is afraid she will be taken prisoner, she can spare a thought in her grief to resent her rival Octavia's triumph, but it ought to be noticed that from the moment she realises that Antony is dying, all her anxiety is to preserve her freedom to die as well. Even at this moment of death, it is very noticeable that the lovers are not crushed by it; they remain creatures of life, reliving together for the last time their joy in each other. Now that their doom has come, there is a note of something not unlike gaiety in the way they accept it.

> CLEOPATRA   Here's sport indeed! How heavy weighs my lord!
> Our strength is all gone into heaviness,

> That makes the weight. Had I great Juno's power
> The strong-wing'd Mercury should fetch thee up,
> And set thee by Jove's side. Yet come a little,
> Wishers were ever fools, O come, come, come.
> And welcome, welcome! Die when thou hast liv'd,
> Quicken with kissing, had my lips that power,
> Thus would I wear them out.
>
> (IV, xv, 32)

The life-enhancing value of their love is very clearly stated, in poetry of great tenderness, which is also poetry that is quite clear-eyed. Cleopatra knows, as Antony does, that of many kisses, this is the 'poor last', that whatever her love and her need for him, she cannot keep him alive. Antony's last words are not a protestation of his love for her, for there is no need for that, but advice, concern for her safety: he wants her to live on, and dies proving that he cares more about her than about himself or anything else in the world. That Cleopatra should brush aside these concerns is testimony of the strength of her love for him; together in these last moments in which they can be together, they recognise that they care wholly for each other, and need express no regret for the lives they have lived. By their concern for each other, they testify that even though they now have been brought to death, they have lived the best of their lives in loving each other.

We should notice that Cleopatra's feeling for Antony does not alter after his death: she has always seen in him something of more than life-size—'this Herculean Roman'—has always seen his manhood as a standard of excellence by which all else is judged. It is this loss of a supreme quality from the world that she feels most keenly, and that her first speeches after his death reveal:

> Noblest of man, woo't die?
> Hast thou no care for me, shall I abide
> In this dull world, which in thy absence is
> No better than a sty? O, see, my women:
> The crown o' the earth doth melt. My lord?
> O withered is the garland of the war,
> The soldier's pole is fall'n: young boys and girls
> Are level now with men: the odds is gone,
> And there is nothing left remarkable
> Beneath the visiting moon.
>
> (IV, xv, 59)

What she feels as the lack of distinction left in the world is most movingly conveyed in this speech, which sees his fall not as her own loss only, but as all the world's. To the soldier he has been like the pole star, by which a course can be charted, an image that suggests both the brightness of his glory and the seeming impossibility of his fall. She has already felt the extinction of her life's sun; the earth without Antony is a dull place, in which it is pointless to argue about rank or precedence among those left, a landscape with all ardour and warmth drained away, fitfully illuminated by the dim and varying light of the 'visiting moon', a phrase which suggests the now meaningless passage of time, bringing variation but no significant event. This feeling of the total meaninglessness of time is taken up in her next speech. 'All's but naught / Patience is sottish, and impatience does / Become a dog that's mad.' Without Antony, there is little to distinguish life from death, tardiness or haste seem equally irrelevant concepts to her. From the moment she has seen his death upon him, her decision has been reached; all that remains is to put it into effect.

> Look,
> Our lamp is spent, it's out. Good sirs, take heart,
> We'll bury him, and then, what's brave, what's noble,
> Let's do it after the high Roman fashion,
> And make death proud to take us. Come, away,
> This case of that huge spirit now is cold.
> Ah women, women! come, we have no friend
> But resolution, and the briefest end.
>
>   IV, xv, 84)

Cleopatra has the whole of the fifth act to herself after Antony's death, but this fact ought not to send us off searching for some Hamlet-inspired reason for her delay. I have no doubt at all that what Shakespeare intends us to see in this last act is Cleopatra's victory, over herself perhaps, but chiefly over the forces that try to prevent her death. She has to struggle to be allowed to die, to prove, in her turn, her fidelity to that ideal of love for which Antony has already given his life. I suggested earlier that the true antagonists in the play are Caesar and Cleopatra: they clash directly here, and the motives of each are very revealing of their respective functions throughout the play.

Octavius has now got what he wants, all except the certainty of Cleopatra's preservation to grace his triumph in Rome, and his plot for the arrangement of this takes precedence over his final comments on his great rival. She must be tricked into thinking that he is her friend, so that she can be paraded through Roman streets. The rigidity of his will is, I think, nowhere more obvious than in his insistence on this apparently trivial final victory: he perjures himself and at the last reveals himself as not only heartless, but stupid in his own self-esteem, for while he thinks he is deceiving Cleopatra, he is himself being deceived.

There are some who read Cleopatra's actions in this last act as a last attempt, Antony being dead, to trick her way out of her predicament, and see her final surrender to death as being made only when no other course remains open to her, but it seems to me very difficult to sustain such a reading from the dramatic course of events. Cleopatra in her message to Caesar may seem to be temporising, but she asks for nothing for herself, and just before Proculeius has entered, she has been musing that

> ... it is great
> To do that thing that ends all other deeds
> Which shackles accidents, and bolts up change ...
>
> (V, ii, 4)

Before she can act, Proculeius, the man whose honesty Antony relied upon, betrays her; she is taken prisoner, and prevented from stabbing herself. The fierceness of her anger, the emphasis of her determination do not sound much like a pretence:

> Sir, I will eat no meat, I'll not drink sir,—
> If idle talk will once be necessary,—
> I'll not sleep either. This mortal house I'll ruin,
> Do Caesar what he can. Know sir, that I
> Will not wait pinion'd at your master's court,
> Nor once be chastis'd with the sober eye
> Of dull Octavia. Shall they hoist me up
> And show me to the shouting varletry
> Of censuring Rome? Rather a ditch in Egypt
> Be gentle grave into me, rather on Nilus' mud
> Lay me stark nak'd, and let the waterflies
> Blow me into abhorring ...
>
> (V, ii, 49)

This is a speech of some power, particularly in that one so concerned with her own appearance as Cleopatra is can face with resolution the prospect of a death that avoids none of the horror of physical corruption. I see no reason to suppose that her reluctance to be led before Octavia, or be shown a captive in Rome, either diminishes the fervour of her resolve or indicates a greater concern with herself than with her love for Antony. Both have been royal: the formality of 'I am dying Egypt, dying' has reminded us of that very recently, and at least part of her concern, as her later discussion with Charmian shows, is that she does not want to appear unworthy of his nobility, or see their love degraded and mocked

> The quick comedians
> Extemporally will stage us, and present

> Our Alexandrian revels: Antony
> Shall be brought drunken forth, and I shall see
> Some squeaking Cleopatra boy my greatness
> I' the posture of a whore.
>
> (V, ii, 215)

Once she is Caesar's captive, and we should remember that he fears
and seeks to prevent exactly what she plans to do, it is not easy for her
to attain to death, and yet it is towards this finality that she must strive,
because only by dying can she prove the worth of her life, and paradoxically, prove for herself and us the vitality of her world, as opposed to
the essential deadness of Caesar's.

What she is dying for emerges most clearly in the scene with
Dolabella, when she confides to him her vision of her Antony. This is
an absolutely crucial scene for the understanding of this last act, and
for the play as a whole, for as Robert Ornstein remarks, 'Nothing less is
at stake in the final scene than the honesty of the imagination and the
superiority of its truths to the facts of imperial conquest'.[21] Shakespeare
presents the clash very openly: can Antony have been to her what her
reverie makes him seem, or is this only a lover's fantasy, beautiful,
touching, but ultimately delusive? Dolabella is a sympathetic hearer;
he addresses her as Empress, thus acknowledging her as Antony's
widow as well as Egypt's queen, but even he, already under the spell of
her charm, feels that he must gently bring her back to reality.

CLEOPATRA   I dreamt there was an Emperor Antony.
            O such another sleep, that I might see
            But such another man!
DOLABELLA   If it might please ye,—
CLEOPATRA   His face was as the heavens, and therein stuck
            A sun and moon, which kept their course, and lighted
            This little O, the earth.
DOLABELLA   Most sovereign creature,—
CLEOPATRA   His legs bestrid the ocean, his rear'd arm
            Crested the world: his voice was propertied
            As all the tuned spheres, and that to friends:
            But when he meant to quail, and shake the orb,
            He was as rattling thunder. For his bounty
            There was no winter in't: an autumn 'twas
            That grew the more by reaping: his delights
            Were dolphin-like, they show'd his back above
            The element they lived in: in his livery
            Walk'd crowns and crownets: realms and islands were
            As plates dropp'd from his pocket.
DOLABELLA   Cleopatra!
CLEOPATRA   Think you there was, or might be such a man
            As this I dreamt of?

DOLABELLA   Gentle madam, no.

                                        (V, ii, 76)

The Colossus-like figure of Antony that her dream recreates is one that Dolabella, for all his sympathy, cannot recognise. He tries to interrupt her, is brushed aside, and when finally he is directly asked to affirm the validity of her heart's truth, he can only answer 'Gentle madam, no', thinking that her mind is wandering. He cannot see that this is her ultimate statement of what her love has meant, her vision of Antony as a man who is both master and in a sense creator of the world, and its finest achievement. Without him, the world, 'this little O' is nothing indeed. In images of god-like size and control, and of the careless generosity of his nature, that made realms and islands coins to be spent, enjoyed, given away, lost, she pays tribute to a greatness that sees the world as an environment to be lived in, used, enjoyed, but not possessed.

Dolabella tries to tell her that no such man could ever exist, but she indignantly denies it, 'You lie, up to the hearing of the Gods', and she is right, for what she speaks of is the value he has had for her, the value that her love for him, and his for her, has lent him, which nobody but she can estimate. We do the play grave injury, I think, if we do not recognise here that this *is* Cleopatra's Antony, that her tribute to him is freed, by his death, of any suspicion of flattery or seeking for effect, and that for her this is the true Antony. Nobody else in the play can see him with her eyes, yet the elements from which her vision has been composed are all recognisably there in the play, and it is clear that this is what he has become for her. As she herself says, this is too heroic a figure for mere fancy; there is nothing that happens in the play to disprove her vision, the truth of which she is prepared to vouch for by her own death.

It is clear that Cleopatra does not really need Dolabella's confirmation of what she has already suspected of Caesar's intentions; her mind is made up, and she has already made the arrangements that will bring her the means to die. Now she must disarm Caesar's suspicions, and I take it that this is her purpose in what follows, rather than any last attempt to save herself or to escape. The stratagem with Seleucus may have been rehearsed, or it may be intended to deceive him as well as Caesar, but whichever is the case, there is no denying the thinly-veiled contempt with which she acknowledges Caesar's conquest of the world that she no longer considers worth living in. 'I'll take my leave' says Caesar, having just threatened to kill her children if she kills herself, and Cleopatra replies:

> And may through all the world: 'tis yours, and we
> Your scutcheons, and your signs of conquest shall
> Hang in what place you please.
>
> (V, ii, 133)

Caesar is delighted by the discovery of her trick (we should notice in passing the wild improbability of Cleopatra's seeking Octavia's intercession on her behalf) and, convinced that she is going to be, in his terms, 'reasonable', allows a little relaxation in his attitude, which communicates itself to the guards, and makes them just that little less vigilant. The confident insensitivity of his final injunction to her to 'Feed and sleep' as if she were a beast being fattened for the market, is a measure of the extent he is deceived into thinking that Cleopatra is of his kind; he can believe it the more easily because if she were, there would be no threat implied to the values by which he himself lives; the love of Antony and Cleopatra could then be dismissed as easily as he tries to dismiss it.

Cleopatra, though, is not only not deceived, she is insulted that he should think her foolish enough, or knavish enough, to be taken in by so obvious a trick and by flattery so gross. Charmian and Iras, who know and love their mistress, appear to have no doubt at all about what she should do, or what she will do. They know that for all of them life is approaching its end:

CLEOPATRA He words me girls, he words me, that I should not
           Be noble to myself. But hark thee Charmian.

                                (Whispers to Charmian)

   IRAS Finish good lady, the bright day is done
           And we are for the dark.

CLEOPATRA   Hie thee again.
           I have spoke already, and it is provided,
           Go put it to the haste.

> (V, ii, 190)

Here the simple contrast between the bright day of life and love (Antony has greeted her as 'thou day of the world') and the dark finality of the tomb falls with chilling effect. Cleopatra knows that the actual choice that faces her is whether to die now in a way of her own choosing, or to endure a mockery that will contaminate and degrade all that has gone before and end in a dishonoured death, but her insistence that she dies for Antony shows that death is more for her than simply an escape from a worldly defeat. As with Antony, death becomes the ultimate way of stating the importance of the love by which she has lived. Iras and Charmian, whose tragedy mirrors that of their mistress, as those of Enobarbus and Eros do that of their master, do not attempt to dissuade her. Again like Antony at the end, Cleopatra, for all the complexity of her life, sees that loyalty to her love demands a very simple integrity. She will die for Antony, though this does not mean that she cannot also feel glad that she will not be subjected to the humiliation of Caesar's triumph, or prevent her from feeling some wry satisfaction at this last outwitting of her enemy. Antony and Cleopatra remain human to the end: the mixture of feelings with which they die enhances their heroic stature by making them credible. There are still traces of vanity and self-deception, but these do not in any way diminish their awareness, or ours, that they die for each other, and that they prove their love by their deaths.

Cleopatra puts on her crown and robes, to play her last part, that of a dying queen, and if she partially deceives herself about what she is doing, at the last, who is to blame her? She does what has to be done, as bravely as she can, with a control and dignity remarkable for who one has feared death, and sought easy ways of dying. There is no chance that the play will allow us to share her delusion, if indeed she is deluded, for besides our memory of her own awareness of death's finality, when she declared her willingness to let the flies of Nile 'blow her into abhorring' there is the scene with the clown who brings the asps to remind us and her that, if death is a sort of victory, it is also a certain defeat. If, at the moment that she must end her life, she remembers her hour of triumph and is again for Cydnus, there is at least half a realisation that she goes, not to be reunited with Antony beyond the grave, but to join him in oblivion. 'Bring our crown and all', she says, which with its childlike tone of one who dresses up to pretend, does not obscure her very real sense of what she has to do, which is something that takes all her courage. She is reminded, as Posthumus is reminded when he declares himself ready to welcome death to prove his love, of the full implications of what death means, so that we cannot say that he or she is unaware of the way most men see death. The resolution in the face of this awareness makes the courage the greater.

CLEOPATRA Has thou the pretty worm of Nilus there,
That kills and pains not?

CLOWN Truly I have him: but I would not be the party that should desire you to touch him, for his biting is immortal: those that do die of it, do seldom or never recover . . .

(V, ii, 242)

and later

CLOWN You must think this, look you, that the worm will do his kind.

CLEOPATRA Ay, ay, farewell.

CLOWN   Look you, the worm is not to be trusted but in the keeping of wise
        people: for indeed, there is no goodness in the worm . . .

                                                              (V, ii, 233)

and finally, ' . . . I wish you joy o' the worm.'

The play does not allow the pathos and the triumph of Cleopatra's
death to obscure our awareness that in one sense all this great love, this
suffering, this nobility and courage end in nothing. The physical horror
of death, the grim reminder of that grave worm that waits, the irony of
that 'immortal', the warning that 'those that do die of it do seldom or
never recover' all serve to remind us, and Cleopatra too, that though
she may have chosen a way of death that is easy, one that will not
disfigure her beauty, the fact of death remains, and it means the end of
the life in which love is rooted. There is indeed 'no goodness in the
worm' and for Antony and Cleopatra to pretend that there is is self-
delusion. Yet they have no other choice, and perhaps as 'wise people'
they have the right to choose death in preference to a life that has lost
all purpose. It is natural enough that Cleopatra should long for an
eternity to spend with Antony, but a very different thing to insist that
she is to be granted it, and the play, I fancy, makes no such promise.

Iras dies of a broken heart, taking leave of her mistress: Charmian
fulfils the soothsayer's prophesy by living long enough to perfect the
tableau that is to confront great Caesar and call him 'Ass, unpolicied'.
Cleopatra's search for ease in dying is rewarded, though it is impossible
to miss the irony of the image she uses to describe it. It is easy to die,
and death may be desired, but it is not like the 'lover's pinch, that hurts
and is desired', for it is the prelude not to the act that creates life, but to
nothing. Cleopatra dies bravely, touchingly, half aware of the irony of
her claim to call Antony 'husband' only in death, as her apostrophe to
the asp perhaps shows:

                Come, thou mortal wretch,
                With thy sharp teeth this knot intrinsicate
                Of life at once untie: poor venomous fool,
                Be angry and dispatch.
                                                              (V, ii, 302)

The asp's untying of life's intricate knot is no real solution, as the
underlying image of Alexander's cutting of the Gordian knot perhaps
hints, however much she may desire it as an ending to her suffering.
What she has at her breast, 'that sucks the nurse asleep' is not new life,
but death, even if it is death for Antony's sake. Charmian, left to
pronounce her epitaph and then to die herself, does not see her royal
mistress as reunited with her love, but as gone, like Juliet, into death's
dominion:

Now boast thee, death, in thy possession lies
A lass unparallel'd . . .

(V, ii, 314)

where the description of her, unexpected in the tragic dignity of the
setting, as 'A lass unparallel'd' looks back to the way that Cleopatra
has lived, rather than forward to anything to come. It is the image of
death and the beautiful woman, again carrying, as it did in *Romeo and
Juliet* the same note of finality, of waste, as the imagination is asked to
contemplate the extinction of a being who, in her capacity for love, was
so brilliantly alive. Caesar's entrance makes the point that he has been
defeated, but not so strongly that we can forget that the victory has only
been won, can only have been won, at the cost of the victors' lives. Love
may have triumphed, but it is at the cost of its own destruction, for it
cannot exist without the lovers.

I hope that I have been able to indicate sufficiently clearly why I
cannot see this as an anti-romantic play, which denies any real value to
the lovers' passion. I cannot see it as a simple romance either, which
sees the world well lost for love, for the love that has been shown can
only exist in the world. Antony and Cleopatra are defeated and
destroyed by death, the more quickly because they care about one
another so intensely. Is the answer to life's problems then, not to care?
Surely not, for on the evidence of this play, Caesar, the man who cares
for nothing outside his own success, is discredited in spite of that success, and Enobarbus, who thought that he, too, was self-sufficient,
found that he cared enough to die because he had betrayed his master.

Not merely the co-existence of love and death, but what can almost
be called their mutual interdependence, is something that this play,
more so even than *Romeo and Juliet*, sees as completely natural. Egypt,
and especially Egypt's queen, have seemed the embodiment of change
and variety; the emphasis on the sensual, on lushness, on the flow and
fall of the Nile that produce the land's fertility, on the frivolity that has
sought to beguile the passage of time, and the acknowledgement that
man and woman can grow old, all these factors show how closely this
way of life fits into that pattern of temporal change of which death is
also an element. It is a way of life that is totally opposed to the
inflexibility, the coldness and the concern with inanimate things, possessions and abstract notions of power, of 'eternal Rome'. Both Antony
and Cleopatra, in their equation of love and death in their dying
scenes—the serious pun again—see nothing incongruous in the concept
of dying for love. Dying is as much a part of being alive as loving, a
price they are prepared to pay for the privilege of having loved while
they have lived, even though the fact of their love makes the price so

much greater. This play, in a way that neither *Romeo and Juliet* nor *Othello*, with their visions of only a brief happiness snatched from a hostile world can do, concentrates on the worth of a love that is allowed both intensity and scope. Its tragic end is the tragedy of all close human relationships, for no matter how strong the love, or what obstacles it has overcome or over what suffering it has triumphed, it cannot survive death. But to love at all, this play seems to say, it is necessary to be fully alive, and since all are doomed to die, it is better to love and die than to be like Caesar, who will die without having lived.

THE ROMANCES

CONSIDERING SHAKESPEARE'S PREOCCUPATION with the subject of the love relationship, it is no surprise that he returns to it in the Romances, the last plays that he wrote. In *Pericles* and *The Tempest* other concerns are obviously more central, but even there the loves between father and daughter or, in *The Tempest*, between the young lovers, Ferdinand and Miranda, provide the regenerative force that helps to bring about the happy endings. In *Cymbeline* and *The Winter's Tale*, both of which in some ways echo *Othello*, sexual love is of much greater importance, and it is with them that this chapter will chiefly be concerned. One has the sense that Shakespeare is taking up and re-examining, from rather different angles, themes and situations that have already concerned him in the love tragedies. Thus both Posthumus and Leontes, in their jealousy, are somewhat like Othello. Their culpability may indeed be greater, but unlike him, they are allowed a second chance for happiness. Circumstances are different, for the magical preservation of Imogen and Hermione that the fairy-tale structure of the Romances allows affords these jealous men the chance to learn from their mistakes. Reunited with their wives, they look forward to a kind of future that was denied to the tragic heroes.

There are perhaps even affinities between *Romeo and Juliet* and *The Tempest*, with the marriage of Ferdinand and Miranda symbolising the kind of reconciliation between Prospero and Alonso, between the warring houses of Milan and Naples, that Romeo and Juliet could only accomplish in their society by their deaths. A similar pattern is discernible in the Perdita–Florizel relationship in *The Winter's Tale,* though there the interest in the young lovers themselves far transcends their function as the reconcilers of Leontes and Polixenes.

In the Romances the potentially tragic consequences of love gone sour, or of seemingly adverse fate, are averted by the fortunate chance that the form allows, but despite this, there is no mitigation of the sense of the suffering that love can exact, nor is there any simple confidence in an arrival at a happy ending simply because of love's good offices. *Pericles, Cymbeline* and *The Winter's Tale* share with the three love tragedies the aim of establishing a value for love which can be maintained in spite of the clearest recognition of the danger of placing one's trust in another person, of the suffering that love may exact, and of the desolation that will follow its loss. It is a value that can only exist within time, for its limits are defined by man's mortality, and man's mortality is something that even the reconciliation and happiness of the endings of the Romances do not allow us to forget. But since, as my commentary on the tragedies has attempted to show, love's happiness depends more on a quality of living than on its duration, it is also to some extent superior to time, for not only can this quality triumph in spite of time, there can even be the suggestion, which many of the Sonnets as well as the love tragedies bear out, that the value may in part depend on an awareness of its transience. The knowledge of impending loss makes the love more precious; the awareness of the joy that has been experienced makes the world more desolate when that joy has been lost.

Something of this sense of desolation is experienced by Pericles, in the play of that name, when he believes he has lost the two people about whom he cares most, his wife Thaisa, and his daughter Marina. But there is little sense that Pericles is being punished for any kind of guilt or inadequacy in his feelings towards them. When, during a storm at sea, his wife dies (or so it seems) in childbirth, and when later those to whom he has done nothing but good turn against him, and plot to have his daughter murdered, it seems sheer bad luck that this should have happened, rather than the outcome of any necessary chain of events. It may possibly be suggested that Pericles' excessive apprehension of his danger from Antiochus, which causes him to leave his home and wander aimlessly around the world, is a cause of his tribulations, but if this is so, the idea is not much developed in the play. It seems more likely that he is presented as an individual subjected to the haphazard buffetings of chance; in any case, it is his reaction to the disasters he suffers that catches Shakespeare's attention in his reworking of the material of this play.[1] Pericles' response to his ill fortune is to retreat into a trance-like state, neither living nor dead, from which he is recalled by the discovery that his daughter is still alive. She, in true fairy-tale fashion, has been preserved by her purity and unselfish love through the successive hazards of a murderous plot, abduction by pirates, and sale to a brothel. Restored to life by his daughter's love,

Pericles is then reunited with Thaisa, who has also miraculously survived. Perhaps the point is being made that it is impossible truly to live without commitment to others, but apart from this general comment, together with the paradoxical reminder of how dangerous it is to centre one's reason for existence in another vulnerable human being, there is little either in theme or situation that relates directly to the love tragedies. What is most moving is the sense of wonder that Pericles feels in his re-awakening to life, but beyond that, one feels that he is lucky to have had his happiness restored to him as arbitrarily as it was taken away. There is little serious exploration of what I have postulated as the great question posed by the love tragedies, of what value can inhere in love in a life where everything that is valued passes away.

A similar sort of question is one of the central concerns of *The Tempest*, but there the answers are sought, in the main, in areas of human experience other than those comprehended by the love relationship.[2] The lovers, Ferdinand and Miranda, have their place, but much more important is the dramatisation of Prospero's consciousness, which looks for its answers in the operation of pure reason. He, for all his encouragement of the match between his daughter and the heir to the throne of Naples, appears to distrust a human emotion that must be founded in the physical elements of man's being. The lovers' feelings for each other, which clearly comprehend the physical, afford a useful balance in the play, for they are set against Prospero's too cerebral approach to life, but their attachment is neither tested severely enough, nor explored deeply enough to displace Prospero from the play's centre of interest.

Miranda's warmth of feeling, her innocence and her inexperience, amounting almost to naivete, are contrasted with Prospero's severity and somewhat weary wisdom. He knows only too well the malice and corruption that exist in the world she hails so excitedly as attractive and wonderful, but her freshness of response is nevertheless a quality that the play endorses, though with some reservations. It is this freshness, rather than Prospero's magic, that makes her fall in love with Ferdinand, and he with her, as soon as they see one another; before, indeed, each knows whether the other is mortal or not. This mutual attraction ripens, in spite of or because of Prospero's feigned opposition, to a love that provides the play's best hope, perhaps its only hope, for a happy future.

One cannot say that Prospero is indifferent to the success of the match, for he expresses his satisfaction several times during the course of the play, and he takes care to test the sincerity of Ferdinand's love by imposing on him such menial tasks as will be naturally repugnant to a young nobleman. But despite his obvious concern for his daughter's happiness, he remains somehow outside the world of mutual trust and joy that the lovers inhabit. There is, after all, a political motive for the match, too, and there is more than a trace of cynicism in some of his comments on Miranda's behaviour. 'Poor worm, thou art infected!' is his aside, when she reveals that she is in love with Ferdinand, and one recognises the same tone of half-mocking, patronising affection in his response to her famous exclamation at the sight of so many fine courtiers before the cell:

> . . . O brave new world
> That has such people in't!
>
> (V, i, 183)

' 'Tis new to thee' he replies, and while one can acknowledge the correctness of the experience that recognises the unregenerate malice of Antonio and Sebastian, and the petty knavery of Stephano and Trinculo, there is nevertheless the feeling that this experience has robbed him of almost all sense of life's enjoyment. He does not seem to care enough about anything to experience joy; the justice which he has achieved is a quality more coldly abstract, and when he is to return to Milan, dukedom restored and daughter married to the son of his old enemy, there is little to which he can look forward. 'Every third thought shall be my grave' is how he sums it up, and this enigmatic utterance seems to fit one who has grown past feeling much for anything.

It is to balance this strain of disillusionment and world-weariness, and to prevent Prospero's 'wisdom' from being thought of as Shakespeare's, that the love of Ferdinand and Miranda exists in the play. Since this is its main dramatic function, it does not need to be subjected to any greater test than will ensure that Ferdinand, the youthful courtier, is worthy of the unspoilt Miranda. The young lovers face no real opposition from within or without; suffering is not really demanded of them. Miranda discovers, without too much distress, that her love for Ferdinand makes her forget her duty of obedience to her father, while Ferdinand finds in the demeaning task of piling logs at Prospero's command that true freedom lies in the service of the woman he loves. In spite of the presence on the island of the unrestrained physicality of Caliban and the unredeemed wickedness of Sebastian and Antonio, any real test of the love of Ferdinand and Miranda lies in the future, and beyond the confines of the play. For the purpose that they serve in the whole dramatic design, it is enough that they are young, attractive and optimistic, that through them new life is to be carried on, and the

opposing houses of Milan and Naples united. The play is more concerned with what Prospero feels than with what they feel.

The two remaining plays of the group, *Cymbeline* and *The Winter's Tale*,
clearly have much closer affinities with the love tragedies, and with the
whole of Shakespeare's continuing examination of the scope and quality of love that I have attempted to trace in this book. For if Posthumus
and Leontes share something of the challenges and sufferings of Othello
and Antony, the heroines, Imogen, Hermione and Perdita seem to have
an all-round awareness and self-possession that relates them to the
heroines of the comedies, just as their situations relate them to the
tragedies. Many of the issues explored before are taken up again, seen
this time in a context in which the learning process that the central
figures undergo is not tragically terminated by death, but where a
second chance for life and happiness is *magically* granted, almost as a
reward for having learned successfully. I stress *magically*, for there is no
suggestion whatsoever that the reward is the necessary consequence of
the learning. These couples have the good fortune to be allowed to put
their knowledge of themselves and each other to further use, and that is
all. This is to say no more than that Shakespeare chose to make these
plays romances or tragi-comedies, rather than tragedies. By doing so,
he gave himself room to explore human responses beyond the point at
which the tragedies stop.[3] In both *Cymbeline* and *The Winter's Tale* the
problem of how to come to terms with an existence from which value
seems to have been extinguished is examined. It is only after this
problem has been faced—not solved, for there is no solution—that the
lovers are reunited.

Posthumus Leonatus, the hero of *Cymbeline*, is somewhat like Othello
in that he is an outsider in the society in which he lives. An orphan,
who for his father's sake has been brought up as a ward of the British
court, he has married Imogen, the King's daughter, so incurring the
enmity of her stepmother, the Queen, who had wanted Imogen to
marry her own son, the boorish Cloten. This fairy-tale structure of
worthy commoner, beautiful princess, and wicked stepmother, which is
the initial situation of the play, helps to prepare one for the improbability of some of the following action, but is less important for the purpose
of this analysis than is the detail of the relationship between Posthumus
and Imogen, which provides an indication of why Posthumus proves
vulnerable to the plottings of the Iago-like Iachimo.

From the first scene, there are indications that Posthumus' worth as
a man and a husband is still to be tried and established. He is worthy,
no doubt, but as the opening conversations between the courtiers make

clear, what distinguishes him most is the fact that Imogen has chosen him as her husband. This measure of his value by hers perhaps causes him a slight uneasiness. Certainly in the scene in which they exchange gifts before parting—for Posthumus has been banished at the insistence of the evil Queen—there is some indication that while Imogen sees her whole happiness in their mutual love, he sees her as a most prized possession, and a possession which may be put in jeopardy by his enforced absence. Posthumus is certainly not conscious that his trust in her may not be as absolute as her trust in him, but when both are put under stress during their separation, her faith proves the stronger.

Like Othello, Posthumus is subjected to the malice of an outsider, who, without even Iago's motive, sets out to destroy the happiness of the marriage for no better reason than that of casual mischief-making. As his name indicates, Iachimo is a version of Iago (though less fully realised) with whom he shares an absolute belief in his own superiority, and the sort of rationality that sees all human affection as mere weakness. Again like Iago, the weapon he uses to undermine Posthumus' trust in Imogen is an assumed air of worldy wisdom, of a sort of 'reasonableness' which, if accepted, will not allow a unique value to any human relationship. When he meets Posthumus in ancient Rome—an odd place to find someone as much a Renaissance Machiavel as Iachimo is—he sets about provoking him, perhaps for no better reason than to pass the time. Posthumus and a young Frenchman have been quarrelling about the merits of their respective ladies; into that quarrel Iachimo inserts his languid provocation

> That lady is not now living, or this gentleman's
> opinion by this worn out.
>
> (I, v, 65)

which has the desired effect of making Posthumus react angrily:

POSTHUMUS   Being so far provoked as I was in France, I would abate her nothing, though I profess myself her adorer, not her friend.

IACHIMO   As fair and as good—a kind of hand-in hand comparison—had been something too fair and too good for any lady in Britain. If she went before others I have seen, as that diamond of yours outlustres many I have beheld I could not but believe she excelled many; but I have not seen the most precious diamond that is, nor you the lady.

> (I, v, 69)

What he says is perfectly reasonable, of course, but it is an attack on love that cannot be met by an equally reasonable defence. Posthumus' mistake is that he tries, and in so doing he tacitly accepts Iachimo's

proposition that Imogen's diamond and Imogen's virtue are equally his
possessions, to be seen as ornaments or proofs of his own worth. His
own pride being now involved, perhaps the more readily because of his
insecurity in his banishment, he is trapped into a wager, the terms of
which are plainly insulting to Imogen. Before he really knows what is
happening, he has wagered his ring against ten thousand ducats, that
Iachimo will not succeed in seducing Imogen.

> IACHIMO   . . . If I bring you no sufficient testimony that I have
> enjoyed the dearest bodily part of your mistress, my ten
> thousand ducats are yours; so is your diamond too: if I
> come off, and leave her in such honour as you have trust
> in, she is your jewel, this your jewel, and my gold are
> yours; provided I have your commendation for more free
> entertainment.
> POSTHUMUS I embrace these conditions.
>   (I, iv, 153)

The irony of that 'embrace' points up how far Posthumus has moved
from any consideration of Imogen as a person. To prove his own 'honour' he is prepared to deceive his wife; by even giving consideration to
Iachimo's proposition he has effectively betrayed her trust. It is therefore no surprise that when Iachimo returns with his lying boasts of
conquest, Posthumus seems only too ready to believe him.

The whole episode is in fact a cruder and more perfunctory treatment of what some critics see as the essential quality of Iago's temptation of Othello. It is Posthumus' pride that makes him vulnerable; he,
unlike Othello, genuinely does care more about his reputation, at least
for the moment, than he does for his wife, but the comparison should
not carry too much condemnatory weight against Posthumus. Shakespeare is much less interested in the reasons for Posthumus' lack of faith
than he is in its consequences, and what was dealt with at length in
Othello is compressed into two brief scenes in *Cymbeline*. In *The Winter's
Tale* there is even less of an attempt to explain Leontes' insanely jealous
imaginings. They occur without warning, irrationally, like the emotion
of jealousy itself.

When Iachimo returns from his unsuccessful attempt on Imogen's
virtue, lying to save his own skin as much as to win the wager, even
Posthumus' friends notice the flimsiness of his proffered 'proofs'. Posthumus alone seems almost eager to accept them; eager, like Leontes, to
derive some importance from his position as a wronged man, the more
so, perhaps, because of his own equivocal situation as the banished
husband of a princess. It is true that the taunting sexuality of Iachimo's
language has made a calm estimation of the evidence impossible for

him, but the way the scene is managed, particularly with Philo's comment on Iachimo's production of the bracelet, which like Othello's
handkerchief is the one piece of objective evidence used to bolster up a
tissue of lies, makes Posthumus' folly clear:

> Have patience, sir
> And take your ring again; 'tis not yet won:
> It may be probable that she lost it; or
> Who knows if one of her women, being corrupted,
> Hath stol'n it from her?
>
> (II, iv, 113)

and

> Sir, be patient:
> This is not strong enough to be believed
> Of one persuaded well of—
>
> (II, iv, 130)

But Posthumus brushes these reassurances aside precisely because he
is, for the moment, not well persuaded of Imogen's virtue. His hurt
pride finds relief in the expression of a desire for revenge; he is deaf and
blind to everything but his own wounded vanity as, doubting the reality of his love, he doubts the reality of everything.

> . . . We are all bastards; all
> And that most venerable man which I
> Did call my father was I know not where
> When I was stamped . . .
>
> (II, iv, 154)

This is very reminiscent of *Othello*, as is the desire for physical
revenge—'O! that I had her here, to tear her limb-meal'—and it is
reminiscent of Troilus, too, who found it easier to believe that all
womankind was corrupt than to admit that his judgement had been
wrong. Like them, and like Leontes in the later play, Posthumus, looking for some notion of abstract justice to replace the lost moral centre
that his love has afforded, sends orders to Pisanio to have Imogen
killed. But since he is far from the scene, and cannot experience even
the spurious satisfaction that action may bring, he is given time to
consider what has happened, instead of being swept along by the
course of events, so that when he next appears he is in a very different
frame of mind.

Of course Imogen is a very different sort of character from Desdemona. She is stronger, more active, more confident and not in the least

disposed to be a victim. She can deal equally efficiently with the leering innuendoes of Iachimo and the bumbling courtship of Cloten and she can retain her charm and her femininity in spite of her vigour. When Pisanio tells her what he has been instructed to do, her first instinctive response is to feel that without her husband's love, life is no longer worth living. Then she feels anger at his betrayal of trust, but her common sense and her love for Posthumus lead her to the right solution, that he has been deceived.

> Thus may poor fools
> Believe false teachers: though those that are betray'd
> Do feel the treason sharply, yet the traitor
> Stands in worse case of woe . . .
>
> (III, iv, 84)

and she feels sympathy for the sorrow he will feel when he discovers the truth. It is from this point that the new direction given to the action by the Romance form shows itself clearly. Imogen makes it abundantly clear that she is *prepared* to die, but circumstances and the whole design of the play do not demand that she does. Instead she accepts Pisanio's suggestion that she disguise herself as a boy and join the service of Caius Lucius, the Roman ambassador, hoping that this will take her to Rome and perhaps eventually reunite her with Posthumus. It is a short-lived hope. For reasons which need not concern us here, she is delayed on her journey through the mountains, falls ill, and is left for dead. When she awakes, it is to find herself next to the headless corpse of Cloten, which she mistakes for that of Posthumus, since it is dressed in his clothes, Cloten having decided to expedite his wooing of her by raping her while dressed in her husband's garments. Summarised in this way, this part of the action sounds like improbable farce, but such is Shakespeare's dramatic tact and poetic power that the scene of her awakening is moving and deeply serious. She is now, she believes, in a hopeless situation: the man she loves has not only cast her off, he is dead, and at the court she has left is only hostility and more danger. Had she been a tragic heroine, this is the point at which she would have killed herself. Instead she feels she must go on living; found weeping next to the body by Caius Lucius, she is accepted into his service, and consequently preserved for the happy reunion.

In a way, the obvious reason for her preservation is the necessity for this happy reunion at the end of the play, but to leave it at that is to beg the question. Shakespeare uses his plot, is not dominated by it, and there is a valid point to be made by Imogen's refusal to extinguish her own life, even though she believes that no hope of personal happiness

remains. It is not that she loves less than did Juliet, or Desdemona, or
Cleopatra, but that these Romance plays offer a wider vision of life than
just that of individual happiness. In *Cymbeline*, Imogen is the symbol of
that wider vision. Her grief is intense, but she can see a value in life
beyond her own individual existence:

> I am nothing: or if not
> Nothing to be were better. This was my master,
> A very valiant Briton and a good
> That here by mountaineers lies slain. Alas!
> There are no more such masters; I may wander
> From east to occident, cry out for service,
> Try many, all good, serve truly, never
> Find such another master.
>
> (IV, ii, 368)

Her dedication of herself to the service of the Roman general, in the
play's terms a good man, seems symbolic of her dedication to the
virtues of fortitude and humility, and it is wholly appropriate that as
the result of this service she is reunited with her husband at the play's
end. Her action in deciding to live on neither invalidates nor is invalidated by the deaths of the lovers in the tragedies, for it is as hard for her
to live on as it is for them to die, and in their different contexts each of
these actions is a testimony to the strength of love.

It is abundantly clear that Imogen's love, her fidelity, her courage
and her reverence for life make her worthy of the reward of happiness.
It is less immediately obvious why Posthumus should be so rewarded,
but I shall argue that he comes to learn what Imogen appears to know
instinctively, and that by learning from his mistakes he proves himself
worthy of her. His action in accepting Iachimo's wager had denied
Imogen's individual worth, and so precipitated all the suffering. It is
therefore appropriate that he should come to a recognition of her worth
as a person even before he discovers that Iachimo has lied to him, and
that he should come to this recognition unaided. In Britain with the
Roman forces to pursue his revenge against the country whose Princess
has betrayed him, he is horrified to receive from Pisanio a bloody cloth,
token, as he thinks, that his order for the killing of Imogen has been
carried out. For the first time since leaving her, he feels a real sense of
loss, and with it comes a much truer estimation of her worth, not only
to him, but in absolute terms.

> Yea, bloody cloth, I'll keep thee, for I wish'd
> Thou should'st be colour'd thus. You married ones,
> If each of you should take this course, how many

> Must murder wives much better than themselves
> For wrying but a little!
>
> (V, i, 1)

In a way which marks the beginning of his process of learning, he accepts the responsibility for what he has done, without seeking in any way to justify or excuse himself. His own part in the affair, he now sees, was much more culpable than hers (for he still believes her guilty) yet he lives and she does not. Faced with this apparently incomprehensible moral situation, and thinking too that all that he cares most about has been destroyed by his own self-centredness, he falls, not into despair exactly, but into a state of passive resignation:

> But alack!
> You snatch some hence for little faults; that's love
> To have them fall no more; you some permit
> To second ills with ills, each elder worse
> And make them dread it, to the doer's thrift.
> But Imogen is your own; do your best wills,
> And make me bless'd to obey.
>
> (V, i, 11)

It seems to me that for Posthumus at this moment to go on living is more difficult than to die, yet for reasons which reflect one of the important differences between the Romances and the love tragedies, he feels that he can best atone by going on living. Though I am aware of how unsatisfactory any abstraction that attempts to capture the central concern of the Romances is, it seems to me that they ask for a recognition of an individual responsibility to life itself. Though these lovers may feel that their own lives are robbed of meaning and value by the loss of the person they love, the whole atmosphere, with its emphasis on the continuation of life, prohibits them from taking their own lives. Hence Posthumus, although he knows atonement is not, in his terms, possible, vows to use what life remains to him in the service of those values which he now sees Imogen represented. He resolves to fight in disguise, for Britain against Rome; he hopes to find death, but will not kill himself.

> I am brought hither
> Among the Italian gentry, and to fight
> Against my lady's kingdom; 'tis enough
> That, Britain, I have kill'd thy mistress: peace,
> I'll give no wound to thee . . .
> . . . so I'll fight
> Against the part I came with, so I'll die

> For thee, O Imogen! even for whom my life
> Is every breath, a death: and thus, unknown,
> Pitied nor hated, to the face of peril
> Myself I'll dedicate.

(V, i, 17)

This essentially disinterested action, for he hopes for nothing for himself save death, turns the tide of the battle, and gives the Britons an
unexpected victory, for which Posthumus refuses to take any credit.
Instead he throws off his disguise and surrenders as an enemy to the
side he has just saved, hoping again to find the death he feels he
deserves.

Nothing is more emotionally moving, or dramatically effective, in
this half of the play (I am leaving aside the part of the plot that deals
with the loss and restoration of the king's heirs, Imogen's brothers)
than Posthumus' speech of renunciation and atonement as he waits for
his execution. It is his testimony that he has achieved that detachment
from the concerns of self, and that reverence for what I must, as a sort
of convenient shorthand, call the values of life.

> Most welcome, bondage! for thou art a way,
> I think, to liberty. Yet am I better
> Than one that's sick o' the gout, since he had rather
> Groan so in perpetuity than be cured
> By the sure physician, death, who is the key
> To unbar these locks. My conscience, thou art fetter'd
> More than my shanks and wrists: you good gods, give me
> The penitent instrument to pick that bolt,
> Then, free for ever! Is't enough I am sorry?
> So children temporal fathers do appease;
> Gods are more full of mercy. Must I repent?
> I cannot do it better than in gyves,
> Desir'd more than constrain'd: to satisfy,
> If of my freedom 'tis the main part, take
> No stricter render of me than my all.
> I know you are more clement than vile men,
> Who of their broken debtors take a third,
> A sixth, a tenth, letting them thrive again
> On their abatement: that's not my desire;
> For Imogen's dear life take mine; and though
> 'Tis not so dear, yet 'tis a life; you coin'd it;
> 'Tween man and man they weigh not every stamp;
> Though light, take pieces for the figure's sake:
> You rather mine, being yours: and so great powers,
> If you will take this audit, take this life,
> And cancel these cold bonds. O Imogen!
> I'll speak to thee in silence.

(V, iv, 3)

This tremendous soliloquy, poetically and thematically one of the high
points of the play, makes very clear the difference between the attitude
of Posthumus, and, say, Othello. Posthumus, like Othello, seeks death,
can contemplate no future without his love, and freely confesses his
own fault in having destroyed what he now realises he most valued. But
there the similarity ends, for his way of atonement lies in surrendering
the concerns of his own will to some greater power, not in achieving
oblivion through another act of the will. The self-defeating quality of
that willed act of extinction, which I noted in the tragedies, is therefore
absent. Posthumus through most of the soliloquy is apostrophising not
Imogen, but the powers of life, the 'gods' who coined it. Since it was
their gift, they must be aware of its value, and so of the absolute value
of what he is prepared to surrender. Notions of freedom and bondage
are taken up, to show his new-found recognition that the surrender of
his will to a purpose outside himself is freedom, as opposed to the
exercise of that will which imprisons within the self. And though his
own life is valueless to him now, and he has no wish to eke it out in
further meaningless years, he is able to see a value in life in the
abstract, which is the surest guarantee that he has the concerns of the
self in perspective, and can therefore face with equanimity that greatest
threat of all to the self, the fact of death. Just as a free acceptance of
Imogen as a person in her own right would have allowed their mutual
happiness, so acceptance of death's inevitability enables life to be
accepted and enjoyed for what it is, not clung to in such fear and misery
that its value is destroyed by the anxiety that it will be lost. So,
paradoxically, his readiness for death is the strongest proof that what
he has learned makes him worthy to go on living.

He has faced, too, the impossibility of making adequate atonement.
No more than does Othello, does he believe that even by making the
ultimate sacrifice of his life will he be able to make up for what he has
done. He cannot put the clock back, and so he sees no nobility in his
gesture. Simply he asks, 'Is't enough I am sorry?' However much he
may wish to do, he can do no more than admit his fault, recognise
finally his own insignificance, and yet in that recognition retain self-
respect, for no one can give more than he is now prepared to give:

> For Imogen's dear life take mine; and though
> 'Tis not so dear, yet 'tis a life; you coin'd it . . .
>
> (V, iv, 22)

The repetition of 'dear' suggests both Imogen's value, with all the
tenderness there was in their love, and his own lack of worth, but the
fact that he can now make the relative judgement is something that his

apprehension of the meaning of his love for Imogen has conferred on
him. To paraphrase the most powerful image of the soliloquy, life is
seen as the currency of the gods, ultimately possessed by no man, but
passing from generation to generation. What matters is the use that is
made of it: its return to its source cancels all individual debts. In seeing
beyond the confines of his own existence Posthumus sounds a note not
stressed in the love tragedies. He explicitly accepts the conditions of
mortality, one of the senses of 'this cold bond', and this acceptance sets
him free. The detachment that enables him to see life for what it is
allows him to see the true value of what he believes he has lost, so that,
when his love is restored to him, it is valued as it deserves to be valued.
This is the major difference between the sort of affirmation of love in
the Romances, and that which distinguishes the love tragedies. The
wider focus of the Romances still allows love an important part in life's
value, but it is there as symbolic of an attitude of unselfishness rather
than in its own right. Posthumus here expects nothing for himself, and
this gives his affirmation an authority, but also a degree of impersonality that is quite absent from the love tragedies, and which indeed would
be impossible, given the intensity of the passion there depicted. There,
the concentration on the nature of love, its joys and its anguish, is
almost the whole purpose; here, and in *The Winter's Tale*, love is one way
to attain that freedom from the concerns of the self that makes one free
of what life has to offer.

Posthumus, then, proves his worthiness to be reunited with Imogen,
and the expected happy ending follows swiftly. Dramatically speaking,
the complexities of the rest of the plot, with the restoration of the lost
heirs, the denunciation of Iachimo, and the multiple recognitions and
reconciliations, tend to distract attention from the lovers, but Imogen's
freely offered forgiveness and her joy at seeing Posthumus alive, are still
poetically and dramatically powerful enough to be the true climax of
the play, even though there are reminders that the suffering that Posthumus' lack of trust has caused cannot be simply expunged.

> IMOGEN   Why did you throw you wedded lady from you?
>   Think that you are upon a rock; and now
>   Throw me again.
> POSTHUMUS   Hang there like fruit, my soul
>   Till the tree die!
>
>   (V, v, 261)

The breach of trust was like a death; their recognition of their need for
each other allows them to stand firmly again, but the inevitable and
tragic conclusion, death itself, is first suggested by the image of fruition,
and then made explicit—'till the tree die!' Because each has experi-

enced what the other's death means, they will not again doubt or risk their love. In that sense they are more fortunate than the lovers of the tragedies, but what the play insists is that while the fortunate chance may have given them more time, this is a remission only. At some time or another, as the dirge recalls,

> All lovers young, all lovers must
> Consign to thee, and come to dust.

In its own way, their victory over time is as equivocal as that of Romeo and Juliet, who had so little time, but who lived and loved with an intensity that made time seem irrelevant.

The Winter's Tale, too, has the happy ending common to the Romances, but it provides an even sterner reminder of what may be lost, of what suffering is involved when self-interest displaces the concern for others that love demands. In this play these issues are the direct source of the plot, for the jealousy of Leontes is the dominant feature of the first half, the unselfish love of Perdita and Florizel the central interest of the second, and there is little that happens that does not have bearing on these two love relationships. However, I shall argue that in this play, though love provides the central image, it is not itself the true subject, as it is in the love tragedies. Here it is through their behaviour in love that the attitudes of the central characters to life itself emerge; in the love tragedies, life outside the charmed circle of love is hardly considered, and there is hardly time to consider it. By contrast, the most immediately noticeable features of the action of *The Winter's Tale* are its great length in time, spanning two generations, and its ending, opening into some future of continuing happiness. Perdita, the child abandoned in the wilds at Leontes' command at the end of Act III is a grown woman, herself in love, in Act IV; through her we are made aware of the way in which life continues, though individuals may be left behind. Leontes in his sorrow and repentance may feel that he occupies a timeless world, but time does not stand still, even though for him its passage may seem meaningless.

The equivocal nature of the consolation that the new generation represents has its bearing on many of the responses the play shows. The first scene has Camillo and Archidamus discussing the heirs to the thrones of their respective countries, but what they say has a more general significance. The young can either be valued for their own qualities, seen, without jealousy, as the heirs to the future, and as some genuine consolation against the destructive ravages of time, or they can be used as extensions of the parents' own personalities, valuable only in that they offer a kind of extension of the individual lifespan, a temporary and illusory immortality, that is as vulnerable to time as is the individual who seeks to use the child as a defence against it.

In *The Winter's Tale* (and to a lesser extent in *Cymbeline*, though I have not discussed this aspect of the play in any detail) the presence of children, and the emphasis given to their role as the inheritors and preservers of the personalities, hopes and fears of their parents are immediate and very significant differences from the love tragedies. Children *are* the future, and the essential fact about the operation of time in the love tragedies is that there is no future. Everything ends with the deaths of the lovers, and the famous graves and golden statues, even the survivors of the tragedy, only emphasise by their insignificance the finality of the loss. Even in *Antony and Cleopatra*, Cleopatra's children only exist as bargaining counters in the last act's clash between Octavius Caesar and Cleopatra, or as a means by which Cleopatra can demonstrate how little she cares, in the last resort, for anything other than Antony's love. The baby at her breast in the final scene is the asp; death, not new life.

Indeed, the concept of the ongoing world is something that all three of the love tragedies deliberately devalue, for whatever survives the lovers is so manifestly inferior to what has been lost. But in *Cymbeline*, *The Winter's Tale* and to a lesser extent *The Tempest* there is more interest in the future. There is certainly no absolute confidence, for life's challenges have to be faced anew in each generation, and the wisdom of experience cannot be passed on. Miranda will have to suffer her own disillusionments, and Perdita and Florizel perhaps will meet a greater threat than Polixenes' opposition. All will need to depend on their integrity, but perhaps this integrity is strengthened by the awareness that they are part of the continuing stream of life. In the Romances, there is not, at all events, the dominance of the note of absolute finality that is characteristic of the tragedies, even though, as I have already remarked of the ending of *Cymbeline*, it is not wholly excluded. Though the great cycle of life offers renewal and continuance, for the individual consciousness there is always a time limit, and even the best of reconciliations and renewals cannot make good time that has been wasted, or extend happiness beyond the limit of mortality. This unity of theme in *The Winter's Tale* makes it a more coherent and artistically satisfying play than *Cymbeline*. Its balances are so deftly managed that it is hard to say which is the more important element in its design, the destructive jealousy of Leontes, or the reconciling love of Perdita and Florizel. Again there are obvious echoes of themes and situations from the love tragedies, again there are important differences in point of view, and it is necessary to keep in mind the overall design of the play if one is to avoid making too much of these similarities. Many critics have found the savage outbursts of Leonte's jealousy the most dramatically satisfying part of the play, and some have gone so far as to argue that the serenity of the pastoral scenes, in which the love of Perdita and Florizel is presented, is a disappointing contrast, and cannot match the tragic force of the play's opening. This seems to me to miss the point: Shakespeare is not rewriting *Othello*, though this play may also threaten a tragic outcome. Even in the most terrifying of Leontes' ravings, there is a suggestion of the ludicrous that hints at some other outcome. Besides, one needs to consider whether or not this preference for the first three acts is not just another instance in which the dramatisation of evil, violence and destruction, by providing a superficially more impressive effect, leads some critics to lose their balance and become fascinated by the evil they contemplate, in a way that they are sometimes eager to attribute to Shakespeare.

If the scenes of love and of reconciliation are read with due attention to their poetic power, the play does achieve a balance. After all, it is in the nature of things for peace, love and happiness to be so much more frail and vulnerable than force and hatred, yet their value is not destroyed even if the situations in which they can exist may be destroyed for individual people. One of the major concerns of this play, and of the other Romances, is to show just how enduring these qualities are in spite of their vulnerability, and to suggest that it is only their existence that prevents individual life from being wholly tragic.

In its final effect *The Winter's Tale* is not tragic, even though for at least half of its duration it threatens to be so. Leontes' sexual jealousy destroys his lifelong friendship with his friend King Polixenes, causes the loss of his most trusted courtier, Camillo, the actual death of his son and heir to the throne, Mamillius, and the supposed deaths of his wife Hermione and his daughter Perdita. To all intents and purposes, Hermione is dead, for although the audience knows of the preservation of the abandoned child, there is no hint until the final scene that Hermione is also alive. Leontes believes that he has destroyed what he has too late discovered he cared for most.

This destructive power of jealousy provides the obvious link with the theme of *Othello*, but the situation is so changed that its significance is radically altered. The careful detail given of Othello's situation, together with the protracted plottings and goadings of Iago may not make Othello's fall excusable, but it is certainly understandable; to a much lesser extent, this is true of Posthumus in *Cymbeline*, too. But in

The Winter's Tale, there is no shielding whatsoever of Leontes from full responsibility for his actions. At the play's opening he is presented as a man who has almost everything that he can desire: a beautiful and loving wife, an heir who is the pattern of what a young prince should be, the continuing friendship of his boyhood companion, King Polixenes, and the respect of his subjects. Yet out of this apparently clear sky comes the sudden destructive storm of his jealousy, unmotivated, inexcusable. The precipitating action is a casual social one. An overzealous host, Leontes has been urging his friend King Polixenes to prolong his visit beyond the appointed time, and calls on Hermione to join her pleas to his. When she does so, and extracts a polite agreement from Polixenes, the self-centredness that is the dominant characteristic of Leontes in this part of the play flames out to full fury. 'At my request he would not' (I, ii, 87) is the line that gives the first inkling that all is not well; then with terrifying speed Leontes passes from the suspicion that his wife and his friend are too fond of each other to the certainty that he has been cuckolded, and the 'knowledge' that the child Hermione is carrying is not his own.

Here, then, is a situation that really does answer to Dr Leavis' account of what happens in *Othello*.[4] Leontes does respond with a promptness that could hardly be improved upon, not to the promptings of a malicious outsider but to what the play reveals as his own essential nature. He views the world as a place created for the unhindered exercise of his will, and his outburst of jealousy is a response to an awareness, dimly comprehended, of the destructive effect of time on that will. Given the freedom that the looser dramatic construction of the romance allows, Shakespeare makes this sudden jealousy credible by the sheer power of the poetry in which it is presented, and does so in such a way that it captures the irrational nature of the emotion, and makes this irrationality the strongest proof of the jealousy's existence. The difference in point of view from *Othello* is very marked, for where that play showed at length how Iago used Othello's own feelings of insecurity, not in themselves vicious or perverted, to subvert his trust in Desdemona, and emphasised that Othello was allowed to hear no other voice than that of his enemy, *The Winter's Tale* shows Leontes as remaining obstinately deaf to the advice of all who try to show him how monstrously he is mistaken. As so often is the case in Shakespeare's work, the ultimate destructive principle is revealed as the unchecked operation of the human will, which in Leontes' case takes him swiftly from suspicion that he has been betrayed, through certainty, to self-pity, even to enjoyment of his plight as a wronged man, and finally to a sadistic and bitterly sexual desire for violent revenge that goes beyond even the incoherent ravings of the stricken Othello.

Although I may in this account have seemed to imply that Leontes' jealousy is quite unmotivated, this is not strictly true, for though in its genesis it may seem inexplicable, as it develops it reveals why Leontes sees the world as an extension of himself and why his response to any indication to the contrary is an irrational and destructive fury. It is clear, in a way reminiscent of Lear, that his authority and privilege have protected him from any opposition to his own desires. In the discussion of the boyhood friendship of the two kings, images not so much of innocence as of inexperience, of unpreparedness to meet any challenge abound. Once only, it seems, did Leontes not get his own way immediately, and that was when Hermione kept him waiting three months for an answer to his proposal of marriage. That delay still rankles, for by some quirk of contrast it feeds his swiftly maturing suspicions of her now. His son's existence he can only conceive of as an extension of his own. Mamillius' admirable qualities are not valuable in themselves, but only inasmuch as they are copies or continuations of Leontes' own, a means to achieve a kind of personal immortality. The idea of living on through one's children is of course a commonplace in Shakespeare's age, but this recognition of it as a potentially destructive force is not. Its extension to the conclusion that life is only valuable to the extent to which it can be possessed by the individual, in some way hoarded and retained by him, is an attitude which rapidly dominates Leontes, and which must be most painfully unlearned by him later in the play. Specifically he is faced with the realisation that he cannot command Hermione's love and fidelity by an act of his own will; love and trust must be mutually accepted and offered, but since he has not yet learned this, and since he cannot really conceive of the independent existence of anyone other than himself, his concept of Hermione is as changeable as his own mind. He knows that the sexual betrayal of which he so rapidly convinces himself is a possible one; wives are sometimes unfaithful, though Hermione is not. It is partly the sudden realisation that Hermione may be beyond his control that is so shattering to him. As he believes only in his own freedom of choice it is easy for him to see the freedom of others as probable licence, and by a sort of process of free association to see what may be possible as first probable, then certain.

> Too hot, too hot!
> To mingle friendship far is mingling bloods.
> I have *tremor cordis* on me: my heart dances;
> But not for joy, not joy. This entertainment
> May a free face put on, derive a liberty

> From heartiness, from bounty, fertile bosom,
> And well become the agent: 't may I grant:
> But to be paddling palms and pinching fingers,
> As now they are, and making practis'd smiles,
> As in a looking-glass; and then to sigh, as 'twere
> The mort o' the deer; O! that is entertainment
> My bosom likes not, nor my brows. Mamillius,
> Art thou my boy?
>
> (I, ii, 108)

What is actually true, the innocence of the friendship between Hermione and Polixenes, is considered only to be dismissed in favour of the diseased imaginings of what may be possible. In disjointed leaps and stops of thought, reflected in the movement of the verse, he progresses from the lover's sigh, which exists in any case only in his own imagination, to the death of the deer, to the cuckold's horns, to doubts about whether Mamillius is indeed his son. Since both Hermione and Mamillius are only valued as his possessions, they are seen, like all possessions, as subject to loss, which destroys their value for him. That being so, his concept of what is valuable fixes itself on what seems its only true object, himself. How little he really cares, in contrast to Othello, for the loss of what is claimed as the central value in his life, is reflected in an obsessive concern with himself, with what people will think and say about him.

> Gone already!
> Inch-thick, knee-deep, o'er head and ears a fork'd one!
> Go play, boy, play; thy mother plays, and I
> Play too, but so disgrac'd a part, whose issue
> Will hiss me to my grave: contempt and clamour
> Will be my knell.
>
> (I, ii, 185)

In his self-induced state of complete disgust with everything outside of himself, he needs no Iago to confuse his mind with crude images of sexual coupling; he can supply them himself. Significantly, they express themselves in terms of property or possessions; no man can successfully guard all his livestock, and Hermione seems to have no higher status:

> And many a man there is (even at the present,
> Now, while I speak this) holds his wife by th' arm,
> That little thinks she has been sluic'd in's absence,
> And his pond fish'd by his next neighbour, by
> Sir Smile, his neighbour: nay, there's comfort in 't
> Whiles other men have gates, and those gates open'd,
> As mine, against their will.   (I, ii, 192)

There is a grim enjoyment in the thought that he is sharing a fate that even if undeserved, is universal; from this he passes to a belief in himself as the one honest man in the midst of this corrupt world. When he looks for sympathy he reveals the extent to which he has isolated himself from all life around him, for he prefers his isolation as the wronged man, he hugs to him his imagined injury, and sees in the horrified denial of his suspicions by his courtiers, from Camillo down, further evidence of his own honesty and of the corrruption of everyone else. The terrible isolation imposed by this negation of all value outside of his own consciousness, of his own will, reaches its climax in the speech following Camillo's attempt to persuade him that his imaginings are completely unfounded. The 'evidence' that he produces exists only in his own mind, but it leads up to the ironically unrecognised statement of the absolute loneliness he has brought on himself.

> Is whispering nothing?
> Is leaning cheek to cheek? is meeting noses?
> Kissing with inside lip? stopping the career
> Of laughter with a sigh (a note infallible
> Of breaking honesty)? horsing foot on foot?
> Skulking in corners? wishing clocks more swift?
> Hours, minutes? noon, midnight? and all eyes
> Blind with the pin and web, but theirs, theirs only.
> That would unseen be wicked? is this nothing?
> Why then the world, and all that's in't, is nothing,
> The covering sky is nothing, Bohemia nothing,
> My wife is nothing, nor nothing have these nothings
> If this be nothing.
>
> (I, ii, 284)

In Acts II and III Leontes' jealousy drives to its tragic outcome. More convinced than ever of the justice of his suspicions by the sudden departure of Polixenes, who has been appraised of the situation by Camillo, he appears to derive active enjoyment from the sense of having been right.

> How blest am I
> In my just censure, in my true opinion!
> Alack for lesser knowledge! How accurs'd
> In being so blessd'! There may be in the cup
> A spider steep'd, and one may drink, depart,
> And yet partake no venom, for his knowledge
> Is not infected; but if one present
> Th' abhorr'd ingredient to his eye, make known
> How he hath drunk, he cracks his gorge, his sides
> With violent hefts. I have drunk, and seen the spider.
>
> (II, i, 36)

This is Leontes' version of Othello's

> I had been happy, if the general camp
> Pioneers and all, had tasted her sweet body,
> So had I nothing known . . .
>
> (III, iii, 351)

but there is a great difference between that despairing look back at
what had seemed perfect happiness, even if based on ignorance, and
what amounts to the relish with which Leontes accepts his own bitter
fantasy. The contrast is strengthened as Leontes proceeds to plan his
revenge, for while Othello could never succeed in forgetting the lost
perfection of Desdemona's love, Leontes looks only ahead to the satisfaction the destruction of Hermione will give him. He cannot even be
said to have destroyed his own love or his own happiness, for there is no
indication that he has ever truly experienced or understood these emotions.

Hermione, like Desdemona, is an innocent victim, but, though her
resources of self-possession and experience of life as well as her position
(for she is a Queen and daughter of the Emperor of Russia) are much
greater than Desdemona's, she cannot save herself from the fury of her
husband, nor does she even wish to do so. Though she can scarcely
credit her senses, she knows of what she is accused and she makes the
only defence she can: she says she is innocent. Yet she cannot convince
Leontes and there is nothing she can do to prove it. Everyone but
Leontes does believe her, but they cannot protect her. Symbolically as
well as actually, Leontes has the power of life and death over her, for all
she cares about in life is their shared love, and without that, life has no
meaning.

For all his power, Leontes is also left without a true purpose. He
believes that there is no peace of mind to be had as long as he is forced
to acknowledge the existence of those who seem to defy his will:

> Nor night, nor day, no rest: it is but weakness
> To bear the matter thus: mere weakness. If
> The cause were not in being,—part o' th' cause
> She th' adultress . . .
>
> . . . say that she were gone,
> Given to the fire, a moiety of my rest
> Might come to me again.
>
> (II, iii,1)

Hysterically he shouts down any opposition to his wishes, and when

Paulina, Hermione's trusted friend and attendant, in a last attempt to move him to reason, shows him his new-born daughter, his response to this image of new life and hope is to order its destruction, not only because he fears it does not belong to him, but also because its very existence communicates a truth to him about his own, that he cannot accept.

So convinced is Leontes of the justice of his cause that he has sent to the Oracle of Apollo for confirmation of Hermione's guilt. When the news comes that his messengers are returning, he impatiently orders the trial of Hermione to begin before their arrival, and so provides the occasion for his ultimate act of solipsistic madness. What he wants is a public demonstration of his own blamelessness, and of his wife's treachery, but the rancour with which he sets himself up as both judge and prosecutor makes the trial convincing to no one but himself. Hermione, bearing herself with patience and dignity, lacks both the means and the inclination to defend herself, though her response to Leontes' promises of torture and death show her steadfastness and the quality of the love she still feels for him.

> Sir, spare your threats:
> The bug which you would fright me with, I seek.
> To me can life be no commodity;
> The crown and comfort of my life, your favour,
> I do give lost, for I do feel it gone,
> But know not how it went. My second joy,
> And first fruits of my body, from his presence
> I am barr'd, like one infectious. My third comfort,
> (Starr'd most unluckily) is from my breast
> (The innocent milk in its most innocent mouth)
> Hal'd out to murder; myself on every post
> Proclaim'd a strumpet, with immodest hatred
> The child-bed privilege denied . . .
>
> (III, ii, 91)

Her obvious sincerity, her composure, her innocence, none of these provides any defence. Even when the message from the Oracle, in what must surely be one of its most explicit utterances, declares her innocence and Leontes' guilt, there is no halting the onrush of his will.

> There is no truth at all i' the Oracle:
> The sessions shall proceed: this is mere falsehood.
>
> (III, ii, 140)

What changes his mind is no sudden illumination, but the recognition, as the punishment for his sins swiftly overtakes him, that he too is vulnerable. News comes that Mamillius is dead, and Hermione falls apparently dying at his feet. Yet the mere reversal of the will is no proof of repentance, as Leontes has to learn, for he shows little understanding in his desire, now that he has been punished, simply to undo what he has done, and start again. There is something pathetically child-like in his catalogue of proposed good deeds, and in his refusal to accept the consequences of his actions. Life is not as easy as this.

> Apollo, pardon
> My great profaneness 'gainst thine Oracle!
> I'll reconcile me to Polixenes,
> New woo my queen, recall the good Camillo,
> Whom I proclaim a man of truth, of mercy...
> (III, ii, 153)

Leontes must accept that Mamillius and Hermione are dead (for there is no suggestion at this point that Hermione is being preserved for a later reunion). Perdita is cast away and probably dead, yet he must go on living, bearing the grief and disgrace of what he has done. Having refused to acknowledge a life beyond himself, his punishment is that he must continue to live in a way which, while demanding his service (for as an heirless king he cannot kill himself and abandon the responsibilities of his state) offers him nothing in the way of personal reward. He must, in other words, live in a way which demonstrates a disinterested acceptance of life's demands. All he can hope for is the fulfilment of the suggestion in the prophesy that his lost daughter may one day be found. Until then, he must live alone, for only by obeying the conditions of the Oracle, whose truth he has publicly denied, can he prove his repentance, and his obedience to something outside of himself.

At this point in the action, Shakespeare simply abandons Leontes. The slow process of his recreation takes place off stage, and at his reappearance in Act V we are shown the result of what he has learned, not the way in which he learned it. Attention shifts to Perdita, but not before, in what is perhaps the most explicit statement of the theme in any of the plays, Time, as Chorus, indicates not only what has happened during that break in the action, but declares himself destroyer as well as creator:

> I that please some, try all: both joy and terror
> Of good and bad, that makes and unfolds error,
> Now take upon me, in the name of Time
> To use my wings...

> ... Let me pass
> The same I am, ere ancient'st order was,
> Or what is now receiv'd. I witness to
> The times that brought them in; so shall I do
> To th' freshest things now reigning, and make stale
> The glistering of this present ...
>
> (IV, i, 1)

Time itself is the only unchanging thing; the chorus offers a reminder and a warning, just before the presentation of what is surely one of the 'freshest things now reigning', the love of Perdita and Florizel, that their youth and vitality, their love too, will be challenged and ultimately destroyed by time's operation.

In fact they must meet this challenge both directly and indirectly, for they have to contend with the bitter opposition of King Polixenes, Florizel's father, to the match, ostensibly because of his objection, reasonable enough in itself, to the throne of Bohemia contracting a marriage to a shepherd's daughter. Underlying his objections though, is a more fundamental cause, his own refusal to accept the passage of time, to acknowledge that he is growing old, and that it is his son who is handsome and young and with whom Perdita is in love. There is a strongly sexual element in the sadism of his threats of what will happen to Perdita, if she does not give Florizel up.

For the play's purposes, Perdita is clearly more important than Florizel, who, if not as cypher-like as Ferdinand in *The Tempest*, is not required to do much more than prove his worthiness as a husband for the heroine. There are obvious dramatic ironies in her situation: a true princess, she has been brought up as a shepherd's daughter, who, in the pastoral scene, is required to play the part of queen of the autumn sheepshearing festival. Many different issues, true nobility and nobility conferred merely by rank, art and nature, court and country, age and youth, responsibility, love and the passage of time are marvellously woven together in the poetry and spectacle of this great scene, though for the purpose of this discussion it will be necessary to isolate and consequently simplify some of its aspects.

Perdita has been brought up away from the potentially corrupting influence of Leontes' court, but her life as a shepherdess has been no idyll. Though the point is repeatedly made that this life is in close contact with the rhythms of nature and the changing of the seasons, with their annual renewal of life, such a contact also insists on those sad and terrifying aspects of time's passage that every individual must feel, though perhaps masked for a while in the artificial life of the court. Perdita knows about death and loss, about the isolation of the indi-

vidual who passes from birth through maturity to death amid the cycle
of life's continuing renewal. Because she accepts this sad awareness,
she is unlikely to be as completely shattered as Leontes was, by any
sudden apprehension of individual insignificance, of individual fate.
The poetic emphasis of these scenes is on youth, on love, on happiness,
but always set against the background of a life where the individual
consciousness must end in death. The point is introduced early. Perdita
is queen of the feast for the first time, for since the last festival, her old
foster-mother has died, and sorrow for that loss mingles with the
excitement of the occasion, to communicate a sense of continuing
responsibility being passed on, as part of the privilege of being alive.

The presence of two strangers, in reality Polixenes and Camillo,
disguised as old men and there to spy on Florizel, gives Shakespeare a
remarkable dramatic opportunity for a poetic exploration of the quality
of a love that will stand the test of time and external malice. Perdita
knows who Florizel is; he, in his careless optimism is in a way like
Romeo, newly in love with Juliet: he believes that love itself will smooth
away all obstacles. Perdita, on the other hand, can foresee all the
dangers and difficulties their love may bring, and loves him in spite of
them. Each guest is greeted with flowers appropriate to his or her age,
and it is worth noticing that Polixenes in disguise is less than delighted
at being treated like an old man by so attractive a young girl, but it is
when Perdita turns to Florizel that she and he reveal the feelings that
lie at the heart of this scene and of the play. Her good sense makes her
turn aside the courtly compliment of Camillo; it is the same clear
sightedness which distinguishes the quality of her feeling for Florizel,
showing it to be a love based on reality and not illusion.

CAMILLO   I should leave grazing, were I of your flock
           And only live by gazing.

PERDITA   Out alas!
           You'd be so lean that blasts of January
           Would blow you through and through. Now my fair'st friend
           I would I had some flowers o' th' spring, that might
           Become your time of day; and yours, and yours,
           That wear upon your virgin branches yet
           Your maidenheads growing: O Proserpina,
           For the flowers now that, frighted, thou let'st fall
           From Dis's waggon; daffodils
           That come before the swallow dares, and take
           The winds of March with beauty; violets dim,
           But sweeter than the lids of Juno's eyes
           Or Cytherea's breath; pale primroses,
           That die unmarried, ere they can behold

> Bright Phoebus in his strength (a malady
> Most incident to maids); bold oxlips and
> The crown imperial; lilies of all kinds,
> The flower-de-luce being one. O, these I lack
> To make you garlands of; and my sweet friend,
> To strew him o'er and o'er!

FLORIZEL   What, like a corpse?

PERDITA No, like a bank, for love to lie and play on:
> Not like a corpse; or if—not to be buried,
> But quick, and in mine arms.

(IV, iv, 109)

Perdita takes up the seasonal imagery that the whole pastoral setting suggests, and, using the story of Proserpina and her abduction by the king of the underworld, softens the recognition of the inescapable lot of all that lives by linking it with the cyclic pattern of the myth. Proserpina is allowed to return to the world above each year, and her return is the coming of spring, the renewal of life. Her delicate beauty is equated with the delicate beauty of the spring flowers, which can oppose their fragility to the last attempts of winter to destroy them. The daffodils, that 'take the winds of March with beauty', oppose the transience of all that lives with the bravery of their beauty, and capture in one marvellous image an attitude that finds a value in life in spite of its transience, in spite of all that threatens it. The seasonal pattern implies fulfilment as part of the cycle that ends in destruction, but Perdita's honesty of vision allows her to see that even this fulfilment is not given to everyone. Some of her young friends may, like the primroses, 'die unmarried' but what matters is that the great cycle is seen to continue, accepted for what it is. No one may try to hold it back, stop it at any stage, no matter how precious or wonderful that stage may be. And since the end of the natural cycle is death, love and death must be accepted together, as they are juxtaposed in the pun that follows. To love one must be alive, and if one lives, then one must die, and the same word means both the act of love and death itself.

Florizel's joking reply states the question quite directly: 'What, like a corpse?' Perdita's instinctive response is to reject this idea, but she immediately returns to the serious acceptance of what has been so light-heartedly suggested. 'Or if' is the qualification that her honesty makes her admit, yet the terror is mastered and fended away by the connotations of rapid movement, of life and joy that are implied by the lovemaking image. It is a point that Florizel in turn accepts, for the speech in which he declares his love for her shows his acceptance of the inevitability of change, the acknowledgement that everything must be esteemed for what it is, and that what it is cannot help but change.

>   What you do
> Still betters what is done. When you speak, sweet,
> I'd have you do it ever: when you sing,
> I'd have you buy and sell so, so give alms;
> Pray so; and, for the ordering of your affairs,
> To sing them too: when you do dance, I wish you
> A wave o' the sea, that you might ever do
> Nothing but that; move still, still so,
> And own no other function: each your doing,
> So singular in each particular,
> Crowns what you are doing in the present deed,
> That all your acts are queens.
>   (IV, iv, 135)

The tenderness of this, the gentle lyrical quality of the verse movement, contains and does not obscure the acceptance of change, for though the change may be regretted, what succeeds will also be valuable. The wave motion, described as well as echoed, suggests the individual's limited share in a process that never ends, gently insisting that life is to be crowned 'in the present deed' accepted as it is, for it cannot be retained. This shared vision of love and of life sustains them even if it cannot protect them, when Polixenes, throwing off his disguise, threatens Florizel with disinheritance, and promises Perdita a death of such savagery that there is clearly something more to his feelings than just the prevention of an unsuitable match by the heir to his throne. After promising to destroy her beauty by having it 'scratch'd with briars' he goes on

>   And you enchantment,——
> Worthy enough a herdsman; yea, him too,
> That makes himself, but for our honour therein,
> Unworthy thee. If ever henceforth thou
> These rural latches to his entrance open,
> Or hoop his body more with thy embraces,
> I will devise a death as cruel for thee
> As thou art tender to 't.
>   (IV, iv, 435)

No doubt he feels that his honour is involved, for like the Leontes of earlier years, he sees his child, even a grown child, as an extension of himself, but the violence of his reaction to the physical relationship between his son and Perdita, the images in which he couches his threats, and his reluctance to accept his own age, all point to a strongly sexual revolt against the fact that it is a young man and not himself that Perdita loves. It is interesting that Leontes, at his first sight of his still unrecognised daughter, has a momentary flash of the same reaction, even though he has better learned to accept what change and the passage of time mean for him.

The young lovers are not protected from the onslaught of this sort of divisive force by their love, but again, as in the other Romances, the potentially tragic situation is redeemed by the fortunate chance, in this case by the sympathy and help of Camillo, who, anxious to return to Sicilia, his own country, offers to give them a ship and letters of introduction to Leontes. He hopes to follow soon with Polixenes, so reconciling him both to the match and to his old friend, but as Florizel does not know this, the sacrifice he makes in giving up his position as heir to the throne is emotionally a real one to him. In the same way, Perdita means what she says when she offers in turn to give him up, though his love for her makes it impossible for him to accept.

Apart from Polixenes' outburst, the pastoral scene lacks the pyrotechnics of the first half of the play, yet it has a quiet serenity that provides an adequate balance to those stormy and tragic acts. The principal impression it makes is perhaps one of tranquillity, but it is a tranquillity that comes from security, and that is pervaded with a vitality, a freshness and a natural strength. The dominant emotions are those of love, happiness and trust, and when evil and malice appear they are steadfastly met, perhaps because the comprehensiveness of the attitude that the lovers share acknowledges the existence of such things, and is therefore not surprised or disconcerted by their appearance. The pastoral atmosphere has no hint in it of an evasion of reality: the world that Perdita knows contains jealousy and foolishness, old age and death, the minor predations of Autolycus, as well as love and joy. The lovers can see all this, and it is this clarity of vision that gives them their strength and makes them worthy bringers of new life and hope to the winter kingdom of Leontes in Sicilia.

The atmosphere of that kingdom, before the arrival of Perdita and Florizel, is still one of penitence and grief, as it was sixteen years before, though the courtiers, anxious for an heir to the kingdom, are urging Leontes to marry again. He, though, remains steadfastly faithful to the memory of his wife, and to the command of the Oracle; he no longer gives way to despair, nor does he complain that life is meaningless, for he finds a kind of satisfaction, or at least a peace of mind, in accepting what he has done, in recognising the worth of what he thinks he has destroyed. Since he believes that Hermione is dead, there is no possibility of his still thinking of her only as a possession, so his tribute to her virtue and her beauty

> Stars, stars!
> And all eyes else, dead coals!
>
> (V, i, 67)

is a disinterested one, though passionate in its sincerity. In all that he
does in his reception of the young lovers, in his reconciliation with
Polixenes, above all in his true estimation of himself, Leontes demonstrates that, like Posthumus in *Cymbeline*, his freedom from the demands
of the self renders him worthy of being reunited with his wife. This
reunion with Hermione marks the dramatic, poetic and thematic
climax of the play.

In this final scene Leontes, the court and his royal visitors are
brought by Paulina to view the newly completed statue of Hermione.
As the play's final action unfolds, it becomes clear that this is no statue,
but the living woman, miraculously restored to life. That, at least, is the
dramatic effect of the scene, for though there is just sufficient information offered to allow the natural explanation to be suggested, that
Paulina has kept the queen hidden for sixteen years, to Leontes and to
Perdita and to the audience it is a miracle that they are witnessing. The
solemn music, Paulina's priestess-like intonations, and particularly
Leontes' own rapt response, combine to produce an atmosphere of
reverence which is, if anything, accentuated by the lack of response
revealed by Polixenes, to whom the statue is merely a very fine work of
art. To Leontes, even before he realises that it is his living wife who
stands before him, the reverence it commands is for life itself

> PAULINA I am sorry sir, I have thus far stirr'd you:
> but I could afflict you further.
> LEONTES   Do, Paulina;
> For this affliction has a taste as sweet
> As any cordial comfort. Still, methinks
> There is an air comes from her: what fine chisel
> Could ever yet cut breath?
>
> (V, iii, 74)

The affliction he has experienced he now recognises as supremely valuable to him, for it has enabled him to recognise what he had previously
taken for granted: 'What fine chisel / Could ever yet cut breath' is his
acknowledgement of the ultimate gift of life itself.

At this climactic moment, the play does not allow us to forget what it
has insisted on throughout. The note is first sounded by Leontes himself, when he comments on how much older the statue of Hermione
seems:

> But yet Paulina
> Hermione was not so much wrinkled, nothing
> So aged as this seems.
>
> (V, ii, 27)

'Wrinkled' and 'aged' are strong words, whose significance is reinforced when Paulina calls the 'statue' back into life.

> Music, awake her: strike!
> 'Tis time; descend, be stone no more: approach;
> Strike all that look with marvel. Come;
> I'll fill your grave up: stir; nay, come away;
> Bequeath to death your numbness, for from him
> Dear life redeems you.
>
> (V, ii, 98)

Death must come, as 'I'll fill your grave up' reminds us, and the only
defence, the only consolation (for this play does not speculate about a
life to come) is the quality of 'dear life' itself. As Leontes takes his wife
in his arms, and realises from her living warmth that she really is
restored to him, he is given a happiness that he has not previously
known, which nevertheless is something that should be available to all
who are truly alive.

> O! she's warm
> If this be magic, let it be an art
> Lawful as eating.
>
> (V, ii, 109)

Yet even in this moment of joy, much of what has been lost remains
lost. Nothing can bring Mamillius back to life, or give back to Paulina
the husband whose death was brought about by Leontes' attempted
destruction of the infant Perdita. For both Leontes and Hermione, the
sixteen lost years cannot be restored. They are no longer young, and
the qualities of youthful joy and love that were theirs have passed to
their daughter and her mate.

In its final effect this astonishing play seems to show Shakespeare at
grips, as he is in all these last plays, with the ultimate problems of
human existence. His conclusions cannot be readily summarised or
abstracted from the play itself, for their dramatic statement has an
emotional truth that no commentary can capture. Nevertheless, one is
obliged to make the attempt, so with these reservations in mind, certain
generalisations can be advanced. The great problem posed by man's
mortality can be answered in two ways, either by believing in a life to
come, or by finding a value in this life that does not depend on perma-

nence. The second of these is the play's answer. The worth of life is that it is life, and not death, even if to be alive is to be exposed to danger and suffering and a certain end. But if this life is not to be merely chaotic, with each individual satisfying his own appetites, then there must be a belief in certain qualities like love, honesty, justice, which have virtue only in so far as they are truly held, and their virtue is that they can liberate the individual from an exclusive concern with the self. If I may quote from what I have said about this play elsewhere:

> Those who live in the self, die in the self...Those who see themselves as something greater, part of a stream of life continually renewing itself, and who defend the values of that life even though they know that they cannot retain or possess them, are those that are most truly alive. The play suggests that to live until one dies is the great affirmation that man is called on to make, and that it carries its own reward.[5]

The Romances, then, provide a more general instance of the theme set forward with such power and intensity in the love tragedies. The main difference in their action is that time, which so relentlessly drives on to the destruction of the main characters in the tragedies, seems in the Romances to relent for a while, and offer another chance to those who have proved their capacity to use it. This second chance, however, foreshadowed to a greater or lesser extent in the different plays, inevitably lessens the sense of urgency, and consequently the intensity of the passion that is depicted. In the end the obvious statement turns out to be a true one, and still worth making, that the Romances and the tragedies deal with different areas of human experience, and therefore complement and do not contradict one another. The lovers in the Romances move on to their allotted spans of happiness not because they are more deserving than their equivalents in the tragedies, but because they are luckier, or in more strictly literary terms, because by using such a plot, Shakespeare could extend his exploration of the human condition, and not duplicate what he had done before.

In the end, these different plays, comedies, tragedies and romances, all share one great concern, that of establishing a value for love, and through love, for life, which can be maintained in spite of the fullest realisation of the hazards, the suffering and the certain end to which men and women expose themselves when they commit themselves to loving someone other than themselves. In the plays that I have considered in the greatest detail, the love tragedies, and this is true even of *Othello*, what destroys the lovers is not so much malice, or misfortune, or ill-governed passions, as the operation of time. The plays are the extreme statement of the tragedy of time, and as such, they seem to me absolute statements of the universal tragedy of human existence. We run out of time; either we die first, or those we love die before us. That is the inescapable human tragedy, to be met with what strength and dignity we can muster. A stronger Macbeth could perhaps have shunned the ambition that led him to his destruction; a different Coriolanus could perhaps have reconciled the pulls of pride and honour. Their tragedies as they exist have their own sense of inevitability, but their falls are produced by the particularities of their characters in the situations in which they are placed, no matter what universal truth may also be communicated. By contrast, the act of committing oneself in love seems not something to be avoided, but perhaps the summit of human experience, and yet whoever does so renders himself at once a potential tragic victim. Even the Romances, with their remissions for good conduct, do not shrink from reminding us that love can neither protect from harm, nor stay the passage of time that leads all to death. They, like the tragedies, affirm the value of living as they acknowledge the inevitability of dying. But it is the love tragedies, *Romeo and Juliet* and *Othello* which show the glory of love so briefly, *Antony and Cleopatra* with its sense of the triumphant achievement of life lived to the full, even if the fullness is self-consuming, that make the most powerful, the most moving affirmation of life's value. As W. B. Yeats has written:[6]

> Man is in love, and loves what vanishes
> What more is there to say?

NOTES

CHAPTER ONE   The tragic strand in the comedies

[1] Rabkin, Norman, *Shakespeare and the Common Understanding*, New York, 1967.

[2] Gardner, Helen, '*Othello:* a retrospect, 1900-67', *Shakespeare Survey 21*, Cambridge, 1968.

[3] Bradbrook, Muriel, *Themes and Conventions in Elizabethan Tragedy*, Cambridge, 1935.

[4] Dickey, F. M., *Not Wisely But Too Well*, San Marino, Calif., 1957.

[5] Campbell, Lily, B., *Shakespeare's Tragic Heroes*, New York, 1930.

[6] Hawkes, T., *Shakespeare and the Reason*, London, 1964.

[7] Marsh, D. R. C., *The Recurring Miracle*, Natal, 1962 and Nebraska, 1969.

[8] See, for example, *Bodenham's Belvedere; or, The Garden of the Muses*, Publications of the Spenser Society No. 17, Manchester, 1875.

[9] Brooks, Harold, 'Theme and structure in *The Comedy of Errors*', Stratford-upon-Avon Studies 3, *Early Shakespeare*, London, 1961.

[10] Though see Brooks, H., *op. cit.*, and Brown, J. R., *Shakespeare and his Comedies*, London, 1957.

[11] See Dickey, F. M., and Rabkin, N., in the works already cited, or Bayley, John, *The Characters of Love*, London, 1960

[12] For example, the treatment of Corvino in Ben Jonson's *Volpone*.

CHAPTER TWO   The problem comedies and *Troilus and Cressida*

[1] See Tillyard, E. M. W., *Shakespeare's Problem Plays*, London, 1950, as a representative example.

[2] For instance, Leavis, F. R. in *The Common Pursuit*, London, 1952, and Knight, G. Wilson, in *The Wheel of Fire*, London, 1949.

[3] For instance, Campbell, Oscar J., *Comicall Satyre and Shakespeare's Troilus and Cressida*, San Marino, Calif., 1938, and Knights, L. C., 'The ambiguity of *Measure for Measure*', in *The Importance of 'Scrutiny'*, ed. E. Bentley, New York, 1964.

[4] Marsh, D. R. C., 'The mood of *Measure for Measure*', *Shakespeare Quarterly* Vol. XIV, 1963, and 'Interpretation and misinterpretation in Shakespeare's *Troilus and Cressida*', *Shakespeare Studies*, vol. 1, 1965.

[5] Now readily available in Spencer, T. J. B. (ed.), *Elizabethan Love Stories*, Harmondsworth, 1968.

[6] 'Interpretation and misinterpretation in Shakespeare's *Troilus and Cressida*', *Shakespeare Studies*, vol. 1, 1965.

[7] Watson, Curtis Brown, *Shakespeare and the Renaissance Concept of Honour*, Princeton, N. J., 1960.

[8] Traversi, D., *An Approach to Shakespeare*, New York, 1956, p. 67.

[9] Knowland, G. S., *'Troilus and Cressida'*, *Shakespeare Quarterly*, vol. X, 1959, p. 364.

[10] See Knowland, G. S., *op. cit.*, p. 365: 'There is disillusion, but disillusion had led to truth, and Troilus is strong enough to survive the shock.'

CHAPTER THREE   *Romeo and Juliet*

[1] Bradley, A. C., *Shakespearean Tragedy*, London, 1952, pp. 3, 29 (first published 1909).

[2] Harrison, G. B., *Shakespeare's Tragedies*, London, 1961 (first published 1951), chapter 3.

[3] Charlton, H. B., *Shakespearean Tragedy*, Cambridge, 1948.

[4] Parrot, T. M., *William Shakespeare: A Handbook*, New York, 1934.

[5] Dickey, F. M., *Not Wisely But Too Well*, San Marino, Calif., 1957.

[6] See Brooke, Nicholas, *Shakespeare's Early Tragedies*, London, 1968, Lawler, John, *'Romeo and Juliet'* in Stratford-upon-Avon Studies 3, *Early Shakespeare*, London, 1961; Stauffer, D. A., *Shakespeare's World of Images*, Indiana, 1949.

[7] Gardner, Helen, *'Othello:* a retrospect, 1900-67', *Shakespeare Survey 21*, Cambridge, 1968.

[8] Brooke, Arthur, *The Tragicall Hystory of Romeus and Juliet* printed by Richard Tottel, in 1562.

[9] Spencer, T. J. B. (ed.), *Romeo and Juliet*, The New Penguin Shakespeare, Harmondsworth, 1967.

[10] Coleridge, S. T., *Shakespearean Criticism*, vol. II, ed. T. M. Raysor, London, 1960, p. 108.

[11] Donne, John, *The Elegies and the Songs and Sonnets*, ed. Helen Gardner, Oxford, 1965, 'The broken heart', p. 51.

[12] Spencer, T. J. B., *op. cit.*

[13] Grierson, H., *Metaphysical, Lyrics and Poems of the Seventeenth Century*, Oxford, 1921, pp. xxvii–xxviii.

[14] Donne, John, *The Elegies and the Songs and Sonnets*, ed. Helen Gardner, Oxford, 1965, 'A Nocturnall upon S. Lucies Day', p. 84.

[15] Coleridge, S. T., *op. cit.*, vol. II. p. 97.

[16] Lawlor, John, *'Romeo and Juliet'*, in Stratford-upon-Avon Studies 3, *Early Shakespeare*, p. 139.

[17] Stauffer, D. A., *op. cit.*, p. 59.

CHAPTER FOUR   *Othello*

[1] Dickey, F. M., *Not Wisely But Too Well*, San Marino, Calif., 1957, p. 8.

[2] Bradley, A. C., *Shakespearean Tragedy*, London, 1952, Lecture VI.

[3] Leavis, F. R., *The Common Pursuit*, 'Diabolic intellect and the noble hero', London, 1952.

[4] *Ibid*, p. 139.

[5] Eliot, T. S., *Selected Essays*, London, 1951, 'Shakespeare and the stoicism of Seneca', p. 130.

[6] Gardner, Helen, *'Othello:* a retrospect, 1900–67', *Shakespeare Survey 21*, Cambridge, 1968.

[7] Gardner, Helen, 'The noble Moor', Lecture of the British Academy 1955 from *Proceedings of the British Academy*, vol XLI, London.

[8] Johnson, S., in *Dr Johnson on Shakespeare*, ed. W. K. Wimsatt, Harmondsworth, 1969, p. 142.

[9] Coleridge, S. T., *Shakespearean Criticism*, ed. T. M. Raysor, London, 1960, vol. I, p. 113.

[10] Muir, K., *Shakespeare's Sources, 1, Comedies and Tragedies*, London, 1957.

[11] Raleigh, W., quoted by Helen Gardner in *'Othello:* a retrospect 1900–67'. The exact quotation is from *All's Well That Ends Well*, Act II, scene iii, 3–6: 'Hence is it that we make trifles of terrors, ensconcing ourselves into seeming knowledge when we should submit ourselves to an unknown fear.'

[12] Bayley, John, *The Characters of Love*, London, 1960, p. 149.

[13] Hunter, G. K., *'Othello* and colour prejudice', Lecture of the British Academy 1967.

[14] Leavis, F. R., *op. cit.*

[15] Knight, G. Wilson, 'The *Othello* Music', in *The Wheel of Fire*, London, 1930.

[16] Gardner, Helen, *'Othello:* a retrospect, 1900–67', p. 10.

[17] I have discussed this at length in *The Recurring Miracle*, Natal, 1962, and Nebraska, 1969.

[18] Coleridge, S. T., *op. cit.*, p. 44.

[19] Leavis, F. R., *op. cit.*

[20] Allen, Ned B., 'The two parts of *Othello*', in *Shakespeare Survey 21*, Cambridge, 1968.

[21] To refer back to Bodenheim's *Belvedere* (see Chapter I, note 8): 'The truest love is most suspicious / The greater love, the greater is the losse.'

[22] Stewart, J. I. M., *Character and Motive in Shakespeare*, London, 1965, pp. 97–110.

[23] Graves, R., *Collected Poems*, London, 1961, 'Pure death', p. 83.

[24] See Marsh, D. R. C., *op. cit.*, p. 194.

[25] Leavis, F. R., *op. cit.*, p. 149.

[26] Eliot, T. S., *op. cit.*, p. 130.

[27] Stewart, J. I. M., *op. cit.*, p. 107.

[28] Gardner, Helen, 'The noble Moor', p. 191.

[29] Holloway, J., *The Story of the Night*, London, 1961, p. 54.

[30] *Ibid.*, p. 55.

[31] Leavis, F. R., *op. cit.*, pp. 151–2.

[32] Ridley, M. R. (ed.), *Othello*, The Arden Shakespeare, London, 1958, p. lvi.

[33] Bradley, A. C., *op. cit.*, Lecture V, p. 192.

[34] Leavis, F. R., *op. cit.*, p. 151.

[35] *Cymbeline*, Act V, scene iv.

[36] Hibbard, G. R., '*Othello* and the pattern of Shakespearean Tragedy', in *Shakespeare, Survey 21*, Cambridge, 1968, p. 39.

CHAPTER FIVE *Antony and Cleopatra*

[1] Reimer, A., '*A Reading of Antony and Cleopatra*', Sydney, 1968.

[2] Dickey, F. M., *Not Wisely But Too Well*, San Marino, Calif., 1957.

[3] *Ibid.*, p. 144.

[4] *Ibid.*, p. 179.

[5] Ribner, I., *Patterns in Shakespearean Tragedy*, London, 1960.

[6] Mason, H. A., *Shakespeare's Tragedies of Love*, London, 1970.

[7] Wilson, H. S., *On the Design of Shakespearean Tragedy*, Toronto, 1958, p. 159.

[8] Knight, G. Wilson, *The Imperial Theme*, Oxford, 1931.

[9] Wimsatt, W., *The Verbal Icon*, New York, 1960, p. 97.

[10] Wilson, J. Dover (ed.), *Antony and Cleopatra*, New Cambridge Shakespeare, 1960, p. xxxvi.

[11] Stauffer, D., *Shakespeare's World of Images*, Indiana, 1949, p. 233.

[12] Reimer, A., *op. cit.* p. 114.

[13] Waith, Eugene M., *The Herculean Hero*, London, 1962.

[14] Rabkin, Norman, *Shakespeare and the Common Understanding*, New York, 1967.

[15] Traversi, D., *An Approach to Shakespeare*, second revised edition, New York, 1956.

[16] Knights, L. C., *Some Shakespearean Themes and an Approach to 'Hamlet'*, Harmondsworth, 1966, p. 124.

[17] Traversi, D., *op. cit.*, p. 261.

[18] Ornstein, R., 'The ethic of the imagination: love and art in *Antony and Cleopatra*', Stratford-upon-Avon Studies 8, *Later Shakespeare*, London, 1966.

[19] Bradley, A. C., *Oxford Lectures on Poetry*, London, 1962, p. 300.

[20] Ridley, M. R., (ed.), *Antony and Cleopatra*, The Arden Shakespeare, London, 1954, p. 261.

[21] Ornstein, R., *op. cit.*, p. 32.

CHAPTER SIX   The Romances

[1] See the Introduction to F. D. Hoeniger's Arden Edition of *Pericles*, lii–lxiii.

[2] Frank Kermode devotes the major part of his Introduction to the Arden Edition of *The Tempest* to a discussion of the major themes of the play. There is also a survey of some of the criticism.

[3] I have discussed these plays in more detail in *The Recurring Miracle*, Natal, 1962 and Nebraska, 1969.

[4] Leavis, F. R., *The Common Pursuit*, 'Diabolical intellect and the noble hero', p. 139.

[5] *The Recurring Miracle*, p. 161.

[6] W. B. Yeats, *Collected Poems* Macmillan, London, second edition, 1950, 'Nineteen hundred and nineteen', p. 234.

INDEX